This issue of *Nimrod* is funded by donations, subscriptions, and sales. *Nimrod* and The University of Tulsa acknowledge with gratitude the many individuals and organizations that support *Nimrod*'s publication, annual prize, and outreach programs: *Nimrod*'s Advisory and Editorial Boards; and *Nimrod*'s Angels, Benefactors, Donors, and Patrons.

ANGEL ($1,000+)

Margery Bird, Gary Brooks, Ivy & Joe Dempsey, Joan Flint, The Herbert & Roseline Gussman Foundation, Susan & Robert Mase, Donna O'Rourke & Tom Twomey, Mary Lee Townsend & Burt Holmes, Randi & Fred Wightman, The Williams Companies on behalf of Elizabeth Joyner, The John Steele Zink Foundation

BENEFACTOR ($500+)

Cynthia Gustavson, Evelyn Hatfield, Bruce Kline, Edwynne & George Krumme, Mary Lhevine & George Schnetzer, Lisa Ransom, Andrea Schlanger, Dorothy & Michael Tramontana, Joy Whitman, Jane Wiseman, Rachel Zebrowski

DONOR ($100+)

Teresa & Alex Adwan, Sandra & Harvey Blumenthal, Colleen Boucher, Katherine Coyle, Harry Cramton, Dianne & Dick Diercks, Kay & F. Daniel Duffy, Marion & Bill Elson, Ken Fergeson, Sherri Goodall, Helen Jo Hardwick, Ellen Hartman, Frank & Bonnie Henke, Nancy Hermann, Mary Kathleen & Douglas Inhofe, Elizabeth & Sam Joyner, Inge Kahn, William Kellough, The Kerr Foundation, Marjorie & David Kroll, Lydia Kronfeld, Robert LaFortune, Sandra & Dobie Langenkamp, Maria Lyda, Daniel & Roberta Marder, Carol McGraw, Geraldine McLoud, Melvin Moran, Catherine Gammie Nielsen, Ruth K. Nelson, Rita Newman, Nancy & Thomas Payne, Kate Reeves, RGF Family Fund, Patricia & Gil Rohleder, R. A. Searcy, Joan Seay, Diane & James Seebass, Glenda & Larry Silvey, Ann Stone, Sarah Theobald-Hall, Fran & Bruce Tibbetts, Renata & Sven Treitel, Melissa & Mark Weiss, The Kathleen Patton Westby Foundation, Penny Williams, Josephine Winters, Paul Woodul, Mary Young & Joseph Gierek, Ann Zoller

PATRON ($50+)

Helen & M. E. Arnold, Margaret Audrain, Mary Cantrell & Jason Brimer, Phyllis Collier, Patricia Eaton, Susan & William Flynn, Carolyn Gardner, Marilu Goodyear & Adrian Alexander, Marilyn Inhofe-Tucker, Living Arts of Tulsa, James Murray, Krista & John Waldron, Ruth Weston, Martin Wing

Alice Price
1927- 2009

This issue of *Nimrod* is dedicated to Alice Price,
artist and poet, whose creations fluttered from
the pages of *Nimrod* in numerous issues starting
in the 1960's and most recently in our *Mexico/USA*
issue, where the cranes and swans she wrote about
in stunning and lovingly respectful books
flew from the pages.

Her spirit, too, always soared.
We cannot imagine the world without her.

TABLE OF CONTENTS

Editor's Note
Awards 31: Words at Play

Words—words at play—allow us, even in the silence, to sound the depths while presenting an infinite variety of surface attractions. Engaging our attention for the sake of "the thing itself" and not for any overt or immediate objective beyond the game, words at play may be distinguished from the words at work in politics, advertising, journalism, as excellent as they may be.

Yet, as Dutch philosopher Johan Huizinga[1] reminds us, play is always serious-fun: it involves both conflict and pleasure, follows the rules of the game, respects time and place, and exercises in an authentic (if not "real" in the usual use of the word) field of play—the very qualities found in poetry and fiction.

So it is not surprising that this issue of *Nimrod, Awards 31,* displays an earnest and playful grappling with basic and contentious questions bound by ties other than those of logic and causality. Lacey Jane Henson's first-prize winning story, "Trigger," with a surface that is bold and tantalizing, plays with interpretation, shifts points of view, taunts our perception of reality, our acknowledgement of the unspeakable. It asks: Why do we tell the stories we tell? Do these stories express our inmost thoughts and actual experiences? Do we inhabit them?

Or do our stories disguise who we are because we feel that we are not cool enough, hip enough, *as* we are? And are we then defined as we tell our tales, change them, embroider them to fit the moment and audience and our own changing perspective?

In short, where is truth, where reality?

Couched so blandly, these basic questions may seem to belabor the obvious, yet they are the trigger for imaginative inventions and link our award-winners and the other writers of quality in this issue. When words are at play, the eternal questions may take on many forms: In Mike Nelson's first-prize winning poem, "Acacia," "its roots gnarled and reaching every-which-way," the speaker grieves for the loss not only of a man but of a principle, and asks in innocence (*akakia*) which would feel more real: "the sound of your friend's voice making you believe, briefly, he was alive? Or his silence?"

---

[1] *Homo Ludens,* 1938

The eloquence of silence and the native properties of trees and gardens—apricot, cedar of Lebanon, Asian pear—provide a metaphorical (hence playful) way of speaking that "plays April" and December, discovers what is real, what is truly valuable, "what to ask for." Thus the Q's "tattooed on our wrists," arterial as the wider system of trees and veins in Maggie Queeney's "Font" and Terry Blackhawk's "Out of the Labyrinth," lead to the gardens of Judy Rowe Michaels's "Saint Luke's Garden" but also to the "weight of the real story" in Patricia Grace King's "Dogs in Guatemala," an exploration that deals with the limits of the imagination's ability to comprehend the extent and reality of suffering, so that all that is left to human feeling is sentimentality, squeezing one's sense of outrage and horror onto a dog or cat.

Once again, this time in Moscow, in Laura Hulthén Thomas's honorable-mention story "Down to the Last Kopek" the central action is ironic. It revolves around the quest for one fragile, precious egg that is not shattered but in fact does crush the main character's perception of reality, just as the memory of *Kristallnacht* (Night of Broken Glass) echoes within Richard Santos's "Charles and Irma," and Elizabeth Fogle's "The Nazi Officer's Wife," where a playful, repetitive use of parentheses adroitly questions each euphemism so that "powder" becomes "(ashes)".

In this issue, playful letters, balloons, hobo signs, mysterious V's carved into prairies of the past as indicators of space and time, seemingly trivial, almost game-show questions regarding roots, Ravenna, memories of a father and husband who went out one morning and never returned—all are like "strands of hair" pulling one back to Bolivia, to Argentina, to the land and the "real" story, to the connection between *then* and *now*, history and the self, as W. Scott Olsen explores in "What Remains."

Surprise too is always a delightful part of any game and with words at play surprise often spikes the search for reality. In Alicia Case's second-prize poem "Ascension," for example, the speaker expects a sad story of loss and receives, instead, a release. In Linda Woolford's finalist story "Bounty," the father's meticulous, painstaking care of rare African violets is contrasted to the daughter's "wild, lush beauty beyond his control" and to the playful, spontaneous—if demonic—game of revenge conceived by the daughter.

Why do we play with words, deal in metaphors, tropes, comparisons and connections of all kinds? Why do we define *love* as a Ferris wheel or a painting or a character in mythology, as in Margaret Kaufman's second-prize winning story "Life Saving Lessons," and speak of the gray tanks and pummeling boots of war as "Elephants," as in Natalie Diaz's honorable-mention poem? For the sheer pleasure? For the challenge? Yes, but isn't it also to allow writers and readers (despite my initial disavowal of intention) to deal with the unspeakable, to preserve ourselves, to add to the store of culture, to understand and make clear that which "ordinary life" hides from daily view? And so we try again—our words at play in the fields of life.

Advisory Board

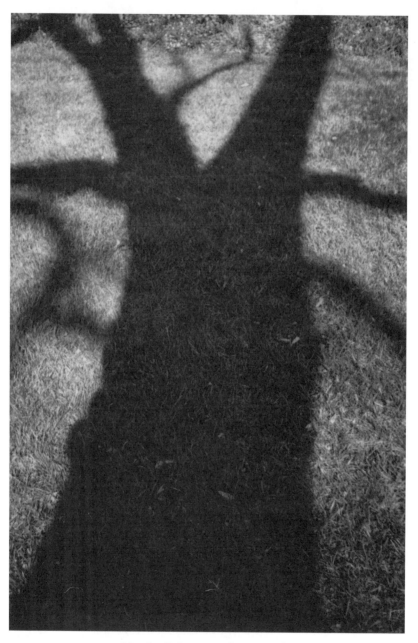

Manly Johnson, photograph

Acacia

Less bullshit, more
con-

viction: that's what my friend said he wanted
from The Crowes. The
Black

Crowes, that is.
And the name of the band they opened for

is Heartbreakers.

And if we were in the Apostles,
my friend would be the one whose name you'll still
see carved in rock, and I the one

called Doubting Thomas.

But it was
Grieving Thomas who spoke

in desperate words, saying unless

he saw the marks
of the nails in the hands, and could put his

finger in them . . .
he

would not believe.

———

What else can you say when everyone's talking
about visions? When your friend is gone;

he hasn't
been buried a week, and someone

says he saw him, in dusty
linens, walking
the same sun-chronicled road

he always walked? And someone else

says he saw him on a clifftop, arms stretched
across the setting sun, his slumped
head bleeding

from the eyes and nostrils? And
someone else

says there was
no sun, no wounds
or garment, that if the form he saw

had been human once,

now it was translated
into crucial light?

———

Sure, you could

believe them. You could believe
those who said they heard their names

on the air behind them, who said it was
his voice calling. His voice,

though one turned and saw a bewildered
silent boy looking back. And another saw an old man

riding a donkey. And
another . . . But didn't you already *know*

what the third one saw? Hadn't
you heard his story? Or others like it?

The third one saw nothing.

Nothing that could have made
that sound, he said,

just as he was passing. There was only
an acacia, its roots gnarled and
reaching every-which-way

and clinging

to the scree and vagrant
soil of a hillside.

———

Akakia, he'd have called it,
if he were speaking Greek—a name
meaning innocence

and thorn.

———

But the story he would tell was
not yet translated
into Greek. And besides,

who'd believe it? How many times

would you have to tell
your story, if

it were your story, before you actually
started to believe
your friend had spoken to you after

death

through a tree? Even

if you'd seen the tree, had seen
how common it is, and how it thrives

on next to nothing: sparse
rain, sunlight,
a little earth crumbling away beneath it?

Even if it occurred
to you that an ordinary tree, on an almost
barren hill, does not

even mock belief,

much less symbolize it?
Even if you

looked closely, and couldn't find a scar
or anything in the natural
shape of its leaves and branches

that someone might read hopefully
or ingeniously
construe as a sign? Even

then, after
you'd told the story ten, twenty,

a hundred times —

which would feel more real: the sound
of your friend's voice making you
believe, briefly, he was alive?

———

Or his silence?

———

Which isn't the silence of doubt,
the silence out of which they

say you, Thomas, spoke.

And isn't the silence of
disbelief, which falls, occasionally, over a room
of hushed gatherers

who have come
to hear you speak, the silence in which you notice,

in a corner, someone uncrossing his arms
and recrossing them, as he looks up

at an unadorned ceiling and
hears, you imagine,

no voice in the wind outside,
no voice from the wooden

beams when they creak,
and so looks back

to the floor again, and scuffs out
the zero or circle
or ouroboros he'd been tracing,

absentmindedly, in the dust
with one of his feet. And isn't

———

the acacia's silence. Or
that longer silence in which an entire language

has ceased to speak, the silence
of all the dead names, some now cloistered

in a quiet, unchanging posthumous life
of scientific appellation

or religious rite, some eking out
a transubstantiation—changed utterly
in sound or nuance

or meaning—as history.

Maybe you should admit it: you never saw
the tree. You made it up because it seemed
to belong in your story. And because

you liked its name, liked the sound of it
even before you learned

any of its history or meaning.

Acacia: it's only a word.

Though it's a word that
helped you tell your story. And couldn't you use
its help now? Couldn't you

use its company?
Doesn't it cast a shade

of truth over the story you tell? —

One day you heard a voice and, when you turned
and were going to answer, but saw
no one there,

felt a thorn in your larynx, something as
guileless and indisputable as a thorn, reminding you
of your friend. Of

the spine in his voice. And the way
he'd hold his fist up, shaking it,
taking the empty

air by the throat. Just

taking it, making out of emptiness a sign
or song, a gesture that

needed no proof or interpretation.

———

It casts a shade . . .

What you mean is, you never
heard your name called like that, with no one

there to call it. Nor have you felt

a thorn where your voice should have been.
Not *really*

a thorn. You mean
that all names —*thorn*, and *acacia*, and
innocence—are abstract, are—

like trees clinging to a barren
hill—empty of

inherent meaning. Yea, even those

names carved and dissolving in marble
on a windswept hill
are abstract, and have become

more and more so until just to
speak

is an exaggeration.

———

Just one
more

exaggeration

among the others. Like pretending
that my friend and I are other
people

who aren't
even people anymore. Who, after all

the stories and interpretations, are just
about anything

you want them to be. Or like suggesting
that my friend is dead, when really
he lost his job,

for no good reason he
or I can see, and found another one

in Missouri.

My friend, the teacher, who didn't lose
his job because he wasn't

a good teacher, who didn't lose
his job because he had done something wrong

or litigable, or even something
questionable, who didn't lose

his job because his ambitions
were Machiavellian, were a clear

and present danger to someone
else in his department. My friend,

the teacher, nearly always
present, nearly

always clear. Whom someone,

in a department meeting, once called
dead weight, because he wanted to live and

teach
where he had always

taught and lived, who didn't think
the name of the university on his degree should

stand in his way. What I mean is,
my friend,

if I called him by name, wouldn't assume that I

mean anything he thinks. How
I miss him.

—*for Greg Smith*

Apricots

It's wrong, I know, shameful to resent
the tree's unstinting act of giving, but
I've had all I can take of this sweet glut,
which will not wait for hands, but must, decadent

flump to the ground with its zither of meddling flies.
For something in my pennywise heart can't let
gold go to waste, but bids me grab all the delicate
ingots I can hold, as I warily rise

on toddling ladder feet. What one life lacks
is another's nuisance. And what does it portend,
this epic crop? Has an old tree, sensing its end,
thrown all its failing strength to stay the axe

of time? Or has nature always tried to cram
her largesse down our throats, deaf to any voice
that dare say no? There was a time I could rejoice
in rot. It's too familiar now. And so I'll jam

and jar until the sweet stench stains my pores
and cupboards all but buckle to contain
too much to spread before May comes again
with more bright gifts than one heart can endure.

Trigger

The first person I tried was Annie, a doctor at Group Health hospital, where I still had coverage through COBRA. She had a thick black braid slung over one shoulder and wore a collared shirt with little seashells ringing the neck and sleeves. Something about her hair and that shirt—its masculine cut, coupled with the sad vanity of the seashells—marked her as an old-school feminist. When I asked to renew my Ortho Tri-Cyclen prescription, she ranted about the ways drug companies market expensive pills, and persuaded me to switch brands. For my Pap, she adjusted the table so I could sit up and hold a little handmirror in front of my vagina, while she gave me an anatomy lesson. It was mostly review, except, with the speculum in, I could see my pea-sized cervix for the first time.

"I have to push a baby through that thing?" I said. "Theoretically, I mean. Like, someday." I was twenty-five.

"Isn't it amazing?" she said, beaming at the mirror.

We both paused for a few beats. My labia gaped silently, almost forlornly, back at us. I thought of a beagle on a leash: sad eyes, fleshy jowls.

Sharing that close-up view with her made the exam more comfortable, somehow, creating a sense of intimacy that I knew was false. Still, I allowed the soothing energy from her fingertips to expand inside me, as she softly kneaded my breasts, searching for lumps. Lulled there, under the flecked white ceiling, it felt almost natural to tell her that I needed an STD check. And then why.

"You were raped," she said. Her fingertips paused at my areola; her mouth began twitching with rage. I became aware of my nipples, exposed in the cool air. "Why didn't you mention this earlier? That's rape," she repeated.

The word reminded me of a TV melodrama: men in suits and the sound of a gavel. Once you define something it can be called into question, examined. What if I was lying? What if I didn't even know whether or not I was lying?

"I'm not sure," I said, dumbly. It was all I knew to say.

I watched her struggle to bring her face under control.

"Well, if you change your mind, there's a place they can examine you for evidence. You've waited a bit long, but they may be able to find something. Will be able to," she amended. She left my side, in search of a pamphlet from a stack on the desk in the corner. "You know, you're not supposed to shower after something like this. You're supposed to go directly to a medical center."

The brochure had a picture of a woman in profile on the front, her hair blowing behind her. I guessed it was supposed to advertise the quiet, inner strength you'd feel after getting your insides scraped for evidence of trauma. "Bruising and that sort of thing will show," she went on. "Ultimately, it's up to you. But remember—your rapist could do this to someone else."

My rapist, I thought, startled.

"I'm putting a note in your chart, in case you change your mind," she said.

I realized that for Annie, the real danger was his status as a predator. She was probably imagining some college-aged boy— white, flipped-up polo collar—with an illegal supply of roofies. The truth was Pierre was my rapist in the purist sense. I didn't think anyone but me would fall for the guy.

As far as Annie was concerned, it was simple: Has the patient ever been a victim of sexual assault?

The answer was precise, a checked box: Yes.

❊ ❊ ❊

In one frame, the box was right, the answer simple and true. In this frame he got me drunk, and slipped me drugs, and I had sex against my will. In another, I got too drunk (as usual), and had sex (as usual), except this time I deeply regretted it the next morning. It could also be said that an older, rich, French-Moroccan man took me out to a fancy restaurant and, afterward, he fucked the shit out of me. By calling it rape Annie had inserted blame into the situation, solidly as a gun in my hand. The problem was that, frame by frame, I kept moving the barrel from my head to his, wondering where the bullet should land.

❊ ❊ ❊

A week or so later, my friend Lauren and I went to a going-away party for a friend we'd known in college. By the time we arrived, his little rental house was so crowded that it seemed impossible to find him. We filled two Pixie cups with beer and escaped to the garden, where we sat on a wooden bench swing, smoking cigarettes end to end.

"Do you ever feel like Seattle's getting old?" I was gearing up for telling her about what had happened with Pierre. "I wouldn't mind starting over."

"Me neither, except I have a tumor. That complicates things."

I paused. "You mean, like, metaphorically?"

Apparently, there was a literal mass forming deep inside her right ear, something I imagined as a tiny, flesh-colored cauliflower. It was still small and benign, she said, but would keep growing until it blocked her hearing completely. Now, I imagined the cauliflower was larger, sprouting from her ear.

"But with surgery," she went on, "I risk hearing loss plus a whole bunch of other shit. The thing I keep thinking is: where will Egore go if I die?"

She smiled. The cauliflower dissolved and I saw Egore's tail lightly thumping the floor, waiting in her apartment with his head on his paws. Lauren and I were swinging in and out between fluorescent light and shadow. When illuminated, her white-bright face seemed to glow, as if lit from within. How becoming, tragedy. I had a palpable desire to kiss her, to touch that light, to suck it out and claim it as my own.

Is that why I told her I was raped?

❁ ❁ ❁

I tried on the word, like a new hat, with my friends. It started the story with a bang, and certainly got a reaction. My male friends, in particular, surprised me. Even the most even-keeled of them got trigger-happy, offering to inflict blame and violence in any way I wished. With a certain gleam in their eye too, like I'd tapped into some deep-seated fantasy.

"I could, you know, take care of him," Jacob said.

"What, beat him up?" I asked. Jacob was best characterized by his boyish, typically Midwestern looks and I'd seen him sob once, at the end of *Chinatown*. He owned rifles, but not handguns. He had lectured me about the stupidity of vigilante justice.

"I mean something permanent," he said.

"No!" I nearly shouted—horrified, thrilled.

❀ ❀ ❀

The story expanded, took on a life of its own. I see myself in a series of scenes during this time, haunting bars and cafés, talking ceaselessly. Only a senseless stream of words, like birdsong, spills from my mouth. I lost track of who and what was appropriate.

I remember a man in a coffee shop who kept licking a white scar on his lip—a tic, or maybe an attempt to hide his disgust. Another man whose broad forehead full of lines kept furrowing the more I talked. A man with tiny bruises on his neck who smiled like a wolf. It was always men that I told. Somehow the incident had become a story, which removed me from it, in a way.

I made it into a story so I could cling to it, as one would grab hold of a bucket to keep from falling completely down a well. And I liked the way my own confession bred others, the darkness of another life was briefly illuminated, clear.

I made it into a story because no one would touch me after I told it; because people would touch me gently after I told it; because I'd get fucked after I told it.

I told the story because it transformed me into a kind of freak, from whom people felt they had nothing to hide.

I told the story because the looks I got afterward never ceased to fascinate.

I told the story because I was scared of what would happen if I were silent.

I think, above all, what I was looking for was an ending or a frame, something I could tack on that would tell me what to do. I would repeat the story as I told it back then, but I can't remember exactly how it went and, honestly, I don't want to.

❀ ❀ ❀

Here's another thing that has something to do with it:

I went to Paris when I was nineteen, for a summer, and one night a man named Luc took me on a date. Luc's father, Tri, was an old family friend. Tri was a devout Vietnamese Buddhist and had driven me and a nun to Versailles one afternoon, where we

toured the hall of mirrors and ate *banh bao* in the gardens. Based
on this, I had developed certain ideas about Luc. He was thirty,
which, at nineteen, I thought was an old and ruined age. On our
date, he took me out for snails and champagne; he bought me
beaded bracelets at a roadside stand; he called me his sister; he
took me for drinks on the Champs Élysées. "I told him I didn't
want any more to drink," I said, telling my mother the story later,
at home, "and got up to go to the bathroom." But when I came
back to the table there were two drinks, set aflame. After drinking
his, he was, conveniently, too drunk to drive home. In the hotel
room he'd asked: Can I touch you here? Will you touch me there?
I refused both times. What you call that, he asked, your princess?
He laughed, afterwards, and, though the laugh sparked a hot, wet
shame at the time, I laughed telling it to my mother. She laughed
too, and had me repeat it at parties, and to my aunts and uncles
and grandparents. I'm good at storytelling—it's kind of my, you
know, *mode*.

❊ ❊ ❊

I have a large, close-knit family full of aunts, uncles and
cousins, all of whom called me after the incident, like normal, from
their homes in Illinois. I imagined their earnest faces as they chat-
ted easily with me from bright, clean kitchens and lounge chairs—a
world in which Pierre seemed impossible. I kept it hidden from
them, relegating Pierre to Seattle, to the dark vault of nightclubs,
and my studio apartment, with its empty wine bottles and dusty
floors. It made me feel as if I were speaking to them from a great
distance, as if they were at the open end of a long well, and I was
falling away from them, towards the ground.

❊ ❊ ❊

Time slipped forward: May bled into June, July, August.
Rain had soaked Seattle until, by sunny August, it was plump as a
breast full of milk, one rosy nipple bared, waiting. "That's the thing
about Seattle," Jacob told me. "In the winter, you're too depressed
to leave and by the time summer rolls around, you forget you
ever wanted to." We were sitting at the little grass beach on Lake
Washington, only minutes from the mansion where Kurt Cobain
had shot himself. The beach where, in May, I'd met Pierre.

Going back could be construed as an act of recouping that place. I'd framed it that way. I am, if not a proper feminist, a believer in Girl Power. A comforting idea, although if I'd been honest with myself, I would have admitted to feeling something closer to curiosity, tinged with fear, something like riding a roller coaster for the first time. Lauren had offered to come with me, but I turned her down. I doubted Pierre would appear, but if he did, I wanted Jacob—all six feet, four inches, 235 pounds of him. Plus, he waited tables at night, so he could show up at noon, wearing board shorts and a pair of BluBlockers.

"Ready to take back this beach?" he said, aping a B-movie thug, though I didn't doubt he had some kind of firearm locked in the glove compartment of his truck.

It *was* my beach. I'd walked two miles there every sunny May morning, once the sun burned off the last clouds, and spent whole days reading, swimming, watching pasty hipsters play Frisbee with ironic smiles. If nothing else, my time at Microsoft had earned me this, I thought, lying flat on a towel, limp from sun. I'd managed to save enough money to coast for months. It only took me one to get bored.

Just bored enough that, hearing French one day, I sat up, blinking, and sought out the speaker. He was talking on his cell, leaning against a tree just a few feet away, wearing white linen pants that offset his ebony skin, which was stretched taut over his entire body: taut over his abs, over his wide, angular face. When he laughed, only his tiny braids shook, just slightly. Late thirties? Or forty? It was impossible to tell. I introduced myself in French when he got off the phone. He raised an eyebrow, walked over, and sat alongside my beach towel. In my head, a film reel began to spin. The young girl in oversized sunglasses and a bikini. The exotic, rich man from Paris. The title sequence of a romantic comedy, perhaps. We spoke only French, subtitles running across the bottom of the screen: You are much friendlier than most American girls.

I suspected him of a lot of things, but that just complicated the plot. I imagined myself arch and aware, even as I giggled when he fingered my bikini, even as I accepted a ride in his Mercedes. Such a beautiful car, and I'm not even into them, really. It was the color of spring—robin's egg blue. He opened the roof and let the air and sun into the car. He dropped me off at Lauren's house, where I was having dinner, and I took his number, happily uncertain as to whether or not I'd see him again.

✿ ✿ ✿

Lauren nicknamed him Pepe Le Pew after dinner, once we'd drunk enough red wine that our lips were stained, purple filling the cracks between our teeth, coating our tongues. I replaced Pierre with Pepe on my phone. "He's probably lying, anyway," I said. "Is anyone actually named Pierre?" I said this! I remember the dirty dishes scattering the table, Lauren's poster of Patti Smith leering at me from the opposite wall. I remember her laugh, our laughter, night blanketing the windows. This clarity seems like proof of my instincts, and yet I ignored them. I wanted to, enamored as I was with the French film version of myself.

I felt stupid each time Pepe sprang up on my phone after the incident. How could I ever seriously say I was raped by someone nicknamed Pepe Le Pew? When he figured out I wasn't answering on purpose, he starting calling from his firm, and then from places that were unrecognizable. "Unknown" called me for weeks until I finally picked up one day, impulsively, as I sat in the passenger seat of Jacob's truck. We were on our way to the firing range, where Jacob had tried to convince me I could learn self-defense. He was persistent and I was bored, jobless, unprepared with any decent excuse. Maybe a little bit curious.

We were speeding up I-5 with the windows down, blaring *Blonde on Blonde*. I screamed hello into the phone, and bit the insides of my cheeks when I recognized Pierre's accent on the other end of the line. "Hang on," I shouted, groping for the volume. Then: silence, the sound of wind filling the car. Hang on, I was thinking. I no longer knew the script. The film was spinning a blank screen.

Jacob reached for the radio and I batted his hand. It's him, I mouthed; and then Jacob was reaching for my phone. I socked him in the shoulder.

"Can I . . . call you back?" I asked Pierre. I leaned towards my window, out of Jacob's reach. My hair blew upward, out of the car.

"Wait. I just . . . I want to know if it's okay what happened between us?"

There were a million words that could have filled this space but I said it was fine, no problem—my chance to confront him dissolving like so much smoke as I hung up the phone. Later, Jacob said the call proved Pierre knew he did something wrong, but it could've equally meant he didn't. All I knew for sure was that I wanted him gone, cleaved neatly from my life, trimmed away like a strip of fat.

❊ ❊ ❊

We like to believe tragedies can mend us somehow. That they are obstacles presented for us to overcome, to clean up after, and to make us change. We play Gloria Gaynor on the jukebox, in bars where our feet stick to the floor, shouting that we, too, will survive. Even more than that, we will be survivor 2.0, become better than what we were. We are the women in Oprah's audience, crying when the pretty guest confesses she once sold herself for heroin, clapping when her miraculous, adorable baby is carried out in a lily-white dress. We wear Oprah's waterproof mascara; it does not run with our tears. We are Oprah. We want to be Oprah. At the very least, we want to believe in Oprah. We want to believe in her story, and that God exists, that there are weapons of mass destruction, that Atticus Finch defended the right person, that women know when they are raped, that only bad men are rapists, that the term "consensual" means something clear and legally binding, that there are true, right, pure and lovely things to dwell on, good reasons and bad, and there is a place where everything will get sorted out in the end.

We want to believe that people can change, but more often than not, they revert back to the same habits they always had. Some habits are just worse than others. There should be an asterisk next to every change referring to the line "Results not typical" in fine print at the bottom of the page. We keep cycling back until we die, or until we've hit the very bottom of the well, and there's nowhere to go but up again. And even then, we'll develop a new set of habits to fill in for the old. Still, we judge the fifteen-year-old for getting her third abortion, particularly if we don't know her—in fact, maybe only if we don't know her, because if we do, we've already pegged her as a fuck-up, not representative of what we would do, given the tragic opportunity.

❊ ❊ ❊

By September of that year, the rain had returned to Seattle, and I was back to living the same lifestyle I had before. Here is the scene: bar, interior. A row of Naugahyde booths, linen tablecloths with a sheet of butcher paper on top, votives flickering in the low light, casting shadows on walls painted red, the color of rust, dried blood. A young woman sits in the back booth, wearing a bell-shaped hat with a scalloped edge, the ends of her curls sticking out from underneath. She is drinking a G&T, reading *War and Peace* in hardback, resting the thick spine on the tabletop, flipping the pages slowly with one hand and dipping the fingertips of the other into the candle wax, letting it build there, capping them. When a man at the bar walks over and interrupts, she accepts his offer of a drink or agrees to give him a cigarette and says of course he can sit down. He looks sometimes like Harry Connick Junior, or sometimes like Jake Gyllenhaal, or sometimes like Beck. He always looks like someone else. He always seems interesting. She will learn that he once lived in a treehouse and watched bugs crawl on the roof before bed, that his sister committed suicide, that he's a Francophile. Half the time, he'll ask, and she'll go home with him . . . why not?

Back at his place, we'd end up making out on a threadbare couch, and then fucking. I'd wake up naked underneath a damp bedsheet, not remembering how I got there in the first place. I felt used and disgusting, like a bad cliché. Why couldn't this be fun, mean nothing? Couldn't I just fuck for the sheer feeling of it? Wasn't it liberating to fuck like this, like a man?

"I mean, technically, there's nothing *wrong* with it," Lauren said, over the phone. "Like, morally, you're fine. I think what you really need to ask yourself is if this is making you happy. If not, then don't force it just because you want to imagine you're sexually liberated." She paused. "Honestly, you could also stand to cut back on drinking."

"I know. I guess I just feel entitled to debauchery, or something. Like I deserve to do whatever the fuck I want."

Lauren snorted. "You deserve a party dress or a large slice of cake. Something . . . actually fun. Listen, I have a fucking tumor in my head. I don't use that as a license to fuck the entire city of Seattle. I just know it would depress me."

"Hey. Have you decided what to do about that?"

"No. I keep putting it off. I have these dreams where Egore offers me advice, but he changes his mind every night."

❖ ❖ ❖

One guy I went home with had pointy ears and a broad smile; he looked kind of like Matt Damon. He was soft-spoken and seemed genuinely sweet, offering me his arm outside the bar, as we walked back to his place. In bed, his whisper took on an aggressive undertone. It was as if he'd been storing little violences all night, and now they were spilling across his tongue, like bullets into my ear. He didn't do much physically but hold my arms down and kind of hit me. I liked it—I've always liked that kind of thing—but the whole time, I couldn't help thinking about how different this felt from what had happened with Pierre, but how it wasn't all that different, too, and what that meant exactly.

❖ ❖ ❖

There was always the threat of seeing him, a small blink-ing light in the periphery of my consciousness whenever I walked around town. I knew it would happen—Seattle is too small for it not to—but I wanted to postpone the meeting as long as possible. My constant sense that he might appear was heightened by the fact that I knew almost nothing about him. He could be anywhere. And he knew where I lived. When I saw a baby-blue Mercedes parked in front of my apartment building, I knew it probably wasn't his, but even as I told myself that, my hands shook opening the front door. I ran upstairs and opened all the doors, and lifted the fur-niture, until there was no place left to look; then, I went into the shower and lay down in my bathtub, letting the water running over me become something redemptive. It felt clichéd, like I was play-ing the victim, following the script of every movie I'd seen, hoping it wouldn't devolve into something out of *Psycho*. But it felt right, too. I listened to the shower until it was all I could hear, until my fingertips became soft and wrinkled, fragile as petals.

❖ ❖ ❖

At the Quality Food Center, I swear I saw a girl from the sex club. That was the insulting thing about the sex club. It was full of people you'd see in the QFC—normal, even ugly people, flaunting skin bruised as overripe fruit, their faces shimmering with desire. It is both horrible and true to admit that I might not have minded as much had the clientele been swanky and lean. Because they were ugly, Pierre's taking me to the club made me feel that I was only a piece of flesh between his teeth. I could have been anyone.

Except, perhaps, that he could not have managed to get just anyone there.

The woman in question was fat and had a mole over her lip, sprouting a single hair. She was squeezing avocados and I was across the veggie island, squeezing tomatoes. I stared at her thick fingers as they worked, and wondered if they'd fondled my breasts the same way.

The lips on the girl at the club were covered in a fine blonde down that almost tickled when we kissed. I remembered the startling coolness of her arms, fleshy as hamhocks. These details troubled me, not in and of themselves, but because they seemed to support an incriminating level of mental clarity. It would be much easier if I could claim that Pierre had given me drugs. Initially, I thought this was what had happened. It was the story I told Annie. But the sensation of the girl's lips and arms, the painfulness of the sex, stuck with me in a way that made me wonder. I had definitely been drunk, but I drank a lot then. I blacked out chunks of the evening. Yet I kept coming to, and when I did, it was with startling lucidity. I would suddenly be *there* — raging, alive. Here is how it went:

He picked me up from a café in his car, and took me to a restaurant by the sea, in Ballard. We sat on the patio, watching the sun bleed out its last light across the water. Even the waitress disapproved of how much wine we were drinking. She looked at us askance when he asked for a third bottle; he kept refilling my glass. I hadn't eaten all day, but he said he only wanted to share a plate of calamari. I was too self-conscious to order dinner alone, so I picked at it with him daintily.

The last thing I remember is returning to the bright table from the bathroom. I took a sip of my wine. It was just enough time for him to slip something into my drink, or just enough time for the alcohol to fully swell within me, or both. The scene fades to black.

Fade in and I'm kneeling on a white mattress, wearing different clothes. My own purple dress, but how has it gotten here? I'm kissing the girl with the downy lips, her tongue like a slick finger prodding my mouth, and Pierre splitting me open from behind. A white sheet hanging beside the bed forms a makeshift door, behind which silhouettes move — a tangle of bodies on what is presumably another bed, arms and legs jerking. People are screaming.

Cut to the street: I'm screaming at Pierre in French, chain-smoking Pall Malls. It is dark, but his teeth and eyes are white. He is laughing. "You are like a pig," I scream, my mediocre French forcing me to articulate things as I never would in English. "You are like pig rolling in shit."

Then, I'm choking on my knees in my kitchen, with the blinds raised and the light on, giving the neighborhood a show.

I slap him so hard my palms sting; he grabs my wrists and holds them above my head. I'm a diver, hands poised, balancing on my toes. Standing there naked, my body is hot to the core, our faces so close he is all I can see. We look at each other for a few long beats. I would spring but there's nowhere to fall.

※ ※ ※

I felt so stupid afterward, like I'd walked into everything he set up. How can you say it was against your will if you could still move around and never actually refused? I fell for all his stupid compliments. When he asked me if I was wearing underwear at the restaurant, I arched an eyebrow, coyly, instead of ordering the check. I was so concerned with not being a "kind of woman." The kind who took herself too seriously, couldn't take a joke, was frigid, did not know what was up. I don't know where I got the idea that being a certain kind of woman was bad, but it concerned me a lot back then. I was so focused on playing the part of not being something that I forgot to look for who I was.

※ ※ ※

One morning, I woke up on my kitchen floor, a thin line of drool crusting my cheek, feeling like my skull had been split in two and stitched back together again. I had hit the bottom of the well. In the next room, Lauren's head was peeking out from underneath my giant down comforter. She put down the book she was reading and said: "You owe me." I crawled into bed and put my head on her chest.

"Tell me everything. Straight up," I said.

We called the previous night "Rumspringa," privately, because it was one of Lauren's last before she went into surgery. In a fit of bold decisiveness she'd called her doctor and agreed to have the tumor removed; directly afterward, she'd asked out a cute boy with Buddy Holly glasses at work, who happened to have a brother. The four of us went to a club, and even before getting there, I drank a full bottle of wine. A full bottle, and I weighed 115 pounds. I lived off cigarettes and bagels. And alcohol.

I remember ordering my third Manhattan at the club and it was this one that sent me deep into the well. Really, I'm surprised how long I lasted. I remember us ordering a table—it was that kind of club, where we had to pay for a purple velvet booth in the back. I saw the amber liquid in the glass, tasted cherry. The rest is a long black fall.

She said it was like someone had flipped a switch and I would not shut up. I insisted on telling everyone about the incident, even as Lauren tried to stop me. "You kept talking about guns," she said. "How his dick felt like the barrel of a gun inside you. Hard and violent and cold." I asked the brothers if they'd ever imagined someone's insides sprayed on a wall. I accused them of wanting to fuck us, both of us. "We are a piece of flesh between your teeth, is what you said. Weird shit like that." When Lauren tried to stop me, I was screaming, ripping my hands from hers. We were kicked out of the club; both boys scurried away into the night. I was sobbing in the cab, all the way home, and threatened to slit my wrists. When I ran into the kitchen, she wrestled me to the ground and sat on me, holding my arms to the floor until I passed out like a child.

"Maybe I should quit drinking," I said, now, lying on the soft pillow of her breast.

"Thank God," Lauren said.

❁ ❁ ❁

Sobriety was fun at first, like anything is. I felt as if a sheet of gauze had been unraveled from my body and I stood, blinking, in the newly exposed world. By this time, it was spring again. I went for long walks in the park by my house, along soft mulch trails carved through dense layers of underbrush and ferns. I saw tiny flowers cascading down tree trunks, amazed I hadn't noticed any of this before. There was so much time to be filled in a day! I ate ice cream and pizza, spent whole days at the movies. I said yes to myself on just about everything. Still, I knew the change was superficial. I hadn't lost my sense of the film. Now I was playing the girl-next-door, while some hot, innermost coil of me throbbed quietly—insistent as a wound.

※ ※ ※

I needed money again and got a job at a national law firm in a big, shiny building downtown. I worked in the records department and spent the whole day listening to NPR while I entered codes into a database. I liked the simplicity of the work, its routine. Taking the bus downtown made me feel like an adult, even though I knew feeling that way made it false—if you're actually an adult, you don't think this. My cubicle faced a window that looked out into an apartment building across the street. I fantasized that I lived in one of the units, which had high ceilings and hardwood floors. There was a man I loved. Sometimes we had sober sex right there, on the floor, in a triangle of sunlight. Sober sex: an elusive and beautiful thing to me at the time. Without the shield of alcohol, I'd become celibate.

※ ※ ※

Pierre receded gradually. Who was he? A dark figure in the distance. The same way, years earlier, I'd forgotten the true shape of my father's face after he died. It happens quickly, the forgetting. Though there were times that things reminded me of Pierre, and those moments were startling, filled with something like awe. Like the time I found one of his business cards under my bed—an artifact. I fingered it gently, smelled it, studied it closely in the dim glow of the overhead light. What I was looking for, I realized, was an ending. This could have been one, but it wasn't.

※ ※ ※

Another possible ending arose in May, on my twenty-sixth birthday. Jacob and I were both still single, and he took me out for a date to a restaurant he kept as a surprise. It turned out to be the same one where Pierre had taken me—nearly a year earlier, I realized. I couldn't believe that I hadn't told Jacob which restaurant it was. Maybe he'd forgotten? Or maybe I hadn't mentioned it? Why wouldn't I have mentioned it, especially considering he's in the restaurant business? He probably would have made some cutting-tender remark about the chef. Why couldn't I think of it?

The questions ballooned in my head while I looked blankly at the menu. We were sitting inside, at a table next to the window. There was a rose on the linen tablecloth, in a little clear vase. I absently picked a few petals and began to rub them between my fingertips.

"Are you okay?" Jacob asked.

"I love the feeling of petals," I said. He kept looking at me, waiting. "You know what it is?" I went on. "I shouldn't mention this now, but sometimes I wonder if I was really raped. Or what happened to me."

"Listen, I think that if a girl thinks she was raped, it's true. No questions asked." He paused. "There's this line, see? A line when you're hooking up with a girl. All guys know it's there. You're just not supposed to cross it. No, you can't cross it. That's why that little French shit pisses me the fuck off. There is no way he didn't know he was crossing that line."

The waiter appeared with his benevolent, tight-lipped smile. He busied us with small talk, and the moment passed. When he left, the conversation shifted to work, and then a girl who'd piqued Jacob's interest, how best to ask her out. In the brief pockets of silence, I thought about what he had said. It comforted me in a way. Perhaps it could be the honest frame I was looking for after all. But I wasn't willing to embrace it. I wasn't sure what the aftermath would be if I decided it was true.

After dinner, as Jacob's truck idled in front of my apartment building, he handed me a small pink box tied with a ribbon. "You're such a good friend," I said, the streetlights briefly blurring, while something tight and coiled inside me unfurled tenderly towards him. "Too bad the sex thing never worked out." Our one attempt to sleep together had been a drunken disaster, something we both continued to be grateful for.

He laughed. "I didn't want to give it to you in public," he said, and the tender thing briefly recoiled. There was a delicate, antique gun inside, its mother of pearl handle gleaming in the truck's dome light. A derringer, Jacob explained. A garter gun for saloon girls. "I never would have given it to you when you actually, you know, went to saloons. But now that you're sober . . . I thought it was cute."

"Does it work?" I asked, picking it up.

"Yep. Mint condition. It's not loaded now, of course. Honestly, I've also been looking for a range partner . . ."

I pointed it at the windshield and squeezed the trigger. Click.

❀ ❀ ❀

The gun distracted me. At first, I hid it on the top shelf of my closet, underneath a pile of winter hats and scarves. I took it down occasionally and posed before my full-length mirror. The film reel began whirring again. In a knit cap, I was Jodie Foster, seeking out vigilante justice, Jane Fonda in my underwear. I was beautiful and bold, my bare feet planted solidly on the hardwood floor. Before, I'd always felt that Hollywood took the whole female power thing too literally. I preferred the high-strung, talky women in screwball comedies—Barbara Stanwyck, Rosalind Russell. They had a different kind of power. But this gun was aesthetically pleasing, in both its size and its detail. I liked how I looked with it, but wasn't sure why.

❀ ❀ ❀

Lauren had kept postponing the surgery she scheduled, but she finally got the tumor successfully removed, months later, and I went to visit her in the hospital. I brought a tin of mints and a big stuffed giraffe that was wearing an "I Love John Lennon" tee.

"You win the award for most random gift ever," she said.

"Not quite," I said. "But I'll tell you about that later. How are you?"

She told me she didn't mind it so much, wearing pajamas all the time and being waited on, even if the food was bad. I told her how I'd missed her, how Jacob had bought me a gun.

"Weird!" she exclaimed.

"Yeah," I said. "And I kind of like it. Do you think that's bad?"

"There are probably healthier fixations. I think you need to do more stuff that involves your body. Start working out or something. Take dance classes."

"That's cheesy," I said, rolling my eyes.

"Well fine. You asked." She crossed her arms.

"Lauren," I said, taking one of her hands away from her chest. "You are my best friend in the world. I appreciate you so much."

"Oh," she said, blushing. "Me too. You're just a pain in the ass sometimes. I mean, Christ, I just had surgery."

       ❖   ❖   ❖

It was an accident, or it wasn't. You could see this first time either way. After going to the shooting range with Jacob one afternoon, I forgot to take the gun out of my giant leather handbag when I got home. At Starbucks, before work the next morning, my fingers brushed the cool handle as I was fishing for my wallet. I physically started and the guy behind the counter cocked his head at me. I just smiled and handed him a five, which quivered in my shaky hands. It only took me until the end of that day to be okay with it, and by the next I was excited — soon I was carrying the gun all the time.

       ❖   ❖   ❖

The ending I was looking for came out of nowhere — like the gun, it fell from the sky. Perhaps you've guessed that I saw Pierre again, this time with the gun in my purse. It happened in the strangest of places: I was waiting for the bus home, and so was he. I recognized him immediately, wearing a swank suit and sunglasses, leaning on the side of the bus shelter. He did not see me and I was able to duck into an alleyway while I considered what to do.

In Annie's version of the ending, I recognize my inner strength. Why hadn't I noticed it before? I am beautiful and bold. Once I have that knowledge, I don't need the weapon anymore. I hide on the back of the bus and discreetly follow Pierre once he disembarks at a garage. I am able to take down his license plate number for the police. The clinic still has a little bag of evidence waiting just for this moment. After my testimony, and the miraculous conviction, I score a guest spot on Oprah's show. The audience cries and cheers. "You're a shero!" Oprah screams.

In Jacob's version, I track Pierre and hold him hostage in his spacious Belltown pad. I bind him with bedsheets and put him in the bathtub, call Jacob on his cell. After killing him, we're able to destroy the body easily, and I run away to Mexico, where I become a waitress in a little beachside café.

In Lauren's version, when I see Pierre, I realize he holds no power over me anymore. I will sign up for yoga classes where I will meet a thin, sweet man. But first, I figure out where Pierre lives and shoot out all the windows of his car, which makes me feel a lot better.

You can frame a story any way you want to: "If a girl thinks she was raped, it's true." Rape is so often a story's truth—one based on perspective and the human heart, rather than hard evidence and fact. Because this is a story, I can write here that I was raped, and who will care if any of the details are true?

Because this is a story, I can give the girl a gun, which makes doing nothing *something*—by choosing nothing, she is granting the man his life. By doing nothing the night of their date, he would have been doing something, too. This is the real ending she wants, the impossible one. The one where, although she gets too drunk at the restaurant, he takes her home—a silly girl in grownup clothes—and tucks her into bed. She'd have woken up thankful and sleepy-eyed; this story would not exist.

If What We Love Turns to Glass, How Do We Keep It Safe

I'd like to make something tender for both of us.   Something, at least, to put into your hands. Something like those flowers I saw by the side of the road in the Polish countryside. Though some might call them weeds, as I might have called them once. But that summer evening, just after the storm, I walked along naming them to myself: *buttercup, thistle, poppy, homely oh lovely dandelion.* I thought them jewel-like, there in the high grass; blue mist rising off the fields. Men on bicycles wobbling home. Everything softening in the blur of twilight: woodsmoke; drizzle; sky. I thought then, as I think now: so where's the line between beauty and sorrow; where's the line between terror and joy? How the small daughter of my friends had run out the open door of the house, screaming and laughing, into the rain. How your mother — still beautiful, still — had hobbled each day down the road to the store. How all those years you watched her disappear until she disappeared for good. How my father, those same years, adrift, drifted too far in his ship of bones; then only the smell of flowers above that bed where he'd lain to die. So I take your suffering, you take mine, we take it up — shall this be a bouquet? That evening in Poland I walked for an hour, away from then back toward the church. I called to no one, and no one called to me — though the warm room was waiting, the bread. I would give you this now: the pale green dome; the meadow; the quiet house, lights coming on. How the child, in her sleep, breathed the breath of birds. How the little boat of my heart goes out.

The Silk of Longing Is Never Worth What We Are Paid

Oh lamb. Oh lonely in your rooms above the childless neighbors,
too. The blue of afternoon went on and on like winter, didn't it?
The first lights flickering at dusk along the street to make you sad.
You took the subway into town, then taxied back, your meager
store of cash diminishing again. And still awake at four a.m.,
you wanted anything but this: the silent bed; the empty kitchen;
birdsong startling the trees. Open your hand and kiss your palm.
That's my kiss, as real as salt. Then turn your head and kiss your
shoulder, pale as snow, then, warm as milk. The day turns over
when we sleep. We need our sleep. Take comfort there. I wish for
you the book of childhood's secrets, love's dark stairs. I climbed
them once to you; would climb again toward you now. And keep
you company awhile. And lie down next to you. Oh lamb.

Manly Johnson, photograph

Font

We had Qs tattooed to our wrists, exploding
the letter to measure ourselves a new font
against our matching tangle of veins.

Distortion, we knew, was inevitable—the wrist
a hinge in almost constant use.

The Q an eyed letter, its descending lick
immediate as the optical nerve
to the brain, the bright pony-tails

we wore as children. They made
our heads into hearts, arteried into the wider

system of trees, the street of families
other than ours that fed and bedded us.
When our mother wanted to kill

and couldn't, she utilized the inanimate,
the unable to scream: a car over a foot,
boot into wall, our bedrooms

rebuilt on the lawn in the careful
framework to a fire. We started to speak
in abstraction—how *glyph* slides

into *nymph*—we burrowed a tunnel
to the dumb, the animal. The mythological
where no one ever turns into a girl.

Always a girl into flame, into bird,
into rock. And our mother in smoke,
her skin a web of vents, in the dark

of her new house slanting south
of a lake. The Q here a noose, a snare
waiting for a triggering foot,

an eyespot we plotted to confuse
our own traitor hands, shaped in her shape,
a seed shooting into any ready break.

Jen Hoppa, photograph

Out of the Labyrinth

Rotten Cotton, Little Yellow Jacket, Slingblade—
when they burst from their chutes, a cowboy gets
eight seconds to ride, else lose to the sawdust floor.

I have seen a bull toss then try to gore its rider
before trotting away elegantly, delicately,
as if sniffing some distant air—as if sensing

smoke or whiffs of lies—the way yours
hung in the air between us those last days
you sat in your chair not speaking—glowering
at the animals lunging on the screen.

Replay bathes the beast in a golden, slowed-down
light—an aura, a cloud, a mythic trick I do not
fall for. No garlands adorn these massive heads

and fringed cowgirl groupies make no ritual
in their name. The whirlwind has no name,
you said of your tribe's dust devils that bore

dead souls across the plains. 8 seconds, more or less,
30 years, more or less, and I'm back in our dissolved
and dappled past—still apt to cringe, weep at the mute
mail you forward, terse notes, interest to be paid.

Little Yellow Jacket, Rotten Cotton, Slingblade.
When does wreckage begin? Your mother threw
your jar of marbles, your childhood's shining prize,

down the outhouse in an outburst of rage.
Mine said she wished I'd never been born. Were we
cradled with neglect? We had no wedding

photo, just a print of a red-faced sculpture
that amused us, a cowry-bedecked tribal couple stuck
in a dimestore frame. I wore a borrowed dress
before the judge that flouting, devil-may-care day.

Loose a bull from its pen, it corkscrews out into
the arena, snorts, contorts, tosses its shit-smeared rump
up into the air. We never spoke of the night

you came home drunk, with a swollen, blackened eye.
I was pregnant by then but I heard you cry, "Baby,
Baby, do you love me?" Had you staggered in,

tried others' doors? The car you would retrieve later
was left blocks away. Afraid to face you, silly,
I thought, of course I do, I sighed, never sensing
how much you needed, how much I denied.

Is this what the ancients tried: to master tons
of mean monster muscle, to worship the bull
from the sea, the power of surges and tides,

to contain its snorts and rolling eyes behind
a slatted grate until—(Say grind, rage, leather
strap; say no, your words were not a wall of fury)

it explodes—(Say no, I did not fling coins
in anger; say no, you did not sneer at me
or lie)—until it explodes outward with a tight-
jawed, bare-handed human clinging to its side.

Rotten Cotton, Slingblade, Blueberry Hill—
they storm out of the labyrinth of fences into
the whirlwind of shame. In the end that unbridled

drama was all we shared. I cheered Wiley Peterson—
Shoshone like you—hero of hanging on. I kept
a false face in the face of your pride and tried

like a clown to divert you, all the while clinging—
clinging still—as if to the brindled back
of Blueberry Hill—a love song I wanted to ride, hold,
however I could, to whatever would connect us.

Saint Luke's Garden, Hudson Street

The wind plays April here.
Bells and songbirds, all sway, all
open mouths, fling down glory
that cracks the earth, stirs
sun breath to slip between
these brick walls and nest
in magnolia virginiana, heart
of our contemplation. Praise
the silver underside of its leaves.

Who's here to learn nesting?
That sparrow tugs a clump of pale grass
twice his size, stiff relic of winter,
another pecks string off some rose canes,
and over there a wren plucks
at her own breast.
                        We five or six strangers,
each having found a half-concealed
bench, are silent. Maybe woolgathering,
lost in the anthem, heedless
of the offering plate.
                        Or kneeling inwardly
in silent cry. My body's a nest
for cancer. Green, green, flows around me.
Beaks open, and the wind shows silver.
Tomorrow's surgery will pluck
and bleed me of cells that spring
called back, that something in me
wanted just as much as these creamy blossoms
want light. Some green bell tolled and woke
what I thought dead.

I'm here
to learn all over what to ask for.
April floods the ear, confuses
breathing, but I know
this garden's mine, an hour's train ride
into city miracle of pomegranate,
fig, rosemary, walled by a church
two hundred years ago. All praise,
miracle of pawpaw, of Asian Pear,
fleur-de-lis, Cedar of Lebanon,
and rosa bracteata, "the mermaid."
Lists are steadying, but *laude*
harrows the whole mouth, delicate touch
of tongue back to the painful
throat howl. Wall and wind
muffle the traffic here. Tomorrow
I'll be on a highway south,
then flat-out loss, no time,
no breath, no mind.
      How can we live
closed and open? Tradition says
look to the sparrow.
      Tug, crack, fling,
I pray my shell and core,
petal and fuse. Tell me the moment
the mix is right. Whoever I am then
will squat down in herself and turn
and turn, shaping the nest again.

Exile

Her bones still hold her and so she lives in them, but my mother
misses the old world, meridian, noon's hot rum to loosen her limbs,
her tongue. She cannot carry the sharp sounds of this place

in her head long enough to say them. One day does not tether
to another, and stories gallop off without their bridles. The ground
is dangerous with fruit and so she gives up walking. Wherever

there is to go, it isn't here. There was once earth soft enough to let
her hands reach down to coax its sticky blooms. There were spices
to arrange from anise to basil, coriander to dill. There were voices

she went to in the night, a white logic of moonlight outlining shapes
she would point to and name. Now all the words are in this changed
language; someone places them, one by one, in her mouth and asks her

to give them back again. The customs here are strange, but she tries
to be gracious — opening when she is asked to open, moving
her hand across blank lines to conjure the name that is still hers.

An Elegy for the Hermetic Sea

Tonight,
amidst the black waves
moon
a whale's eye,
stars like silver fish
breathing in a mesh of tar
such is the wasteful hunt of a fisherman:
his tattered nets
hauled in the emptiness of all directions.

Jen Hoppa, photograph

Dogs in Guatemala

All the dogs in Guatemala are like this. It's what Laurie wants to tell her, this college sophomore crying in the street over yet another brutalized puppy, except she can't imagine a worse moment for explanations.

"Come on, Arabella." Laurie touches the girl's sharp-boned back. "We can't just hang around out here. Not in the dark."

But Arabella falls to her knees on the sidewalk, stretching tremulous fingertips toward the dog. Scuttling down the edge of this no-name park, the puppy is oblivious of them, his muzzle thrust inside an old bean can. There's no sound but the amplified banging of his can on the hard-packed dirt, his once-lush tail rustling behind him like a sullied white train. Cocker spaniel, most likely: one of the cuddly types the dog vendors specialize in. By day, they camp out in this park, middle-aged women who stand on the curb with crates of small wriggling dogs at their feet. Or they dangle a fat furry handful of cocker spaniel or poodle out over the street, as morning traffic grinds past. They make a couple of pups sit together on top of a high stack of boxes, so high the dogs can't jump down.

Every morning for two years, Laurie has seen this. Normally, after the sun's up—when it's safer—she walks out from the Peace Action house in Zona 1, Guatemala City's decrepit old heart, to buy the paper in Parque Central. She reads it aloud to her teammates, though they've all come to Guatemala to stay and are no longer shocked by the news: University students kidnapped as they step off their campus, a leading journalist's house set on fire, a judge on the Constitutional Court shot through the head in his driveway. Reporting these matters—or teaching them to students like Arabella, who come on brief learning tours—is Laurie's job. *Here's what happened, and how, and to whom.* The follow-up question must be, *What can we do about it?* It keeps the bad news just bearable.

Explanations are Laurie's strong suit, part of her work. But the dog hawkers don't fit into any Peace Action report or lecture to visiting students. They are one of those things she sees but tries not to see. Most days, however, she still thinks of the dogs, how they quiver together on their wobbly box towers, stranded in air.

Now here, before sunrise, is one of their lot—a stray?—snuffling among the day-old tabloids and empty Tortrix bags that litter the park, and nobody else is around. Only Laurie, who wants to keep moving, and this teary twenty-year-old who won't listen to her.

"I can't leave you out here alone." Laurie tries to keep the apprehension out of her voice.

It's the end of the third decade of war, the tenth year of the Army's scorched-earth campaign. They have burned whole towns to the ground, with people in them. *Draining the ocean to get rid of certain fish,* as one general put it. The Army's death squads patrol these streets every night, their black Chevy vans with dark-tinted windows hunting down writers, union leaders, students: anyone who might still support the guerrilla.

"Poor puppy, can't we help him?" Arabella wails from the pavement. "He must be lost."

Ten minutes earlier, Laurie showed up at the guesthouse where the visitors in her charge are staying, to share early breakfast with them. But the first thing the other kids told her was that Arabella had left for a jog. "*What?*" Laurie said. "Who let her do that?" She banged out the front door before it shut behind her, and didn't stop running till she saw the pony-tailed figure in a silver-gray Gore-Tex tracksuit, on her knees at the edge of the park.

"Arabella. We can't do anything for him. We need to get in off the street."

The dog shakes the can loose and notices them. His forelock is matted, his jowl smeared with beans. He cowers and whines, then shrinks away into the park, and Laurie's chest tightens with pity. She could pick him up in one sweep, zip him into the front of her sweatshirt.

The dog's retreat seems to unlock Arabella. "Oh my *god,*" she breathes and, before Laurie can stop her, hastens after him into the darkness. The park's trees close around her and blot out the shine of her tracksuit.

Squinting after her, Laurie hesitates on the sidewalk. "Give me a fucking *break.*"

Normally she wouldn't enjoy being out in Zona 1 at quarter till six; normally she'd walk fast and hold onto her Mace or her knife. But today she ran after Arabella with nothing at all in her hands, nothing in her head but the notion of bringing her back. And the guilty image she's pushed down this past hour won't leave her alone any longer: an image of the man who secretly slept last night in her house. A guerrilla, who arrived after supper, bedded down on the spare cot, and slipped out before dawn, before she did. Laurie had said Yes to him, and endangered them all.

"He's on his way through," Ruben told her, when she answered his knock yesterday. "He needs a hiding place in the city just for tonight."

The skin beneath Ruben's eyes was pulled tight, pale as the color of scars. He'd come all the way from his human rights office in Zona 9—one of the city's new neighborhoods, wheeling out from the center like a graph of centrifugal force—to ask for this favor in person.

"Ruben, *no sé*," stammered Laurie. "We're here to do education, to work with civilians. We have to act like we're neutral."

"Please, *compañera*. We would do it ourselves, but—but we can't keep him this time." Ruben's voice sank to a whisper. "We think he's been seen at our place before."

"Bring him, then," Laurie said blindly. "Just for one night."

The guerrilla had not remained long. He came at nightfall, looking half-starved and strained in civilian clothing, borrowed khakis and a washed-out polo. He slept a few hours and left under cover of darkness, presumably looking the same. During his refuge with them, the man barely opened his mouth, and Laurie and her teammates, tense as he was, hadn't tried to make conversation.

Now the guerrilla won't stay quiet inside Laurie's mind; he keeps moving around just in back of her eyes. *Oh, please please be gone by now, please be out of the city again. Please have left without anyone knowing you stayed here with us.* She might as well be walking around with her skin peeled back from her bones, she feels so exposed this morning.

"Arabella," she calls. The girl's torso is a thin silver wedge, ten or twelve yards into the park. "Let that dog go, and get back here."

She can see, as if from a distance, how all of this looks: the moon scraping the roofs of the buildings behind them, throwing the last of its light on the backs of a dog and two foreign women, none of whom should be out at this hour. Laurie takes one step, then another, into the park. It's like wading into cold water. Arabella crouches in front of a park bench; the dog's eyes are two frightened glimmers beneath it. Laurie can feel the street sneering behind them.

"What were you thinking, coming out at this hour?"

"I needed to get *out*. To do something, you know, on my own."

"Well, you can't." This seems so self-evident, Laurie is blunt. She's supposed to be teaching—supposed to take care of—short-term visitors like Arabella, but she's clearly neglected to explain a few things.

Arabella wipes her nose with the back of her wrist and sinks to all fours, so as to get her head under the bench. Another thing Laurie's forgotten to explain is that Guatemalan men view parks as urinals.

"You *can't* just go out on your own," Laurie insists. "Not here. Not without one of us."

She hears the morning's first buses, a few blocks away, grind past the stops on Parque del Centenario. Though she can't see them from here, she knows how the passengers throng against the bus's bright windows like a Hydra in silhouette; before daybreak, drivers burn their interior lights, to fend off hijackers and thieves. Traveling in city buses is never a picnic, but Laurie envies those riders for the way they are inside, together. Marimba music drifts from an apartment window across the street.

Then she hears something else, a sound less expected—*Psst, psst*. A human voice, just behind her.

"*Grin-guiiitas.*"

Laurie spins on her heels, her skin prickling. The man sounds so close, she ought to detect his outline. But all she can see is the shifting penumbra of the park's furzy edge and behind it, the street, narrow as a tight-lipped mouth.

"*Váyanse a casa, gringas.*" Go home, gringas.

Surely this antagonist at the edge of the park is just another Guatemala City catcaller. Surely nobody's been watching *her* house.

"Better go home, *gringuitas*," sings the man in the dark. "We know you're up to no good."

Laurie's whole scalp seems to vibrate, like a cap that might leap off her head. But she balls her hands into fists; she points herself toward the man's voice.

"Fuck off," Laurie says. "Fuck you, and your mother, and fuck *off*."

Arabella withdraws her head from under the bench, her face a smudgy white thumbprint on the thick air. "What are you saying? What's going on?"

"Nothing," says Laurie. It's a mercy this girl speaks no Spanish. Laurie takes a final step forward and hauls her up by both elbows. She does not release her again until they're well out of the park and making for Casa San Juan, still three blocks away. As far as Laurie can tell, no one follows.

For the first block, Arabella keeps crying. "It's not fair, it's not fair. I *hate* how people treat their animals in this country."

She's tired, of course. She's overwhelmed. Laurie tries to recall how this feels. In another corner of her mind, she calculates how much longer she has to work with this group of students. Six days down, four more to go.

Helping North Americans to see Guatemala is how Peace Action describes their learning tours—to refugee camps on the Mexican border, through Guatemala City's orphan-filled slums—but for some people it is too much. There's always one, toward the end of their time with Peace Action, who ends up like Arabella: fixating on animal life. It's as if they give up, Laurie secretly thinks. They squeeze a week or ten days' accumulation of horror and grief onto these objects of suffering—the dogs or the cats—that still make some sense, whose pain is just small enough to imagine.

Even some of her Peace Action teammates, though they've lived here so long they all dream in Spanish, have started to weaken. Last month, Dean had to dash from the theater in the middle of watching *Platoon*, to throw up in the manicured bushes of Zona 10. And now Yvette won't leave the house after dark, not at all: not since she saw a death squad chase down a student outside Universidad de San Carlos.

"He froze when he saw them," Yvette kept saying, when she got home. "Like a deer in the fucking headlights. Just froze."

"You'd have to be crazy, reacting like that," Laurie said.

But Yvette slapped the table, open-handed, so hard Laurie started. "You don't know. You don't know what you'd do. If you try to fight them, those death squad guys just break your legs first. *Then* they can get you into their van."

"But you could *try* to run away, couldn't you?" Laurie snapped. She felt she'd been struck herself. Yvette was over-reacting.

The next day, however, when Yvette wouldn't get out of bed — not even to eat — Laurie tried praying again, a practice she thought she'd abandoned once and for all, along with her sorry-ass backwoods hometown.

"We ought to think about leaving," Yvette said, when she finally got up. "It's getting too dangerous here."

No, Laurie thinks now, hustling Arabella along the last blocks to the guesthouse. Joining Peace Action, she signed on for three years; they all did. She won't, she can't, back out now. No matter what Yvette says. *No.* You have to grow a new skin to live here; have to tell yourself, "My life in this country is going to be different." That's all.

All the dogs in Guatemala are like this. Laurie's neighbors downstairs, Silvia and Tomás, have a new dog, a Rottweiler; they unleash the dog in the foyer, whenever they leave, unshutter the window in their front door. When someone walks by within twenty feet, the dog hits that door like a cannonball. He dives — as far as his huge head will let him — through the window, eyes rolling, fangs bared, drool flying past the metal bars. He doesn't just bark; he roars. Adrenaline blazes through Laurie's veins every time. When he's not playing guard, the dog is kept locked, alone — Silvia and Tomás freely admit — in a small airless room in the basement.

Laurie pats Arabella on the back, where a reflective stripe glints, passing under this block's single streetlight. Then she lowers her gaze to the gutter that runs beside them, and for one long cold moment she feels her heart stop.

There's just enough light to tell that she sees this: a man in the gutter, sprawling face-up, a huge open welt where his throat used to be. His yellow shirt flushing with blood, from collar almost to belt. His eyes are still open, but open like the eyes of a fish boned and gutted and laid out on ice.

Oh my lord. Laurie sucks air in so hard, her sinuses burn. She staggers to a halt, her body choosing to do this before her mind catches up. She can't move; she can't feel her heartbeat. Then it comes back, a wild bird in her throat. *Oh my lord. Jesus Lord.* A dead man: She's sure of it now, though she won't look again.

A murdered man, in the same zona where Laurie lives with her teammates, practically at the doorstep of Casa San Juan, the guesthouse they use for their tours. It's true, dead bodies show up every day, at this hour, in this city—street kids by the municipal dump, activists in the gorge behind National Cemetery—but so far, not here. Not in her neighborhood. Laurie lurches forward again.

"What is it?" Arabella blinks like a sleepwalker jerked awake.

The man lies a few yards behind them; Laurie twists her back toward him, angling Arabella away; she makes them both walk faster. I can't let her see this, thinks Laurie, her first cogent thought since she saw what she saw in the gutter. But the image has stained her whole field of vision. His shirtfront was soaked, it shone in the streetlight.

Yellow shirt, yellow shirt still yellow along the waistline, above the line of his belt, yellow shirt turning black-red. Was *he* wearing a yellow shirt this morning? Bile stings Laurie's tongue; her stomach is empty, but something inside wants to come up. Has she just seen him, the clandestine soldier? Through her horror she tries to recall the man's face, tell who he might have been. But he was so covered in blood, all she saw of his face were the eyes. Dark brown, almond-shaped: the eyes of most Guatemalans.

The word Laurie has not said aloud in two years throbs in her brain. *Guerrilla, guerrilla.* If the guerrilla she harbored has had his throat slit, the same hour he stepped out her door, who's to say the Army's henchmen have not traced him back to her house? Who's to say they aren't stalking her now?

So this is it. This is how Laurie might die, on a street she knows well, before breakfast, taking an innocent bystander in a tracksuit down with her.

Because these might be her last conscious moments, she sees everything too clearly now—the crenellated roofline of the triple-X movie theater, a sheaf of bougainvillea bursting over the top of a wall: their outlines so sharp and hard, it's as if they've been razor-cut from cardstock and held up against floodlights. She's illuminated, too—she must be—she and Arabella alike, glaring in their shared strangeness. White women: one beginning, one ending, their twenties; Arabella shimmering in Gore-Tex, Laurie almost six feet tall. How could they be less than conspicuous? Anyone can find them, like this.

But then the old moviehouse, the wall with its cascade of flowers, slide past her, slowly, and she can still feel her heart in her head, pounding down her arms and her legs, can still feel Arabella's elbow inside one of her hands.

"You're hurting me," Arabella protests. She tries to shrug Laurie off. "What's wrong with you?"

Laurie shakes her head; she holds on even harder. Two blocks to go. One streetlight and then one more, faint green orbs against a black sky fading to smoggy brown: Morning. Laurie says nothing at all, down these last blocks, sees nothing save the blue fluorescent light seeping through a distant grilled window, clearer now with each step, that she knows to be Casa San Juan's.

❀ ❀ ❀

Laurie's friends at home worry about her. "Come back," they say when they call. Their letters end with a plaintive *Haven't you had enough yet?*

"You'll be back soon," Caleb predicted, when she left South Carolina. But Laurie's been proving him wrong, month by month for two years, till it's clear he was badly mistaken, that she'd known, after all, what she wanted—the risk and the rush, the adventure interknit with good-doing—and was getting it here, had made the right choice all along.

No one back home seems to grasp this. Even her old Spanish professor, when Laurie went to tell her goodbye, clutched Laurie hard by both wrists. "I'll picket and protest till I turn blue, up here. But going to Guatemala, these days? Not on your life." Doctora Nuñez tightened her grip. "You're either incredibly brave or you're out of your mind. Which is it?"

"Neither," Laurie said, believing this. "I just think it will feel—well, *worthwhile*, you know? Plus, it's got to be more exciting than teaching high school."

Her professor shook Laurie's arms like a loose pair of reins. "It must be all those damn cowboy movies. You white people think you're invincible."

Laurie had walked away flushed and resentful. Who was Doctora Nuñez to tell her she wasn't bright enough to be scared, or was too innocent to measure the danger?

❀ ❀ ❀

Stucco over cinderblock; one square, louvered window behind an ornate grid of bars: Casa San Juan looks like all the other buildings on Sexta Calle. Laurie leans on the buzzer until the housekeeper, Gregoria, slides open an eye-level panel in the door, as if the place were a speakeasy. Visitors give their names through this slot, to be checked against a list the guesthouse updates every day. But Gregoria knows Laurie by sight.

"*Adelante.*" She holds the front door ajar, her gaze scouring the street behind Laurie and Arabella.

"I need to make a phone call," says Laurie.

The telephone is black, rotary-dial, hanging in back of the kitchen. One shoulder against the cold wall, Laurie listens to the bleat on the other end of her phone line. *It's happening*, is all she can think. The worst thing, the thing she has dreaded.

"*¿A-ló?*" Yvette sounds drowsy, answering the phone.

"It's me," Laurie says. She can see, as if they were drawn on the cinderblock wall before her, the central images from her story, the news she needs to convey. But silence wells in her throat.

"Laurie? Is that you? What's going on?"

I saw a dead man—a murdered man—near our house this morning. It's not something one says out loud, not on the phone. Even inside their own house, she and her teammates evade certain words. "G" for *guerrilla*, "Smurfs" for *the cops*. But what do they call a dead body? Laurie mashes the teacup against her forehead, hoping to force out the right code word. Something about Edgar Allan Poe. Raven? *Ah.*

"I saw a—a blackbird this morning."

The line between Laurie and Yvette buzzes for one lengthy beat. Empty air. Except, most likely, not empty at all.

"Excuse me?"

"A blackbird. I saw a blackbird."

The repetition makes Laurie feel slightly insane. Then she hears or feels the meaning slam into Yvette.

"Holy Mother of God—"

It's too strong a response; they both know it. Laurie pictures some eavesdropping *oreja* in a dark government office jerking upright in his hard little chair.

"Not—not the G? Was it the G?" Yvette sounds muffled, like she's speaking through her hand clamped over her mouth.

The line crackles, a long hollow sound, and Laurie blinks, fighting tears. *Send me a sign*, she started to pray, a few months ago. *Show me I'm still doing the right thing here, not making any irrevocable mistakes.* And now it's happening, here it comes: just as she was daring to believe it never would.

"I don't know," Laurie says. "I couldn't see. It might have been."

"Oh holy Mother," whispers Yvette.

Laurie hears Yvette swallow; the *oreja* must hear it too. Only now can she see where this conversation might end. Downplay it, she thinks, play it down as far as you can. Laurie leans with her hairline pressed to the cinderblock, pushing until her skin burns. She concentrates on that pain, gathers herself around it.

"Listen. We can't jump to conclusions. In fact"—the lie appears in her mouth like it's been waiting for her all along—"in fact, I'm 99% sure it had nothing to do with us. Okay? I just wanted to tell you to stay put this morning. You and Dean both. And, uh, don't let anyone in. Just to be on the safe side."

"But—but—where was he? I mean, where was this? The blackbird."

In the gutter. Suddenly these verbal stratagems seem pathetic. Can't a well-trained *oreja* see—or hear—right through their code? *At the corner of Third Avenue and Ninth Street.* That's not any better, giving the coordinates over the phone.

"Listen. Yvette? I should tell you the details in person."

"Right, right, I'm sorry. What am I thinking? I can't think, I don't know what to think."

"Just breathe, okay? I'm sure we're fine." Laurie begins to believe this is true; already she's standing up straighter. "Try to get hold of yourself."

"But still—still we should *do* something—*tell* someone— shouldn't we?"

"Yvette. Right now you should get off the phone. You should, I don't know, go lie down." Laurie grimaces; it's the wrong thing to say to Yvette, of all people. "Or go do some *work*."

"But you're coming home now? I'll send Dean over, to walk you back here."

"No. *No.* For God's sake, it's only six blocks. I don't need that."

Laurie hangs up the phone harder than necessary. She heads for the front door again, rings for Gregoria to let her out. But here comes Arabella instead, changed into chinos and a bright Mayan vest from the city market, her face washed and avid.

"Just now, in the kitchen. I overheard you. You were reporting what you and I saw?"

Laurie cranes down the hallway, but Gregoria is nowhere in sight. "Something like that."

"We saw a puppy, though. Why did you keep saying *bird?*"

Laurie doesn't look at Arabella. She jiggles the doorknob instead.

"Don't you trust me?" asks Arabella. "Is it because I freaked out this morning?"

"It's not that," Laurie says. "That happens."

"Listen." Like a conspirator, Arabella leans closer. "I know there was something out there. I know you saw something. What was it?"

Her eyes are too dark, a brown moving toward black; Laurie sees again, superimposed on them, the eyes of that other—the man in the ditch—as the streetlight caught them, brown and wide with surprise. Laurie puts her fingertips to her temples; she pushes until bolts of pain shoot down both cheekbones.

"Why can't you cut me some slack?" Arabella insists. "I didn't travel this far to have someone cover my ears half the time. I didn't come here to be *protected*."

"That's not always a bad thing," Laurie says.

This, at least, is the truth. When someone broke into Tomás and Silvia's apartment last month and wrecked it—dashed cups and plates to the floor, split the sofa cushions with a machete—everyone in their building knew this was no random violence. Tomás, who works for a union, has received threats before; the break-in might have been one last warning. No one called the cops; the cops are as corrupt as—controlled by—the Army. The next day, however, the enraged Rottweiler showed up in the foyer.

Arabella scowls. "I came to Guatemala to *know* things."

Like a godsend, Gregoria rounds the hall corner, her ring of keys chiming. She hurries toward Laurie. "*Ai, perdón, señorita, perdón.* So sorry to keep you here waiting."

When the housekeeper clasps her elbow, Laurie realizes she must look as bad as she feels.

"*¿Cómo se encuentra?* Are you all right?" The gray-streaked top of Gregoria's head doesn't reach Laurie's shoulder, but she's trying to hold Laurie up. "When you went after the *jovencita*"—she cuts her eyes sideways at Arabella—"did something—happen out there?"

"Oh—" Laurie gropes for an answer. She can feel her bones shifting inside of her skin. "I saw a—we saw a—a lost dog in the park."

In a way, it's the truth: the part she's able to tell. She can still see the man's startled mouth above the raw wound of his neck. The weight of the real story, the one she'll leave out, pushes against the insides of her skull.

"Are you sure you're all right?"

"The dog made us feel sad," Laurie says weakly.

Gregoria nods, grim but unfazed. "You just sit here a minute. You should rest."

"Please, no," Laurie says. "I'll be fine."

Gregoria should not worry for her. Gregoria, who left her own hometown in the mountains six years ago, when all the rest of her family were slaughtered there in one morning.

"Well, take these, at least." Gregoria produces a small compact bundle, wrapped in a striped *servilleta*. "Tortillas. Still warm from breakfast. Your *estudiantes* didn't eat them."

"*De veras. Gringos* don't eat many tortillas."

"But you do. The *compañeros* in Peace Action do."

We're not your average *gringos*, thinks Laurie. "That's right," she says. "Thank you for these."

She looks past the tortillas to the housekeeper's vivid *huipil*, embroidered with blue and green birds, the way women from Gregoria's mountain town always make them. Perhaps this *huipil* is the one she put on that very last morning, not yet guessing what the day held.

"How do you do it?" Laurie blurts out. "How do you stand this?"

She'd bet a thousand *quetzales* Gregoria knows what she means. But Gregoria looks down and shakes her head slightly. She fits the bundle into Laurie's hand, folds Laurie's fingers around it.

"Hold onto this," she instructs, as if that's one possible answer, because there's no possible answer. And lets Laurie outside again.

At her feet, Sexta Calle lies deep in blue shadow; across the street, however, the tops of the buildings are slashed with pink light. Laurie inhales the morning: parched corn and woodsmoke from *elote* stands; a chemical whiff of the city dump, heating up; papaya and pineapple rinds shedding their distinctive fruit smells, putrescence and syrup. And underneath this torrent of odors, something else, something new, a fetor like mud and wet ink, like the smell of fish after you catch them. Laurie's free hand moves to her throat.

The guesthouse door clangs open behind her; Arabella stands, arms akimbo, inside the frame. "I know you're keeping secrets," she says.

Laurie says, "I don't think that's your business."

Arabella pursues her as far as the last step toward the street. Maybe she is one of the signs Laurie's seeking: an accusatory spirit in a red Mayan vest, come to tell Laurie she can't do much good here anymore.

"It just seems like you're picking and choosing what the rest of us do or don't know."

"Don't be silly," Laurie says, leaving her. "You don't always get to choose what you know."

❀ ❀ ❀

Laurie goes home a roundabout way: through the intersection where street kids juggle limes, past the corner of teenaged fire-eaters whose trick is washing their mouths out with lighter fluid first. On the next block she says *No thanks* but nods to the flower vendors who walk with arms stretched to hold paper cones full of roses, like the wings of birds spread to show their pied undersides. *Rosas, rosas, muy finas rosas.* Roses in all the colors of the top half of the rainbow.

Laurie walks without hurrying down the street lined with optical shops, then the *calle* of Chinese restaurants. On purpose she cuts through Parque Central, to see the kids who hang out at the taxi station. *¿Taxi? ¿Taxi?* they cry, each time Laurie crosses the plaza. *¿Le ayudo, señorita?* Need any help, ma'am, need a taxi? They seem to live for the purpose of hailing any passerby who might be on her way somewhere else.

At this hour of the day, as Guate comes alive, Laurie understands again why she lives here. Parts of this life still hold her in place, go on giving her pleasure. When someone asks what these are—as visitors do, once the rush of arrival wears off—what does she say? Semana Santa, for one: the whole decadent week. Fog on the Cuchumatanes. That time she and Yvette watched a sea turtle lay her eggs on the black sand at Monterrico. Lake Atitlán: That one's easy. Any place, really, on the Lake. The way people here take her into their homes so easily. The bus ride from Guate to Huehue, when she gets a seat by the window.

Maybe these are reasons enough to stay. They'd seemed an endless plenty, at first. Arriving, she'd felt brave and excited. Pleased with herself. No one back home knew what mattered; they talked of their cars and their shoes and cholesterol levels. They didn't know there was anything else.

At the corner of Séptima Avenida and Novena Calle, Laurie's feet drag to a standstill. There it is again: a trace of blood on the air. An hour ago, up this street, she saw the dead man. Had he seen her, too? She can't shake the feeling that he had stared back. His eyes were open; perhaps they had shifted inside their sockets. Even now she can see how the streetlight bounced off them, wetly. Laurie feels her thigh muscles go slack.

"*¿Señorita?* Are you unwell?"

She has collapsed on the front steps of Pizza City, a hole in the wall where she sometimes eats lunch. Pizza City's proprietress, broom in hand, stares down at Laurie.

"*Con permiso*, Doña Marta, I'm sorry." Laurie struggles back to her feet; the bundle of tortillas seems to weigh more than it should. "I guess I felt faint. I'm all right."

Another few minutes' walk, and she'll be home. Laurie wants to think only of this: deliberate, physical action. "Get a grip," she mutters aloud. Most of her time in Guatemala, she has held herself together quite firmly; she has believed in the work, in herself. In her own inviolability, to some degree, which has helped. But this morning she is coming to pieces.

Once upon a time I was falling in love, now I'm only falling apart. What was that song, and why does she know it? It's not music she'd ever own. Something from one of Caleb's albums, then: music to coax Laurie into a suggestible mood. "We should've warned you," she heard her mother confide once to Caleb. "That girl has a mind of her own." Her mother considered this dangerous. "Maybe, though, Caleb honey, you'll wear her down."

Glancing up now, Laurie sees Yvette walking toward her, gripping a red plastic dustpan. She holds it out at arm's length, as if it's a tray she must balance, the dustpan's brush laid flat across it. Yvette's been sweeping the steps of their apartment again. "It makes me feel like a Guatemalan housewife," Yvette has been known to explain. "Like I'm fitting into the landscape." It used to be one of her little jokes. Lately, though, Yvette's humor, like her step-sweeping routine, has grown erratic.

Laurie eyes the dustpan with hope. "Feeling better?"

But up close, she sees Yvette's pinched mouth, her bloodless face under the suntan. With her unoccupied hand Yvette grabs Laurie's wrist.

"Come with me."

She hustles Laurie back toward Pizza City, then right in the door. Together they dodge tables of Zona 1 office workers eating breakfast, step over the resident black cat who prowls the floor eating scraps. They're heading for the back, for the bathroom, and Laurie begins to guess why. There are things they can't discuss in the Peace Action house: things someone could hear through the walls. Nothing in their house absorbs sound; it's all cement and rebar and tile.

What now? Laurie holds back the question as she and Yvette duck past Doña Marta, producing self-exculpating smiles—*Con permiso; ya regresamos*—and swing open the bathroom door. Every year there are a half-dozen kittens growing up somehow, back there, since the room opens out, past the toilet, onto a small weedy back lot. The kittens meet you as you unlatch the door. This morning they pop up at the threshold, only to scatter like leaves on the wind as Laurie and Yvette whirl in.

Enveloped in the tang of Pine-Sol and damp cinderblock, Laurie watches Yvette slide the door's rusty bolt, holding the dust-pan perpendicular to her chest.

Yvette's gaze lights on Laurie's own unusual cargo. "What's that?"

"Tortillas. From Casa San Juan."

As if in response, Yvette gives her dustpan a brief nervous shake; something rattles against its hard plastic sides.

"What's *that?*" Laurie asks.

"Ah," says Yvette, and then doesn't say anything else. In-stead she lowers the dustpan, extends it so Laurie can see, and lifts the brush off what it's hiding.

Teeth. Human teeth? Five—no, six of them. Teeth, all by themselves. For a single humming second Laurie can't make sense of this. Then she stumbles away from the sight. She bumps into the sink, something mercifully solid.

"I just went down to sweep the front steps, and there they were." Yvette's voice is flat, her gaze stuck to the dustpan, as if she hasn't quite seen these teeth until now. "They were arranged. In a little half-circle. A little half-moon."

"No," Laurie hears herself say. "*No.*" She wants to retreat in time thirty seconds, choose a different revelation.

"Molars, mostly. Although I think that one's an incisor." Yvette pokes it with the end of the brush.

Underneath the sight of six teeth in a red plastic dustpan, Laurie feels something else, a new calm in Yvette—a bright brittle hardness like the edge of something just freezing. How can this be? How can *any* of it be? Dry and square, the teeth are light yellow, their roots brown and jagged. By themselves, they seem small, too dirty. They look obscene. They belong to someone, should be inside someone's head. What has she done to summon such evil to her door?

"It's a threat," says Yvette. "Someone threatening us. Isn't it."

"It happens," Laurie whispers. But so far, only to others. "You don't know they're for *us*," she adds, somewhat hoarsely. "We're not the only ones who live in that building."

"You mean, it's like getting someone else's mail by mistake?" Yvette shifts the dustpan from one hand to another; sliding across the pan's bottom, the teeth make a sizzling noise. "Well, *there's* one cultural sensitivity issue they didn't address in our training."

"God, Yvette. This is no time to joke."

"I know it's no joke. Believe me. The Army wants us gone? I'm gone. I'm outta here."

Now Laurie recognizes it: the cold, crystalline weight bearing down, flattening out, Yvette's voice and demeanor. This, too, is something that happens: once you've come through a hard decision, once you've made up your mind for good.

"No," Laurie says. "That can't be right."

"Not right? You think they're for Silvia and Tomás, instead?"

"They could be. As likely for them as for us."

For the first time since they entered the bathroom, Yvette looks at Laurie. "Except," she says, her voice dropping lower. "Except they didn't just have a G spend the night at their house."

Laurie is falling again; her spine clouts the wall, the tortillas crushed to the front of her sweatshirt. Yesterday, when Ruben showed up with his urgent request, she hadn't asked how he knew his own house was less safe for harboring guerrilla than theirs. Maybe Ruben understood then what Laurie is just starting to: No matter what thoughts fly through your mind, when you find a half-circle of human teeth at your door—no matter if you respond with revulsion or pity—the impression that lingers is, *It might be me, next time.*

"It's time to stop fooling ourselves," says Yvette. "I'm buying a plane ticket back home. Buying it today."

"No," Laurie whispers. "Please, no. Just a minute."

But they are on borrowed time, locked inside Pizza City's only bathroom. Someone is jostling the lock. Gingerly holding the dustpan behind her, Yvette moves to open the door.

"No," Laurie repeats. She lunges after Yvette; she thrusts out a hand, catching the edge of the dustpan. *"Espérese un momento, por fa',"* she calls toward the door. Through clenched jaws she says to Yvette, "Just please fucking wait one minute."

Laurie scans the space behind them, seeking she doesn't know what. Despite its astringent bouquet of cleansers, Pizza City's bathroom is partly jungle; beyond sink and toilet, the floor drops off into dirt, and the roof ends. It's as if the builders of this room tired of pouring cement and ran out of the corrugated tin used for roofing at the same time. The result is this odd slice of land, unused, wedged between the john and the back of some-one else's building, overgrown with birds of paradise and banana trees—plants that will spring up on their own, anywhere.

"What?" Yvette says. "Make up your mind."

They are holding the dustpan between them, and Laurie forces herself to look in it again. Man or woman? Chosen for hav-ing done what? The teeth seem to demand a response.

"We should bury them," Laurie decides.

She squats at the edge of the bathroom's tiny back lot, bal-ancing the *bulto* of tortillas on her thighs. With her nails she digs out a hole at the base of a yard-high banana sapling. In another year, the tree will be two or three times as tall; its roots will spread out and embrace the teeth, protect them down there in the dirt.

"You'll get rid of the evidence," murmurs Yvette.

But Laurie keeps digging. The ground is hard on the surface, bruising the pads of her fingers, but inches down it gives way, coming up in damp loamy clumps.

"Evidence?"

"If we're all leaving Guate, the thing to do, just before we get on the plane, is hand these things over to—someone. So they could make a report. Go after the perpetrators."

"*Someone*? *They*? Who do you think would do it?" Laurie hears it in her own voice, too: a steely unflappability that says you're past all debating.

Even now, they both speak under their breaths. The diners close to this thin metal door are surely aware of as much. What kind of people run into a public bathroom and whisper together? People generally up to no good. Someone outside rattles the door once again.

"*Un momento*," shouts Laurie. She gropes for the dustpan. "It's the right thing to do."

"I don't know," Yvette mutters. But she hands the pan over.

Laurie pours the teeth into the hole that she's made. They crowd and click against one another and spatter into the earth; down there, they look harmless, like pebbles. "I do know," she says. "I know."

She scoops the dirt, gritty and cool, back into place; she tamps it down with her fingers. There. She thinks of saying a few words over the teeth—some sort of prayer? *I know. I know.* The words beat in her head. She doesn't have any others. The person outside is banging now with his knuckles; the door jangles and skips in its frame.

"*Ya vamos*," calls Laurie. "Okay, already." They have run out of time.

She and Yvette buy Cokes from Doña Marta, repayment for the use of her bathroom, but in the street, they set them down by a couple of sleepy adolescent glue-sniffers. They drift among small fleets of schoolgirls in kneesocks and kilts, heading to class, some holding hands the way girls back at home seldom do.

Laurie's mind stays on what she's just buried. She will always know where those teeth are; she will always see the man in the gutter. "You don't always choose what you know," she told Arabella an hour ago, outside Casa San Juan. But she'd heard the word, "Bullshit," as she walked away: Arabella's challenge, thrown at her back. Maybe at home—where you can flick the evening news on and off at a whim, watch the world's miseries from your futon—Laurie would take her point. Maybe, in that world, Arabella is right. Arabella, who is luckier and unluckier than she understands.

With her free hand, Laurie reaches to hold onto Yvette's. At first, Yvette stares; then she shoves the dustpan under one arm and reaches back. For the last block to their house, they walk with linked fingers, their arms in a tight V between them, like two Guatemalan schoolgirls.

"We'll be all right," Yvette says. "Now that we'll be home again soon."

Home, Laurie thinks. She can see the living room in her old apartment, the television set and the futon—see Caleb stretched out beside her, remote control in his hand, clicking through channels. *Go home*, the teeth tell her. But what part of home does she want anymore?

On the steps of their building, Laurie looks up. The second-story windows slant open, their panes yellow with light. Music from her own Sting album drifts down to the street. *¿Por qué están aquí, danzando solas? ¿Por qué hay tristeza en sus miradas?* It's one of the songs that moved her, two years ago, that sent her headlong into Latin America. Sting's Spanish sounded off, but Laurie respected the effort. *Why are these women here, dancing all alone? Why is there this sadness in their eyes?* It was as good a place as any for an outsider to start: with a question, and then another.

When she left South Carolina to come here, her mother had sighed, "I hope you get that wanderlust out of your system." "You'd better," Caleb added. He was somewhat less dismissive of Laurie's intentions. "I'm worried about you, you know. Worried you'll get yourself hurt."

From the Peace Action apartment above Laurie's head, the song keeps unspooling; its words sift through the air like the aftermath of a dream. Then Yvette fits her key into their building's front door, and Tomás and Silvia's dog bursts into his outraged-lion act. *RrrooOOOWWWRRR!* It drowns out all other sounds.

"God." Yvette twists her key in the lock. "Brace yourself."

But Laurie stands where she is and lets it hit her. In this space between the gutter and her doorway, she listens to the roar, and beneath it the wild kennel of her own heart, clamoring and thrashing like all frightened things. Gregoria's tortillas, hugged to her chest, have the weight and density—and almost, she thinks, the warmth—of a very small living creature.

M. Teresa Valero, from *The Levant: Lebanon and Syria Through Western Eyes*, photograph

Tikal

We climbed Temple IV
and leaned against the ancient
stone and watched the dark list from tree
to tree, the silhouettes of other towers
climbing towards the idea of the stars
as the stars floated deeper into
the sky's dark well, and we were cold
but knew this was something we could suffer,
and as the sun began to stain the dark
it happened suddenly, one hollow howl,
long and light, like metal being scraped
by metal, then the return of other calls,
howler monkeys opening the door
into another time.
                    It was easy
to get there, to imagine Mayan
life a thousand years before when
so much was still being learned
and their temples
were compass and map, star
charts and calendars of sun and moon.

And then a camera flash and electric whir,
the distrust of memory and desire for proof
splitting the moment open and making
it nothing less or more than ordinary. A bunch
of tourists with bottled water and sunburned skin
breathing the cool damp air, leaning back
into stone slabs, wondering if anything
was happening. If this was what it felt like
to be transformed.

Finco Paraiso, Guatemala

Even in paradise we didn't
trust the locals, we left
one person with the bags
while the water fell hot
from the sulfur spring over
the mushroomed rocks &
the cold river below
was clear & kept between
jungled walls & our time
was like this—always between
the hot & the cold &
never really a part of either.

The Second Third

for Jason, Matt, and Ryan

Since I left you, tromping puddled sidewalks
    trying to stomp our ontological "IT" out of Danville's introspective cement
    carrying on to where town ended without grace in railhead hinterland
    walking elsewhere now & muttering to myself as if the shadow behind me
    listened as you listened, hearing your voice in the creak of pedestrian shoes
I have seen some of the sights then dreamily supposed by conversational sketches
    bequeathed forever in secret ink to the stranded walls of school buildings
    and businesses

I have seen—

the all-night insect light & speedball buses rushing loose in the main vein
    of Mexico
the jungles vaporizing green, bloody-staired ruins on a cliff, beaches depressed
    w/ sand and underground rivers of Yucatan
the bridges, gypsy wax museums, parks trimmed in parsley, tea-puckered nostrils
    water-warped books browned & abandoned on benches at Piccadilly Circus
    clockwork pigeons, reveille escalators, and Ripper Walks to Ten Bells
    then riverside coupled along the wrung shroud of London
the salons & cafes, milling galleries, metal bone towers, firefly sky of flashbulbs
    above the Arc, thin alley vistas, compact cars which cut & corner over cobblestone
    cubist cityscapes near swept piles of Nazi dust, shepherds on leashes of *savoir-faire*
    and graves spray-painted w/ beastly red-grit appellations for god
    in the cemeteries of Paris
the spare apartments, songs in Dumpsters, last-call dives, courthouses & constipated
    psychologists, pinch of hetero-sex in bucket seats & whispered park hill penumbras
    of manly love, flashing barricades, broken sapling boulevards, fire-pokers & muskets
    strolls in mud made holy by Chernobyl glow of homegrown stash, & the ghostly
    shadow-grip of fingers bygone cast against a mushroom-pink motel & beneath
    lost trestles of the devil train in Louisville
the girls of Louisville, porch doors gone slam in Richmond, strapless shoulders of
    Lexington courtyard, Indianapolis parking lots laid for love in allotted spaces
    skinny-dip pools public or private where played waists upward in moonlight bare
    what may have been mermaids beneath the water; & later, on peninsula shore
    cream skirts espied at dusk followed hopelessly from crab-shacks in Destin.
And who could have conceived the great crisscross of roads spread over the continent

like screen on a green window—American highways, some sunning themselves
south straight through Georgia, others having leaked northwest before coming of
Great Plains winter: farm equipment frozen in gentle deep-freeze of white groves
tumbleweeds held in fences like giant vascular snowflakes—traveling in twenty-foot
trucks where each weary driver is sung softly along by the Kansas kettle-whistle of
wind & tires' goodbye hiss
Colorado. It's in Colorado now—
at home in easy yawning mouth of the west w/ its pool halls, ale, wanderlust crafts
contortionists & poor street magicians, elk & coyote, eagle & stone perch of ram
and everywhere in town girls wonderfully tall as if conceived by the spume
of mountain water cascading from falls into their beautiful mothers—
the ghosts of old Denver Five Points beatniks hearing all they want of jazz
and there are incomprehensible parks here w/ roads 12,000 feet high & no guardrails
just a harum-scarum view of wood crosses at the curve set blinding by argentine
reflected sun on thaw of snowdrifts plowed aside, calling forth in end-all flash
tipsy tears, trembling skids, and emboldened by last thought reenactment of those
dead—sure to have been young also—no brakes
and there are fewer churches or bumper-sticker chiliasm caveats
and it seems everyone is outdoors toting tents or skating campus rails
biking w/ whizzing spokes down dirt paths, or on blankets lying out
reading Kerouac in the grass
But most of all, more than any repeatable thing, the figure of drama is clipped by
distance here conveniently away from the discord of home, & contagious memory
of discord, & the Mason-Dixon lynch-mob of mothers who hang their sons w/
apron strings or beat them to death w/ a rolling pin in sad whiteouts of flour
and Old Man Time, that life-sentence cellmate who always held his shiv to my throat
has eased up & we're puffing peace-pipes, sitting around gesturing & writing together
awake most days before the sun, who often beds down in a screwdriver haze
touches the sky.

Since I left, that lame gray Danville sidewalk has stretched into many things
and I have thought of you, wished you along, confiding thoughts to tabletops instead
counters & chairs; writing in notebooks rebound w/ black tape, on receipts, envelopes
cocktail napkins & hotel stationeries—notching marks, burying tokens—saying all
otherwise untellable.

Darren Dirksen, *Time (4-Way Stop, Muskogee County, OK)*,
oil on panel, 42" x 42"

On a Visit Home to Buenos Aires, I Ask My Mother Whereabouts in Emilia-Romagna —Italy—Her Grandparents Came from

I
She says call Uncle Julio,
he'll be the one to know,
but Julio's mind is wrapped
around what to do about the family
vault, in the cemetery of the forever
middle-classed; who to will
the scrolled iron key to—once he is gone.
No one wants to deal with the small catastrophes
of hail the size of grapefruits smashing
the little windows through which
our dead peek and watch
the polluted seasons of Buenos Aires.

Moreover, Julio adds,
the 99-year lease has expired
and the cemetery wants money or
its little house back—crumbling cement,
the unbearable mustiness, three flights
of stairs down to rooms furnished
with the hard beds where the coffins sleep.

II
Uncle Julio who looks like Uncle
Enrique who looks like Roque and Rafael
who looks like Aunt Ani who mirrors Mom,
all nosed with eagle beaks, hair straighter
than an old Roman road, not one

as wrinkled as Great Uncle Emilio but
give them time. All meant to last long,
clinging to their teeth, eyes buried
under plies of crow's feet.

III
Questions about emptying the vault:

what to do about, say, Antonio and Esther,
whose own two daughters are dead, how to track
down elusive cousins to present them
with reductions to ash, small urns
carrying a kilo of bone brittle.

Or Emilio himself, passed away at a thousand or so,
obdurately single, who of us will take
wrinkled Great Uncle Emilio under
our reluctant wing, burn him, find him
an unmoveable place of rest. Who will claim

Great Aunt Assunta, married
for exactly one day before she left
that never-described sinner—the day-old
husband—and went home to pray,
and pray, and pray, her room
under the perpetual fog
of candles she burned to the saints.

IV
When Julio says, "Ravenna!"
I believe it's another Italian curse, but

no, he says, "Ravenna!" and
I see the place where Dante

died of the wide ache of exile;
somehow I know this is not right,

not Ravenna where the old *abuelos*
came from, too lofty for the kind

of amiable peasants who'd become
grocers in the New World, who,

at night, made children joyously,
as if following an ancient recipe.

"Ravenna . . . " says Julio, cupolas
covered in gilded mosaics of flat Christs,

flat Madonnas, Ravenna, says Julio
walking through the skinny roads

that separate the houses of the dead,
where it is moving day for our departed:

how will I leave this place with three urns
under my arm, grandparents, infant uncle,

will I have to take a taxi or can I hop
on the #44 bus and walk the rest of the way,

me and them, our little family procession,
will I keep singing, "Ravenna, Ravenna . . ."

as a dirge to them, especially the little one,
the boy my Mother was conceived to replace.

This garage sale of relatives, we the dour
and uncomfortable, live ones, who resent

the siblings who sent us here to collect
rotten coffins and metal containers

of whom we don't remember, the ones
that came from a mythic Ravenna,

the ones who now have to be placed
somewhere as we leave Uncle Julio

to gather all the lost, unclaimed *muertos*
who had once come to dinner and would tell

Julio about the lime-white dawns of Ravenna,
the honest truth of what never happened. Ever.

Anne Thompson, photograph

My Last Memory of My Father, 1989

He went out at dawn,
a shotgun slung over one shoulder, knife in hand,
and, waking to the clap of the screen door,
I watched from my window as he walked away,
fixing my eyes on the deep green of his flannel shirt,
knowing how it smelled, like oak and sleep,
when I pressed my face against him.
Perhaps it was the steadfastness of that scent,
or the thought, not wholly unfounded,
that once out of sight, he would never come back,
but something inside me for the first time struck open,
and with those early, clouded rays angled upon my face,
I crawled out the window, and barefoot,
oblivious in a pink nightgown, followed him.
I ran along our bog, red with fruit,
through a field of grass grown taller than I was,
and down the rutted path through the woods,
where suddenly and finally he stopped.
I stood close behind, excited and a little unsure
of just how far I had come in his footsteps,
and I almost allowed myself to call out to him,
except something about the crease of his mouth
at that moment silenced me. The thin sound
of brushed leaves drew my eyes instead
toward a young doe, standing smooth and unmoving
on the path ahead. He lifted his gun, took aim.
It was midsummer, two weeks before my birthday,
my mother had already bought candy to put in the piñata,
and at that moment in the woods I closed my eyes,
imagined everything turning, turning,
imagined the doe made of pink and blue papier-mâché,
imagined the world falling down around me
was nothing but sugar and ribbons and rainbows.

River

It's not that I imagined making love to a river,
to the three cold peaks of Illimani
and the waters that flow from the city,
down, down to the valley where you were born,
but I may have gotten carried away
once or twice, looking out
your bedroom window at that mountain.

You first took me to your village in mid-December,
and while we ran off behind the abandoned chapel,
your mother beheaded her fattest hen in my honor,
hung it by its feet over a tin pan in the courtyard.
Before dinner, you held me quick in the cusp of your arm,
swirled me through eddies of white feathers.
Is this what snow is like? you asked.

I did not love you so much
as the rise and fall of your voice when you would say *mi vida*.
I liked the thought of it—your life,
the wool cloth your mother carried you in as a baby.
Once, I wrapped your nephew in that cloth,
tied him to my back the way Bolivian women do,
and stood before the mirror, imagining he was mine.

On Sunday, your mother brought me to church,
dressed me up like a dream she had before you were born,
in shining silver sandals and that low-slung
blue dress she bought twenty-five years before.
As the only guest, and an American, I sat in the front pew,
so close I could feel the air brush against my bare thigh
each time the priest swung his heavy, vested arm.

That night I let you make love to me
hard against the dresser.
I remember the moon was full against Illimani,
its snowcaps reflected back the blue
of an unbeating heart, and I thought nothing
was ever so brazen, so beautiful
as that moon and that mountain repelling each other.

Losing La Paz, June 2005

At an international call center on the corner of Sargánaga and Loza,
I have my mother on the other end, and I'm not telling the truth.
I'm staying out of principle. The Bolivian people
don't have five a.m. government flights to whisk them away from here.
Outside there is the incessant, childlike pop of rubber bullets.
I hold my hand over the receiver so she won't hear.
But when tear gas curls itself under the glass walls around me,
there's no covering up anymore. *Are you crying?*
I think you should come home. Mom, I'll call in a couple weeks,
my only answer. *Once the president is overturned, I'll be fine.*

Out on the street, I force my way through the crowd
that has filled Plaza San Francisco for seven days.
They come from as far as Huachacalla on foot, wool *aguayos* full
of babies and fruit on their backs. Their cheeks are stained
the violent purple of open *altiplano* wind,
and they look me in the eye as I walk past, as a horse does
when you put your palm to its neck, not allowing you to relax.
Once I near Peréz Velasco, I can't breathe. It must be the thin air,
the tear gas, these thousands of people, my mother's voice. It must be
the sadness, like thick jute rope, of needing something so much.

That afternoon, my boyfriend had boiled pasta for lunch,
cut up *ají* peppers for the sauce, and told me of the meals his mother made
back in that red clay valley on the Argentine border.
I observed the angle of his jaw, the arc of his tongue
as he ate those peppers whole, a sword-swallower
trained in the art of self-preservation. And I laughed
at stories of him and his sister hiding in the garden until dark,
daring each other to eat *ají* until even their nostrils went numb.
But with one mouthful, fat tears were coming fast down my face,
and tentatively, as if I would break, he moved the plate away.

At a dusty, outskirts school in the mornings, I teach the nuances
of Spanish to young Aymara children who, for this miraculous moment in time,
cannot mouth the word *indígena*. But that morning, Karem, the boldest
of them all, had put forward one hand, placed it flat against my head

in small defiance. *Does everyone in your village have hair like that?*
Now, surrounded by these people who may be her parents,
holding on for dear life to a country they can't keep,
I can feel her fingertips, the muscles tightening in my neck.
I can feel each strand too easily separating from the next,
the weakest of them breaking off under the pressure of her palm.

Juan Franco, photograph

Down to the Last Kopek

On the day the ruble crashed, Sveta and I took the #7 bus to Moscow's Central Market to buy an egg. Back then, that's the way you bought eggs in a Russian produce market, not by the dozen, but one at a time.

The following August, Gorbachev would be under house arrest at his vacation dacha. Yeltsin, suddenly beloved, would clamber up a tank and silence the guns firing upon the White House. A new Russia would rise from the rubble of the imploded Soviet empire. But the autumn I was in Moscow, scouring the city for eggs, the Russians still had a long winter ahead of them. Future freedom felt like fear, not hope.

Sveta was dead set against going to Central, the best stocked of the Moscow markets. Central's vendors weren't babushkas and the farm boys they bossed around, but tough guys from Down South trafficking in good food and black money, more mafia thugs than tillers of the land. Since I'd arrived in Moscow, there had been one shooting death there and any number of reports of gunplay. I'd never consider going in without Sveta, but it had been a hard sell at the bus stop, in the chill November wind, to persuade her to take me. She was still protesting as the #7, drooping on deflated tires, rattled to a stop in front of my apartment building.

"Today is simply not a good day to shop," she insisted yet again. Her narrow eyes submerged briefly in a cloud of asphalt-tinted exhaust.

"Maybe it is," I argued. "Who'll be out spending money?" The Kremlin had opened that morning's commerce with another currency devaluation, part of a bumpy strategy to coax the ruble into the global exchange. On top of triple-digit, fast-spiraling inflation, by midmorning the ruble had lost so much value state banks were refusing customers at the door.

"People might not come out to spend money."

"I need those eggs, you know I do. Just think how short the lines will be. We'll be in and out in no time."

Sveta frowned at my hopeless naiveté. "It has to be eggs?" she asked for the hundredth time that week.

It had to be eggs, and fast. My dinner for the journalist next door, and a bunch of her friends, was beginning in a few hours. She'd invited herself over, really. The writer knew I loved Pushkin's poems. Her friends would bring poetry and vodka. What could I say? But conjuring up a meal for ten in those lean times was a magician's feat. Meat had disappeared entirely from desiccated state stores, hijacked to the black market. Then my stove crapped out, and I couldn't get the landlord to so much as whiff the astringent odor of gas leaking from the pilot. I had nothing to cook and no means to cook it. I decided to tell my neighbor our salon was off. When I stopped her in the hall, however, she pressed her fingers to my lips and pulled me into a cove at the end of the hall. Whispering, she told me she'd been fired for investigating Yeltsin's recent car crash. I'd read about it, of course. Medics had rushed to the scene to find the smashed sedan and bloodied bodyguards, but not Yeltsin himself. When he resurfaced three days later, dazed and wandering alone in an alley miles from the crash site, he refused to explain what happened. The article I'd read implied he'd gone on another bender. My new writer friend had tried to find out the truth, whatever that was.

"But doesn't the Kremlin want to discredit Yeltsin?" I asked her. She shushed me again. I saw then the shift in her fear, from those in power to those who would soon win it. You could tell by that fear who was really in charge.

After hearing she'd been sacked with no hope of future employment as a journalist, I couldn't very well cancel dinner on her. I had a hot plate. I could scramble eggs, at least, serve them with malted black bread. It would have to do.

To prepare even this spare supper I had to gather eggs one at a time from markets all across Moscow, unless I wanted to buy a whole dozen all together for a small fortune at the joint-venture supermarket. Which I didn't. I detested the Western-currency-only shops, with glaring white-tiled aisles and listing columns of shelves crammed full of the same soulless merchandise that overwhelmed me in superstores back in the States. So all that past week, while the ruble's value fluctuated so wildly that prices changed every hour and you never really knew what anything would cost, Sveta and I rode overstuffed buses to all the markets in Moscow. I'd managed to procure all of nine eggs that way. Dangerous or not, Central Market was my last option. Sveta, thank God, would do the haggling for me, and wouldn't be intimidated one bit by those menacing farmer-gangsters. She would get the job done despite the fact I wouldn't invite her to dinner.

I couldn't, knowing who she was.

"Of course. It has to be eggs." For a moment, as her gaze flickered to the soot-stained bus doors wheezing open to admit us, I thought she would refuse to get on, but with a small sigh she followed me up the steps.

There was certainly no pulse of unrest on the overcrowded bus. Elderly women bundled in heavy woolen scarves and unemployed men stripped of shaves and hope slumped tiredly in their seats or slouched against the poles; somber and solitary, just like any other weekday. As we pushed our way to the bus's articulated midsection, where one seat was open, I turned to give her a thumbs-up. She ignored both my thumb and my cheerful grin. When I offered her the seat, she shook her head. No matter how often I insisted she be the one to sit, she always refused. Part of keeping tabs on me, apparently, was to put my comfort before hers. I shrugged and sat down. Sveta stood rigidly in the aisle, grasping an overhead strap as the bus peeled across five lanes of dense traffic to take a sharp turn.

"We should go to the hard currency store for your eggs," Sveta said to me. "I think Central will be volatile."

I winced at the mention of hard-currency in her formal English clip and the glances it attracted from the other passengers. I had learned how to blend with Moscow by dressing down—beater boots, heavy black polyester overcoat, a traditional Russian fur cap made of cat, not mink—but in public Sveta liked to give me away. She claimed she wanted to practice her English, and in fairness to her, the only Russian I spoke without flubbing was "Pleased to meet you" and "Forgive me," but I had the sense that she liked the attention I attracted.

"'Crowded,' I think you mean," I corrected.

"No, I quite meant to say 'volatile.' If we depart at the next stop, we can board the trolley and attend a proper supermarket."

"Not 'attend.' 'Go to,' or 'shop at'," I said automatically.

"For me, 'attend' is more precise." She smiled, a fatigued flattening of her lips. Her verbal correctness was matched by her formal bearing. She liked to dress in tweed skirts and linen tops, even now when the first blast of winter had plunged the air temperature below zero. Her short hair was frizzy, chafed by a succession of harsh perms. Curiously, she reeked of maple syrup, although I hadn't seen a pancake anywhere in Moscow. That odd sweet odor announced her when she first knocked on my door with some story about the building welcoming committee reaching out to foreign guests, and would I like an escort for the new Futurism exhibit at the Museum of Modern Art? It didn't take me long to learn she didn't even live in the building. After our first week of daily excursions, when I didn't avoid her or ask pointed questions, she abandoned the subterfuge of hesitating at the door of a ground floor apartment while I climbed the stairs to mine. From then on, I was never without her. She kept up a running commentary on all we saw, corrected me patiently with a gentle explanation if I unwittingly offended a babushka or ordered beets instead of ice cream at a restaurant. She could quote Pushkin fluently, any poem I threw her way.

We never discussed politics, or money, or who we really were.

She was consummately polite. The only glimmer of impatience I ever caught, when I made an error she deemed intentional—a graceless flash of temper I couldn't help when I was tired of her steady, sugared presence—was in the cast of her lips, the way she tucked them together into a straight, unhappy line. Like she was tucking them in now as the bus careened onto Tsvetnoy Boulevard and lurched to a halt.

"I don't want a proper supermarket. I want to go to Central," I replied, too loudly, into the tired silence and muted growl of the idling engine.

No one disembarked when the doors creaked open. The only passenger to board was an exhausted babushka. Her thin polyester coat was fraying at the shoulders. Swollen ankles spilled from the tops of her beat-up boots. She shuffled towards us, dragging behind her a string bag full of wilted apples and stunted potatoes. Her day's meal, probably purchased from a cheap street vendor who had grown the potatoes in a window box and pilfered the apples from the back of a truck. I leaned forward to catch her attention, but like all the old women in Moscow, she wore her paisley scarf knotted tightly around her cheeks, the triangular fold at her hairline flopping over her eyes. I leaped up, stretched out my hand to guide her into my seat, but just then the bus pounced away from the curb with a violent jolt. The articulated belly buckled and heaved. I pitched forward straight into the poor old woman's chest. With a cry, she flailed backwards. The string bag catapulted from her wilted fingers and landed hard on the vinyl tread. As the bus raced on, her dinner thumped slackly down the aisle.

"Oh, I am so sorry," I mumbled, staggering, my cheek mashed in the cheap fabric of her coat. We were going down. Toby always said that Russia's old women endured all crises, mopped up every mess, plucked the shards of order from any chaos. Not this time. Not this babushka. Anyway, for all his expertise, Toby had never even been to Russia, so who was he to say nothing could topple Moscow's women?

But Sveta had us both; me roughly by the shoulder, the babushka gently by the arm. She lifted me up, pushed me back into the seat, held fast to the old woman's arm. The bus was rocking alarmingly. Sveta planted her short legs firmly between two rivets jutting from the floor and hugged the babushka tightly as she reached up for the strap.

"Excuse my friend," Sveta murmured calmly, as if the scuffle was an ordinary example of well-meaning foreign interference. The other passengers avoided looking at us altogether.

"Clumsy girl." The babushka patted Sveta's arm gratefully. "Who has my bag?" She glared at me. The angled flap of her scarf had flipped up to expose her gray widow's peak. And sharp metallic blue eyes. She didn't look exhausted. She looked pissed. Christ. This woman had probably lost everything today. Whatever meager sum of rubles she'd dared to deposit in a bank had dissolved, and whatever money she'd kept in her mattress for safety was as deflated as the near-rotten produce she carried. Had been carrying.

Even Sveta was thrown by the bus's next maneuver. From a cruising speed of at least fifty the bus screeched to a sudden halt. This time, everyone flew forward. Sveta kept hold of the babushka, but I flopped to my knees in the muddy streams of the treads. As the bus hiccuped and lurched back, I raised my head to see the red string bag thumping back down the aisle, rolling end over end like somersaulting circus tumblers, skipping past a gauntlet of skidding boots. The bag rolled straight into my hands. Triumphant, I struggled to my feet.

"Here you go," I attempted to say in Russian. The babushka blanched. God knows what I had actually said. But as I handed her the bag, the sodden strings dripping mud, she turned pale. It was the condition of her meal that upset her, of course, not the condition of my language skills. A muddy sheen shellacked her apples and potatoes. I flushed and tried to stammer another apology.

The bus-driver stood up and bellowed something. I tapped Sveta's shoulder.

"Should I offer to pay for these?" I asked, in English. The babushka eyed me warily and hugged her bag to her chest. Dirt streaked her poor coat.

Sveta turned to me, her gray eyes distracted. Wary. It wasn't like her to look nervous. "We have to get off," she told me. "Mechanical failure, the driver is saying."

"The food," I repeated, pointing to the babushka's bag. "I've ruined it. Should I reimburse her?"

"And how much would you propose to give her?" Sveta asked evenly as a crush of impatient passengers swept us down the aisle. Sveta tried to keep her steady hand on the babushka, I tried to clutch the back of Sveta's coat, but by the time we reached the front doors we were on our own. On the top step I felt an elbow jab my spine. I tripped, tumbled down to the curb under the tide of boots sweeping from the bus. Sveta reached in to grasp my hand. She hauled me easily up out of the crowd to the sidewalk.

She was half my size but twice my strength. When she let go of my hand—at once, decorously; we had never touched—I had the sudden impulse to take her hand back in mine.

Black exhaust billowed from the bus's engine. Coughing, we jogged away from the smelly thing.

"That must happen a lot," I commented. All the buses in Moscow seemed to run on grace alone, the way they wheezed and hacked crookedly through town.

"What?"

"The bus breaking down."

Sveta shook her head slowly. "Never before. Moscow buses are completely reliable." Not a hint of irony. Her voice was even, but an undercurrent of worry laced her flat tone.

I saw the babushka emerge from the thick pillow of soot and

shamble down the walk.

"I think I should do something for her," I insisted as I watched her inch past the ivory skeletons of birch trees and floppy stalks of withered tulips in the planters lining the walk.

"She will wash them," Sveta said. "Anyway, those potatoes can hardly be in any worse shape than when she bought them."

With a tug of shame, I watched the old woman shuffle away. "Well, at least we can walk to Central from here. Can't we?"

"We can. It is down the block. But I think we should not."

"I need those eggs."

She hesitated at my urgent tone, glanced at me. Wary again. Suspicious. She was always suspicious of me. I glared at her in exasperation. I had no idea who she thought I was. If she'd ever asked me directly, I'd have told her I was as innocent as I seemed. I didn't know a soul in Moscow. I didn't want to make friends, let alone spy. I was there to escape.

Well, really I was in Moscow because I was angry with Toby. Toby. An incongruous name for a Russia freak. Like Prudence, my own improbable name. We used to laugh about how the most avid Russophiles often had no ethnic connection, in name or lineage, to the place. What made us Russia freaks was usually something simple, something pure, entirely unrelated to our own personal backgrounds. Like Pushkin or Tolstoy, Turgenev or Fet. Or a national history in which good and evil were absolutes, kept always to their own sides.

Like me, Toby had never traveled in Russia. In his case, lack of worldliness led him to sleep with a Russian foreign exchange student who was assisting with his university course on Russian Romanticism. She got a green card out of the whole thing. I got this trip. It was her Zamoskvoreche District apartment I was staying in. Toby suggested it, as if I wanted to see Russia as badly as he did. He actually suggested we travel together, as the Russian girl certainly didn't want to go back. A swap. Our apartment for hers. I left them in ours and took hers.

Sveta never asked me outright who I really was. Even if she had, maybe she wouldn't have believed that I was just jilted and miserable and licking my wounds in Moscow, of all places. It was an unlikely story, as the truth generally is.

"It is worth it to you? If something happens?"

"Is something going to happen?" I asked her sharply.

Sveta had a canny prescience for trouble, I had learned. Two weeks ago, for the Revolution Day parade, the Kremlin had closed the city center at the last minute and ordered tanks to ring the old part of the city around Red Square. In the days leading up to the celebration there had been currency exchange rate fluctuations, spontaneous demonstrations, a general air of descending revolt. The authorities weren't taking any chances. Neither did they give advance warning. Not knowing about the tanks, I set out for downtown. For once, Sveta wasn't with me. She said she wanted to watch the parade on television with her father. I reached Pushkin Square before being turned back by a young soldier wagging a Kalashnikov at me like a reproving babushka. He was polite but firm when I told him I had come for the parade. As I turned to leave, I saw him light a match against Pushkin's bronze boot.

Neat trick, I thought.

While I had been talking with the young soldier, a tank had rumbled to the far end of the square, dwarfing Pushkin. Its guns were trained on the pedestrian boulevard leading to Red Square, cleared by then of all pedestrians. Over the Kremlin's walls floated the boom of a cannon salute and the strains of a military band playing a march. As I started the long hike down Tverskaya Avenue—the subways had all been shut down—I saw Sveta approaching me, her lips flat-lining impatience. Since then I'd been certain. She had to be who I thought she was. How else would she know to fetch me in the middle of Tverskaya Street on Revolution Day to take me safely home?

"But don't you see it will be cheaper now, after all, to buy them for dollars at the hard-currency shop?" she said simply, avoiding my question.

"It'll cost me twenty-five bucks for a dozen."

"The single egg you will find at Central—if you find any—today, it will cost perhaps a hundred rubles."

"Which is like fifty cents to me," I said without thinking, and she drew in her lips. A flash of anger sparked her narrow gray eyes. A first. I deserved it. It was a shitty thing to say. And I didn't want her to guess that I'd exchanged five dollars for a fistful of rubles that morning with the building's resident black market dealer, a blue-eyed, sandy-haired young man who always wore a jeans jacket and claimed to be the building maintenance guy. I'd figured out who he really was the time I'd asked him to fix my stove and he'd looked at me blankly. It was my first illegal exchange. But I was running out of cash, and after the morning headlines I knew I could get a tremendous deal. "Anyway, we're here. It won't take long."

"It really has to be eggs?"

I didn't answer.

She was furious, I could tell. Her shoulders hunched under her thin coat. She didn't have a scarf. Even in the cold air her maple syrup odor poured from her collar, bitterly sweet. Years later, when I was back in the States, I would solve the mystery of that strange odor. By then I was living alone. Toby had married his Russian girl. I'd left her apartment, but she never did leave mine. I read murder mysteries, not Pushkin. I came across one mystery in which the crime scenes reeked of maple syrup. The twist was that the murderer had something called maple syrup urine disease. Related to diabetes. The odor secretes through sweat. That must be what's wrong with Sveta, I would think. Rotting sweetly from the inside out.

She swept her flat gray eyes over me to take in the nubs of mud on my knees, my sodden jeans and bedraggled hair. The mess of me she faced every day. Why had I thought Moscow would pull me together? I was a disaster. I couldn't even forage for food without destroying an old woman's dinner. All I had of Pushkin so far was a soldier's match against his bronze boot. And I'd alienated Sveta, whose job it was to be my friend. "All right," she said stiffly. "Let's get the task done."

She usually walked a few steps behind me, another deferential habit I couldn't get her to change, but now she struck out ahead of me. Two blocks later I saw the market's arched entryway. Central Market's bloated, Quonset hut structure intruded rudely on the surrounding historic buildings. I tailed Sveta's angry back to the market's concrete steps. To my surprise, a steady stream of shoppers clutching string bags flowed into the market. At the entrance to the buttercup-yellow Old Circus building next door, a large group of men gathered under the prancing pony cutouts toeing the beach ball-red Circus sign. A guy raised a bullhorn, on the cusp of an announcement.

"Is the show about to start?" I called to Sveta. She glanced over at the circus. "Maybe we can catch it after we're done shopping."

"It's a show, all right," Sveta replied grimly. "A circus of a different sort."

A demonstration, then. Reflexively I looked around for cops. They always seemed to find even the smallest pockets of dissension. I didn't see any. Not yet.

"It's more crowded than I thought it would be." I jogged to catch up with Sveta under the market's entry arch. "Just like any other day at market."

"Central Market is always busy during a crisis," Sveta said shortly.

"Why?"

"It has the best food."

I didn't know whether she meant to convey hope or despair, but the market was alive with neither emotion, just the swell of haggling voices echoing in the great domed ceiling. A thousand bargains, down to the last kopek. We pushed our way through the crowd from stall to stall, watching babushkas waggle their fingers at stone-faced, sun-kissed men who smoked stoically over their fruit, dripping ash on their apples. The occasional carton of cigarettes or bottle of name-brand gin appeared from secret stashes, illegal sales at premium prices. Babushkas bundled in cheap coats and scarves flashed Rolexes as they paid for bags of tomatoes or pears with wads of rubles. It was chaos, but it was controlled. Although I saw a number of poorly dressed men and a few young girls wearing neon blush and flamingo-pink lipstick openly begging for food, from the Rolexes and Sveta's tension I knew for certain that this was a market for the wealthy black market operators and government officials that the crash would never turn into paupers.

"Look." Sveta pointed to a stall loaded with peaches and cantaloupe impossibly stacked into perfect pyramids. "Are those blueberries?"

I moved closer. Lined up along the base of the fruit pyramids, I saw pint boxes brimming with the biggest blueberries I'd ever seen. The vendor, a thick-haired muscular guy with a pack of cigarettes rolled up in his t-shirt sleeve, glanced at me briefly before glaring at Sveta. She usually attracted suspicion, with the sharp lines of her face, her narrow eyes, as if anyone could tell she was a tag-along. I resented anyone scrutinizing her. What followed was usually an unkind comment about her shabby clothes that she tried so hard to make presentable, or her strange odor. I was much the worse dressed of the two of us, but the newness of my ugly clothes, my height, and my obvious glow of health pegged me as foreign as certainly as Sveta's slight build and gray skin identified her as having no business with me that wasn't official.

"I'll buy some for you," I said to her. Loudly. In English. While I stared the guy down and drew closer to Sveta. "Ask him how much."

The guy lit a cigarette, never breaking his stare.

Sveta folded her arms. "I don't want them."

"Come on. They're beautiful. I haven't seen a blueberry since leaving home."

"Forget it," she said in Russian, and moved away. Behind us a swell of sound rose from the direction of the entry arch. The vendor's black eyes flickered briefly from Sveta to the source of the noise. I turned around, craned my neck. Nothing out of the ordinary. A tide of greedy shoppers. A cacophony of barter. I turned back to the seller.

"How much blueberries?" I stammered in Russian, butchering the syntax even worse than usual under that black, dead stare.

He played with me by answering in his native language, whatever that was.

Sveta was back at my elbow. Now she wasn't avoiding his gaze as she answered him fluently in whatever he was speaking. The guy twitched an eyebrow, but remained impassive as he shrugged and said something short. Probably a price. Non-negotiable.

Sveta argued calmly. His replies were brief. He finished the cigarette and lit another. Again came a tide of new noise from the entrance, a cascade of shouts; a rumble. Sveta followed my gaze, although she was too short to see anything. A shadow of concern crossed her face.

"What is it?" she asked.

"I can't tell. Look, let's forget this guy."

"He wants dollars for the fruit. He knows you're foreign."

"I just wanted to get you the berries as a gift. Let's go."

"If you have ten dollars, he'll sell you three eggs."

"I don't see any eggs."

"He keeps them behind his stand," Sveta said impatiently. "Did you bring any real money with you?"

In fact, I did have thirty dollars I'd kept out of my morning transaction, tucked in my pants pocket. Dollars were the easy way out, but Sveta was fed up with my egg chase. Another ground-swell of noise rolled our way. "Okay. Have him show me."

Sveta spoke to the guy, and he brought out the eggs, each nestled in a tri-legged metal stand. He lined them up neatly on the pine board so I could inspect for cracks. I looked them over and nodded. While he wrapped them in tissue paper I slid a pint of blueberries over and draped my ten dollars on top of them.

"Okay?" I said.

He looked me over, then shrugged. "Okay, sure." He bagged the berries and placed the eggs in gently. I smiled trium-phantly at Sveta.

"Look. My first bargain."

If she hadn't been so proper, she would have rolled her eyes.

We threaded down the aisles towards the arch. I cradled the bag under my arm to protect the eggs. Not one market had ever had an egg carton, but then, it was no use having a whole carton on hand to pack a single egg. As we drew closer to the exit, I was jostled and elbowed sharply. Sveta was nearly swallowed by the crowds. Once, I lost sight of her and had to push one of those poor painted girls out of my way to catch her again. I tugged at the back of her coat.

"I'm going to lose you," I shouted when she turned.

Her narrow eyes were filled with fear.

Suddenly the crowd before us parted. Sveta drew back, crashing into my belly. I nearly dropped my bag. Her maple odor washed over me as I wrapped my free arm around her shoulders. I held onto her as first one stall, then another, crashed to the con-crete floor near the market's entry. Heaps of produce collapsed and rolled along the ground. Someone had overturned a pickle barrel nearby; white vinegar, reeking of garlic, splashed my boots. The crowd surged forward. I was pushed hard from behind; I stumbled, knocked Sveta down, but kept hold of her coat and hauled her back up roughly. The floor was slick with ruined food. The stinging aroma of garlic and crushed oranges made my eyes water. It seemed everyone had dropped to their hands and knees to pounce on the goods, gather up anything they could into their bags and pockets, even the fruit that was flattened to pulp.

Sveta was shaken, but she found a way through the mess, stepping over people, slipping on the wet concrete. I kept my eyes on her as we struggled towards the entryway. The guy with the bullhorn we'd seen earlier was leaning against the steel-cased jamb of the arch, the horn tucked under his arm, watching the mêlée calmly. The rumblings I'd heard before the riot began must have been his amplified voice. He'd corralled the demonstrators into the market. They were hungry. They'd lost everything that day. They were going after the crooks' market, and there wasn't a cop in sight.

We had almost made it outside when shots rang out at our backs. The guy with the bullhorn flopped down right into a patch of pulverized tomatoes. Screams engulfed me like a swift lick of flame, and suddenly Sveta and I were in exactly the wrong place, in the middle of the only way out. I was knocked down and hit the floor, hard. I curled up, knees to chest, pressed my arms to my head. Over the thump of pounding boots and the siren of screams, I heard more shots, felt the fever of crowd panic. I was to be trampled to death in oranges and pickles, months before the real revolution, breathing in Sveta's sugared odor; so she must be near me, nearly crushed.

Suddenly a pressure eased, like an iron lid lifted from my head, and I sat up. The front of my coat was soaked. Dazed, I rubbed the mess with the palms of my hands as I stared in at the market. The vendors whose stalls had been raided were hefting assault rifles, ready to fire again at the first twitch of theft. Bodies lay splayed in clumps of spoiled fruit. Incredibly, some babushkas were already at work, on their knees mopping up the mess, while a crew of men righted the plundered stalls and began the chore of restocking the produce as calmly as if unloading a new shipment.

"Come on." Sveta had my arm. I stared at her. Her cheek was gashed and seeping blood. She should have looked panicked; or surprised, as I was, to find herself alive. But all I saw in her expression was that dusting of impatience she revealed when I wasn't moving fast enough for her.

"They'll shoot us if we move," I said dully.

"Not if we're moving *away*," she hissed.

She tugged me right out of there. We crawled out, scuttled to the side of the building. Outside the market the street was strangely quiet. Anyone who could flee had done so. The small plaza in front of the circus was empty. Even the traffic on Tsvetnoy had evaporated.

Sveta sat up straight, frizzy hair pressed flat against the wall, and squeezed her shoulder. I saw then that her coat was wetter than mine, and shredded at the seam, and it wasn't fruit juice and vinegar staining her sleeve.

"You're shot?" I cried.

"Keep it down," she snapped.

"Oh shit."

"Just shut up. I am not shot. I am not. Nicked, that's all."

She looked at me, and her gaze dropped to my lap. Suddenly she began to laugh. In all the months she'd been attached to me, I'd never seen her laugh. Her eyes flashed and filled with tears. Her teeth were pearl white, perfectly straight.

"Christ," she said in Russian. "You've still got those god-damn eggs."

I realized then that my bag was nestled safely between my legs.

"That is very funny." Sveta doubled over with laughter, clutching her shoulder. "Goddamn blueberries. You can bake a pie. A fucking pie. For your fucking subversives."

A babushka emerged from the market, wielding a bucket and brush. She glanced at us suspiciously before dropping to her knees to scrub the concrete under the arch. I waited for Sveta to calm down.

"Will the police come?" I asked, wondering, if they didn't, how I was going to get her home.

Sveta watched the old woman wash the steps with broad, muscular strokes. "I have no idea." All in a breath her skin paled, gray to ivory, and her stale sweet odor washed over me, stronger than ever. Sweat bubbled on her cheeks and brow.

I swallowed hard, trying to submerge panic. "You have a dangerous job," I murmured, my first, and only, hint at who she really was.

"You make it so." Her quick admission surprised me. "Buying cheap eggs for your journalist friend to sell to that black market creep."

"You're kidding."

She shot me a sharp look. Not kidding. "You are not so naïve. You changed money with him, didn't you?"

I flushed. She didn't miss anything I did. "My journalist friend, as you call her, doesn't even know what I'm cooking for dinner!"

"Why else would you traipse all over town to find them for rubles? You can afford supermarket eggs. You know how our food is being trafficked."

"An egg at a time?" I protested. Sveta shrugged, wincing. "It's all for nothing, you know," I whispered. "Following me around. I'm nobody."

"Nobody is nobody," Sveta sighed. "Anyway, it's not for me to say who is who, and to whom." She closed her eyes. "Why don't you give those fucking berries to that poor old woman? Make up for knocking into that old woman on the bus."

"I don't want to get shot, that's why."

"It's me or those eggs. You can't carry both."

It was down to that; me rescuing her. I crawled to the edge of the arched entry, but I wasn't about to be seen by the thugs standing over those bodies in the ruined fruit. I whistled softly at the babushka's back. She looked over her shoulder, frowning; annoyed, as women are with interruptions to their efforts to mop up mess.

"For you," I whispered hoarsely, and pushed the bag towards her with my foot.

When I had scooted back to Sveta, I saw that she was laughing again. "For the love of God," she breathed, and shook her head.

I looked over to see the babushka unwrap one of my eggs and cradle it, unbroken, in her hand.

At Last It Snows

Muted singularities.
Like words,
They settle upon
My tongue
What is unsayable:
How one loves,
Then goes on.
Even here, even
In this cold.

A Night Poem

Darkness stretches
Over the riverbanks.
What happens next
Happens as before;
Moths swirl to light,
An owl cries,
A dog dreams of running.

First Snow

It was December, morning dark, first
snow, you called and wanted to go
for a drive. You came before the plows,
and I remember we went down the hill,
then over, there was the stream, black against
white, the blacker trees. We didn't get far.
Did you see the car, the girl, or was it
me, was she already standing or did
she open the door? She flagged us down.
We pulled him out, her grandfather, our coats,
we put them under, you stepped beside him,
and she, was she sixteen, we were eighteen
or nineteen, she must have gone for help.
I don't remember what happened next,
but I see his hair and her shoes, your mouth
on his, the blue house set back from the road.
I was standing, I don't think I moved.
And then years later, this took me years,
I knew he was dead, he was when we got there,
you already knew and there was nothing
you could do but breathe, wait and breathe
until the police came, until they came
and we got in the car and you tried to drive away.

Massachusetts Avenue Tableau

Two small blonde boys
are circling the statue of Gandhi.
Their hair is like new corn.

They circle and circle him, arching
toward the red garland at his hip. He is all bronze
on a granite slab.

Across the street, on the steps
of the Cosmos club, the liveried concierge
is putting a yellow apple

into the hand of a woman wearing
doeskin gloves. The boys go round and round.
They keep their eyes on the red garland.

It would be good to say
we are in Vienna. The year is 1939.
It is spring, and on a side street

an organ grinder plays a mazurka. In the bake-shop
the cook's assistant pounds the almonds
and boils the jam for a Linzer torte.

The lady of some big house buys the torte.
She brings it home in the afternoon
in a white waxed box, takes off her gloves, cuts

the cotton string from the lid
with a kitchen knife and serves it
with cups of strong Darjeeling.

Everyone takes care to have small bites,
sour raspberry, brown nut,
because they suspect they might not have torte and tea again

for a very long time. After the tea
has cooled, the guests refuse cognac
and go home early.

It is not Vienna. It is not
1939. We are in America.
The boys in the park are laughing. It is overcast

and a fine mist has collected on Gandhi's brow.
The boys go around and around.
Their hair is like wet hay.

The marble steps of the Cosmos club flash
with navy serge and gabardine. There is no jam,
no almonds, no hot black tea.

Labor Day

High Point, NC

Four weeks on the picket line,
ears full of lint, and you can only
ever think about being little.
Winter in Krakow. Beet soup,
cold for dinner, hot for supper.
The pogroms, three times
in two months, stridulating
crackle of broken glass;
a window, a jam jar, a glug
of kerosene with a paper wick.
Everything goes orange.

Twenty-three years later and work
grows you old young,
lobbing the same crude shrapnel
at a knot of scabs. They scatter
like popcorn in a hot kettle.
They dance outward
to the rim of the explosion
but they high-step back when they know
you've run out of jars.
They walk through your doors
to do your work.

You finally stand up
to be a man and you can only
think about being little.
You were seven. In the grayness,
you found yourself under the table.
The baby's face was covered
with beet soup, scarlet dripping down
her fat cheeks.
You pressed your nose against hers
and tasted beets and salt,
and behind it
the dull tin of blood.

Night fell but you stayed
with the baby under the table.
Your hands were pinned around her ribs.
You couldn't move them. You couldn't move.
It was fully dark. You covered
her mouth with your hand. You probed
with your tongue all over her face
from brow to chin until you found
the little x of flesh opened up
underneath her left eye
and then you bit her there, hard,
and she screamed silently
but you kept gnawing at her face
chewing her like a chicken bone
until you bit down
on the shard of glass lodged there
and pulled it out with your teeth and spat it
onto the carpet. And her little head
fell against your chest and she was still,
shocked into sleep
by the sudden absence of pain.

When the bosses come
to break up the picket
they go for the weakest first.
They choose the oldest man.
As they carry him away
his head thumps against their chests.
"I am a physician! Why will you lock me up?
I can practice medicine! There
is work I can do! What if
you should get sick someday?
What if you should need a doctor?"

from *Counting the Body*

Poor Dear

I don't like penises
very much, she said.
It's life with a two-year-old:
ME, ME.

You're trying to cook
or sleep or read,
and here's Sir Penis
plump with need,

poking the folds
of your skirt, whopping
your leg, begging.
Men are okay,

she said, *but penises*
make me tired.
It's the stare
I don't care for,

that one glistening
eye. Thank God
I don't have one
except by marriage.

Imagine the drag:
trailing it around
like some third leg
or a mailing tube

packed with explosives,
a dumb joke.
But he looked so sad,
her heart broke.

Aw, Sweetie, she said,
I didn't mean it —
what I just said,
and took him to bed.   93

The Elephants

Hast thou not seen what thy Lord did with the possessors of the elephant?
—*Al-Fil, Chapter 105, Qur'an*

My brother still hears the tanks
    when he is angry—they rumble like a herd of hot green
        elephants over the plowed streets inside him, crash through

the white oleanders lining my parents' yard
    during family barbecues, great scarred ears flapping, commanding
        a dust storm that shakes blooms from the stalks like wrecked stars.

One thousand and one sleepless nights
    bulge their thick skulls, gross elephant boots pummel
        ice-chests, the long barrels of their trunks crush cans of cheap beer

and soda pop in quick, sparkling bursts of froth,
    and the meat on the grill goes to debris in the flames
        while the rest of us cower beneath lawn chairs.

When the tusked animals in my brother's miserable eyes
    finally fall asleep standing up, I find the nerve to ask him
        what they sound like, and he tells me, *It's no hat dance,*

and says that unless I've felt the bright beaks of ancient Stymphalian birds,
    unless I've felt the color red raining from Heaven and marching
        in my veins, I'll never know the sound of war.

But I do know that since my brother's been back,
    orange clouds hang above him like fruit made of smoke,
        and he sways in trance-like pachyderm rhythm

to the sweet tings of death music circling
    circling his head like an explosion of bluebottle flies
        haloing him—*I'm no saint*, he sighs, flicking each one away.

He doesn't sit in chairs anymore and is always on his feet,
    hovering by the window, peeking out the door, *Because,*
        he explains, *everyone is the enemy, even you, even me.*

The heat from guns he'll never let go
    rises up from his fists like a desert mirage, blurring
        everything he tries to touch or hold—If we cry

when his hands disappear like that, he laughs,
    Those hands, he tells us, *Those little Frankensteins*
        were never my friends.

But before all this, I waited for him
    as he floated down the airport escalator in his camouflage BDUs.
        An Army-issued duffel bag dangled from his shoulders—

hot green elephants,
    their arsenal of memory, rocking inside.
        He was home. He was gone.

Manly Johnson, photograph

Hymns for Sailors

The lock workers went on strike somewhere upriver around Cornwall
And in the fall of 1984
All the shipping trapped in the Great Lakes
Was anchored in the St. Lawrence Seaway
Right below my window
The Big Rose Window
On the third floor of the old monastery
Which was the boys' dormitory at the time.
I was 17 years old
Away at boarding school
And the ships were there for months
Or maybe it was just weeks . . .
It seemed like a long time
But when you're a kid
Time works differently
And memory doesn't serve.
They were there all through the fall, though,
There until early winter and the snow came.

At night I'd lie awake in my bunk
Each ship lit up like Christmas
For miles and miles up and down the river
Reflecting in the water
Silhouetted against the darkness of the far shore.
The American side.
Starboard shining green
And port is glowing red
I can see the barges from my bed.

Talk was, because of something political and Canada Customs laws
The crews weren't allowed shore leave
Stuck on their ships in the middle of the river.
We had a pair of binoculars and a pocket book of flags
And one afternoon between last class and dinner
We matched each ship to its country
Greece and Panama and Morocco
A dozen different nations

Chained in the current on our doorstep.
So one morning after breakfast
Our headmaster got this idea.
He was an American
From somewhere in the South.
An old-school Episcopalian priest
Who loved the Pope
And, according to rumor,
Kept a revolver in the drawer by his bed.
He cancelled our morning classes
And took the whole student body down to the river,
One of those crisp fall mornings
When everything is bright and clear
And the sky so blue it's painful.
And we stood on the shore and sang hymns to the sailors trapped on their ships
The boys in our navy blazers and plaid ties
The girls in their white blouses and tartan skirts.
300 teenagers belting out *This is my Father's World*
And all the other old hymns from the Anglican Hymnal
While the French horns of the faculty orchestra
Flashed and rippled gold with bits of light
From the sun on the water.

I don't remember the day the ships left.
It was one of those things that literally happened overnight.
Woke up one morning and the ships were gone,
The river empty.

Charles and Irma

It was their wrists. That was the only reference she ever made. She hugged me, kissed me, picked up my right hand and said, "Oh, look hez like a pensill—so thin. And theze vrists—look you've got Jewz vrists you do."

My grandmother was 16 when the Americans marched through. It was a small village, fewer than a thousand people— more before the war of course. I've never been there, and have always pictured it as rows of cobblestone and white-corniced shops and brownstones with flower boxes. The May sun beaming down through the clear air. I see the women dressed in white shirts with puffy *Sound of Music* sleeves, their blonde hair in pigtails. The men with bushy moustaches piled under their noses, and straight ginger hair beneath their green bowlers. A Butcher with a bone-clean apron stretched taut over his belly. A Mayor and his Frau heading the welcoming committee. And I picture a Teacher clutching a grammar book and weeping for joy.

I see them watching the Yankees march down Main Street. A slow-motion invasion that's only possible at the end. Yet, they're still scared—they're all scared, the soon-to-be-conquerors and the soon-to-be-conquered.

The Butcher, the Mayor, the Teacher, my grandmother and all the others decided not to fight. They put away the few guns that hadn't been confiscated, and they sheathed the dull cleavers they were holding in their right hands as their left hands waved out their windows. They knew it was over. They knew the Americans were here to stay and they didn't have the energy or the patriotism to fight them off.

But I want to think that there was someone—just one person—blindingly proud enough to know they needed to keep fighting. This was a time of nonsense and there would be a gap in this story without at least one man determined to turn back the entire Allied army. A lonely and scared man who didn't know what "empire" meant but couldn't believe the empire was falling. He climbs to his attic, I think, with a rusted and dull bolt-action rifle issued three decades earlier to a British soldier who was bayoneted somewhere in northern France. He doesn't know if it will even fire. It worked in the trenches, but since then it had moved from its place on the wall to a hiding space behind a panel next to the bedroom door.

So the British rifle rusts until this man decides he has to make a stand. His country needs him. This is his moment. He could be the one, the martyr, the hero whose bravery turns everything around. I picture him hobbled by a bad hip or maybe cataracts, something severe enough to keep him out of battle even when they were putting twelve-year-olds on the front line. Maybe lung scars from mustard gas. The same scars killed my great-grandfather eventually and I'm sure he would have dragged his oxygen tank up a flight of stairs for one last shot at redemption.

By now the Americans have stopped in the center of the village. They're gathered around a well—or perhaps it's a fountain with a moss-coated angel looking to the sky—and they're collecting their breath, and waiting and resting.

I can see the villagers hiding behind the curtains. They've heard the stories. They know what victors can do. They all have Dresden dolls on their mantels and they're waiting for the flames or the tanks to descend.

But the Americans are tired. They've come too far and most of them are fresh off the transport plane and haven't fired their guns in battle; the few that have been there since Omaha are so skeletal that the recoil alone might knock them over. The last mile of a marathon isn't the most difficult because it's the hardest, it's because you're so tired that you begin to wonder why you're running at all.

So they collapse against the town fountain and try to stretch the knots out of their backs while the Sergeant looks at a map or the radio guy calls someone somewhere to get some sort of information or direction.

I see a private, someone with young clean skin, maybe from the Midwest, who's worried he's not going to see any "action" and won't have any stories to tell the guys back home. He tries to move near the Sergeant because standing there is better than standing with the Polish guy or that quiet guy who never shaves. Midwest lights a cigarette. Lucky Strike of course, standard issue, nine per C-ration. Probably using the Zippo that his "girl" gave him just before he "shipped out." Midwest still can't get used to the taste. Flakes of tobacco stick to his lips, and when he tries to spit them out they just end up on the roof of his mouth.

But we've almost forgotten our hero hiding in the attic. The hopes of the Germanic people rest on his curved shoulders. The pride of his race, the purity of his bloodline, and his strength as a man will be immortalized if he leads the revolt. It takes him about thirty seconds of pulling and quietly swearing before he can draw back the dusty bolt and lock the mechanism into place.

He's sizing up his options, sliding the tip of his gun from one man to the next when the first faint hint of the cigarette reaches him. It's too far away for him to taste the depths of the tobacco; all he gets is a hint, a blue cloying tease. The Virginia tobacco fills him with pity and disgust for the cheap sawdust imitation he has been smoking for years. The American cigarettes are dizzyingly impractical. This is what the world smelled like before rations and factories and the black smoke to the east and the war smoke to the west. This is cleansing smoke that could only come from a country where thousands, or maybe millions, of men have nothing else to do, no other duty in the world, but to refine their tobacco into the strongest and coolest and most satisfying tobacco in the world. Leisure. Defeat slips into his mouth and settles deep into his lungs. He sets the gun behind a pile of boxes in the attic and starts down the stairs.

They all do.

They bring out flowers and steins of watery beer. The teenage girls run up and kiss the soldiers on the cheeks, calling them all "Johnny" and trying to wrap their tongues around the vowel-laden and soft-palated "Roozevhelt." The men clap them on their back and say, "Joe Loudis," "Joe Loudis," "Babe Vuth," "Babe Vuth."

The soldiers slowly relax and then smile. They distribute Luckies and chocolate. The people want them to stay and rest and drink and flirt with their daughters. The soldiers wonder how a conquered people could be so pathetically grateful.

My grandfather did more than flirt with the daughters.

❖   ❖   ❖

Charles and Irma.

A classic love story built by the Army PR guys. After the war, "Operation Reunification" tried to spread the word of the new American-German alliance. Now that those troublemakers in the black boots were gone, these two countries could finally move forward hand in hand.

My grandparents would go on tours of VFW halls and speak at receptions and pose for the cameras. They'd hold hands and her blue eyes would gaze adoringly into his strong brown American eyes. He'd talk of "liberating" the Germans who had been through so much suffering; they were asked not to use the words "conquered" and to avoid the term "Nazi." She'd call him a hero and say how dreadful it was before "the American rescue." She would always shed a tear when she got to the phrase "American saviors."

My grandmother always hated my grandfather. They made her drop her accent. She had to mouth those long vowels and get rid of her natural inflections. The day after the last show, she brought back her Germanic zzzs and vvvvvs and would never let them be pried out of her mouth again. My grandmother turned into a bad Marlene Dietrich impersonator. Eventually she couldn't talk any other way.

On the VFW tour they never got into too much detail. The fliers read "Charlie and his Fraulein…Hear their love story worthy of Tracy and Hepburn. Hear his brave exploits! Hear her tale of suffering and rescue! A true fable of compassion and unity!"

I have to admit it's a great story. There was never a dry eye in the house. The women would fall all over themselves. The men would set their jaws and wish they had been there. Charlie and the boys liberate Germany town by town. Freeing minds, feeding the hungry, rebuilding a great country. And oh how the Germans suffered oh so very very much. "They had lived in the hell we were fighting against," my grandfather would whisper at the beginning of his performance. They were innocent. The real criminals were dead, or in prison, or they were, he would come to the edge of the crowd and make a fist, *"living hunted lives of anguished guilt like the mangy curs they are."* The crowd always clapped at the *"cur"* line. Those balding men in the bulletproof cages were the evil ones. That mustache with the voice like broken knives was the real enemy. Dictators trample the people—the people don't support dictators. How could they? Obviously.

"Oh I thought he was very handsome. We had been waiting for a very very long time for them and when we saw them march into the village we all jumped for joy." She would beam her capped teeth across the audience. They loved her and they couldn't help it. "Our long long nachtmare was over. And thank God the Americans came through my little village and not the Red

Army. I thank God every night that the Communists didn't get to me first."

Cheers! Applause! God Bless America AND Germany!

I bought it for years. I still believe it; I can't help it.

I was used to seeing old film footage of my grandparents. They were in small green film canisters on a living room bookshelf full of dolls and picture frames. My grandfather would pull the canisters out after Thanksgiving dinner. Sometimes he would stand next to the screen so he could point out details and describe where they were or what kind of food they served. He'd get excited and bounce from one side of the screen to the other trying to convince us how popular they were, and how proud he was to stand next to her. My grandmother would only walk into the living room occasionally to pour some more coffee. He would turn to her and ask if she remembered this person or that person. She always shook her head and said, "Oh I don't know. So long ago." And then she would walk out without looking at the screen. He'd pretend not to notice and tell stories of meeting generals and the one time Eisenhower almost came to one of the receptions. And sometimes he'd just quietly put the films on and walk out of the room. Leaving their younger selves silently dancing and smiling on the living room wall for anyone who wanted to see.

❈ ❈ ❈

Instead of taking a risk in the new half of her old country, she decided to live with the conqueror that got her pregnant. Most of the time I think she should have stayed. She should have accepted her guilt and tried to rebuild. Instead she came here and had kids who had kids, she ate her sour candy, watched soap operas and gave her children and grandchildren haircuts in the kitchen. And she grew to hate everything about the country that ruined hers.

The pipe was old; a deep rosewood with natural brown grain that stretched down the barrel and swirled up into the bowl, it looked warm and soft, but was old and hardened. The tip was black hard plastic covered in tiny teeth marks.

I don't remember seeing her ever smoke a pipe in her own house, but she would always have it lit when she was anywhere else. My mom had to buy an ashtray that she would pull out only when my grandparents came over; my grandmother would carry it around with her from the couch to the dining room table and back to the couch. At first, my father would cough and try to drop hints, open windows and say something vague about "smoke around the kids"; my grandmother would look at him, smile slightly and send two puffs of her cedar-smelling smoke out of her pipe.

Some older women make quilts or collect small porcelain dolls, but the only thing my grandmother collected was stories about pissing people off. She once lit her pipe in the middle of a movie theater; when the ushers came bobbing up with their red flashlights she blew smoke in their faces and said, "You charge nine dollars? I smoke." My grandmother has gotten us kicked out of more places than a drunken sailor on shore leave. Long after all restaurants in the state had banned smoking she would pull out her pipe and light up; we had learned not even to bother asking her to put it out. Instead, we'd just tense up and quietly wait for the owner to walk over and ask her to put out her pipe. It was classic rebellion; whenever she didn't like a place, or whenever someone made her mad, or if she didn't like the direction a conversation was going, she could shut it all down by pulling out her velvet pouch of tobacco and her well-chewed brown pipe.

"So ve vere dere, in the funeral, back row of course, so I go for a puff. Then thiz American priest tellz me to put it out."

Or

"I vas minding my own business on the tour bus to Atlantic City, and the American driver stops on the highway and tells me to put it out because of the oxygen tanks."

She saw it as a uniquely American conspiracy, designed to keep her from enjoying: "The one thing I love."

My grandfather would look at her, put a hand on her forearm and say, "Irma, it's against the law. And smoking is bad for you; you should stop, for my sake if not yours." She would grit her teeth and stare at him until he lowered his eyes.

We were used to it, and I liked the thick, peaty smoke. She would even smoke while cutting my hair. It was always the same chair, no cushion, with a tall back that came to a rounded point like a V2 rocket. The chair was so stiff and uncomfortable that it forced you to sit up straight while she snipped away. I remember hearing her teeth gnaw on the tip of her pipe and her old-woman slippers squawking across the linoleum. In my memories I always got my haircut in the late afternoon and there were always twin sunbeams floating in the smoke. She cut my hair for years. Always the same generic boy's haircut—I try not to look for parallels in the old newsreels of youth camps.

In middle school, the other kids didn't have haircutting grandmothers. I made my mom tell her that I didn't need a haircut that month. I wasn't sure it hurt her feelings until we went over for dinner a couple of weeks later. She hugged me and kissed my cheeks and picked up my hand and said I had Jew's wrists. I didn't understand her, and my mother pretended not to hear and pushed us both towards the dining room.

❊ ❊ ❊

They had to keep marching. The soldiers kissed the girls, pulled up their pants, put out their cigarettes, handed out the last of their Hershey Bars, and got back into formation. The young women held onto the soldiers' arms and pouted and tried to pull them back into the lofts and barns they had just emerged from.

I see them standing in a line weeping and calling the soldiers back to their open and conquered arms. Begging them not to leave. Throwing their bodies between the soldiers and what lay ahead. Part of me wants to see Charles look back over his shoulder and lock eyes with Irma and silently promise to return to her. But I can't quite bring myself to think that's how it went. They were never that romantic.

My grandfather only talked about this once, and it wasn't to me. But this part isn't my imagination or old movies filling in the gaps in the narrative. This is how it happened.

The platoon was about ten miles out of town following a dirt road that was deeply rutted by the large convoys of supply trucks that had connected the town to the rest of the Empire. They were under large oak trees and there were birds in the trees.

Then they heard a noise from the woods to their right. Something was coming towards them; branches were snapping and being torn. They braced and brought their M1s up to shoulder level ready for the Stormtroopers or whatever German monster was about to descend upon them.

About ten yards up the road one gray-uniformed member of the Schutzstaffel burst through the trees and tripped on a root and went sprawling into the middle of the road. His breathing was throaty and ragged; he quickly pushed himself up, glanced to the left and kept running into the woods. He was a few yards away before his brain processed what he saw and he turned around and ran screaming towards the Americans with his hands up and his palms facing the soldiers.

The men kept their guns trained on him but no one moved. This was one man. Individual men aren't supposed to fight in wars. Soldiers move in squads, squads move in platoons, platoons move in companies, companies move in brigades, brigades move in divisions, divisions move in armies and *armies* fight wars, not individual men. He ran closer and wouldn't stop screaming and pointing towards the woods and he came closer and someone in the platoon got nervous and let out a single bullet that caught the SS officer on his left cheekbone. He stopped, stared forward with suddenly waxy eyes, folded onto his knees and, with a puzzled look, fell face-first onto the dirt road.

The Americans were braced for more. They scanned the woods. They were sure this was the first wave of a last-ditch suicide attack on Allied forces. One private thought he heard tanks, and another was scanning the forest to his right convinced he could see uniforms in the branches.

Then the three of them silently appeared on the side of the road where the SS officer had come from. One carrying a shovel, one carrying a hammer and another with a loop of barbed wire. No one heard them approach and their gray-striped uniforms blended into the woods, rendering them almost invisible.

The Americans didn't lower their weapons.

Slowly, with their shaved heads hunched forward, each tendon in their necks pushing out through their skin, the three men moved towards the fallen body. My grandfather said the one with the barbed wire met his gaze and looked at him with a questioning hollowness that he couldn't see the end of. Their yellow skin and impossible cheekbones slowly stumbled towards the Americans; the soldiers saw the sores on their ankles and the thin rope pulled tight across their waists.

They got to the corpse, looked up at the Americans and started to shake. The man with the shovel at the front of their group opened his mouth in a scream but nothing came out, not even a rattle. He brought his face forward and stared at the Americans with his lips curled back in anger. The man with the

barbed wire mimicked the dead Nazi and fell to his knees, then
he sat down hard and his head sunk between his knees. He let go
of his barbed wire and his breathing and his blinking slowed as
he slipped into a waking sleep. The man with the hammer calmly
walked towards the dead man, straddled the corpse and brought
the hammer down on the skull. He brought the hammer up, lifting
the head off the ground with his upward swing, shook his hammer
free and brought it down again and again on the back of the dead
man's head and neck.

The soldiers lowered their weapons and ran; someone picked
up the man with the hammer and, maybe not knowing how light he
would be, threw him to the ground shattering the bones in both of
his legs.

❋ ❋ ❋

Besides the 16mm footage of my grandparents on tour, there
was one other film my grandmother starred in. She was only on
camera for six seconds, but she stood out the first time I saw it and
I couldn't take my eyes off her. The other people in the film melted
away—the very definition of star power. I stood in the museum
waiting for the film to start over again, and again, and again, and
every time it was her. It was one panning shot of women marching
along the edge of a mass grave. I've dug through other pictures
and I've watched other footage, but I can find her only in these six
seconds.

It's her. Her black hair hangs limply on her shoulders, a
primitive shadow of the bounce and curls of her VFW posters.
She used to squint her eyes into small slits when she was chopping
onions, but she would never rub her eyes; she used to tell us that
rubbing our eyes when they stung would just make it worse because it would press the stinging in deeper. I recognized the way
she lowered her head but raised her eyes just like she used to when
she was lifting my grandfather out of his chair. I saw her walking along the edge of the grave with her eyes scrunched together
against the stench and the fumes from the lye. I see her walking
along the edge of the grave with her neck bent and her eyes lifted
because she knows she can't show submission or hesitation or the
Americans will make her get back in line and walk through it all
over again.

She never talked about it. The family never talks about it.

When I was old enough to ask questions only my Aunt Karenna would talk to me about this, but even she hardly knew anything. Karenna and my grandmother were sitting at the kitchen table drinking coffee and talking about whatever middle-aged children talk to their parents about. Karenna said there was no transition, no warning, she just started, "You know ve never even knew it was happening of course. Zey only came at night. The trains, painted black—you couldn't see zem if you vere looking." My grandmother looked into and through Karenna's eyes, but didn't wait for a response. Instead, she collected their cups, placed them in the sink and picked up the thread of the conversation where they had left it before her digression into a past none of us knew existed.

Karenna didn't tell anyone and she couldn't find the words to ask her mother what she meant. It was just one more memory that no one wanted to pick up and examine too closely. Just before my grandfather died, Karenna asked for more detail about the war, but he just started into the Charlie and Irma star-crossed lovers routine that had established a beachhead in his memories. It wasn't deliberately misleading, it was just the slow calcification of an old memory until it transformed itself into something else.

He told the museum the story about the three men descending on the fallen SS officer, but that's where his story ended. I accidentally found his testimony, long after he was dead, in a museum archive. I'm not sure if he didn't want to tell us, if he couldn't tell us, or if over the years the truth had simply slipped into the comfortable fog of heroism.

❖ ❖ ❖

At the end of their lives, my grandmother was stronger than my grandfather. We used to joke that if her pallbearers were having a hard time, then she would get out and carry herself into her own grave. He could feed himself and push himself out of his chair into a slow laborious stand. Limbs and tendons stretching with the dust and nails of old age. A nurse would come in a few days a week, but the rest of the time it was up to my grandmother and one of her daughters, who took turns helping with him.

I would visit them on Saturday afternoons and we would have sandwiches and play dominoes. About a year before he died I walked in one morning, a few hours earlier than usual, and saw them in the backyard. She was leading him in a circle around her brick-lined flowerbed. There was a breeze and it was cool outside, but I could see the shirt clinging to my grandfather's back; two dark half-circles of sweat ran down from his shoulders and up from his waist. She stood to his right, her left arm stretched across his back and supporting his left elbow, and her right arm holding his hand for balance. I could see her mouth whispering. His face was tightened with exhaustion and obese beads of sweat had collected on his earlobes and the tip of his nose. He was pushing his feet forward, just barely lifting them off the ground. I slid open the back door and my grandmother jumped when she saw me. I took his right arm and started moving him back into the house.

"Exercise . . . is good for him."

"Not right now."

I got him into bed and brought him a glass of water; he clutched the glass and drank too fast. He coughed some water back up, opened his mouth and took a long rattling breath and brought a hand up to rub the bridge of his nose.

"See, he's okay. Stronger."

I looked down at my grandfather, his eyes bloodshot and his breathing finally slowing.

"Are you okay?"

"Yeah," he coughed. "Yeah . . . good . . . stronger."

"You see? It's okay."

He fell asleep and my grandmother and I walked into the kitchen.

"Do you do this every day?"

"No. It's good to be strong." She looked me straight in the eyes and didn't blink even once.

"You saw him sweating; he was about to pass out."

"He could have gone a little longer. Is good to test the heart."

"I think you should stop."

She smiled and looked at me softly. "You don't understand." She leaned over, squeezed my hand and turned towards the refrigerator, closing the door on the rest of this conversation. I would come by at different times from then on, never entirely sure what I would find, but I never saw them in the backyard again.

❖ ❖ ❖

There were approximately four hundred prisoners still alive; more than one hundred died after liberation, with many over-eating and drowning their brains in water until they went into shock and died. At a certain point, even water can become an indignity. Some succumbed to old wounds and infection. There were only a handful of guards left at the camp; they stayed behind to burn the documents and they didn't get out in time. A few guards tried to escape into the woods and some probably got away; the rest were hunted down and killed by the prisoners. When a guard was healthy enough to fight back, one of the Americans would shoot him in the knee. There were more than two hundred corpses inside the camp when the Americans walked through the front gate. They were stacked in the main courtyard, they were left to rot in their barracks, there were a few dozen in a sealed truck where they had been left to asphyxiate, they were tangled in barbed wire after they were shot trying to escape. There were thirty carbonized corpses in a barracks that the guards had set fire to as they were abandoning the camp; the ashes were still smoking.

Of course there are pictures of all of this; newsreel footage, photo correspondents, official government photographers, Army Signal Corps cameramen and GI pocket cameras. You can find the images if you want. Most people don't of course. Most of these pictures haven't been looked at in years, and some of the film is still undeveloped.

They've been archived. It's worse than death; at least the dead have cemeteries—you can't avoid cemeteries, they're built in plain sight next to highways and restaurants. But archives are buried in basements and sub-basements. Anyone can walk into a cemetery; any animal can stroll through the front gate and piss on your great-uncle and no one will stop it. But you have to earn your way into an archive. You must navigate through a maze of forms and fees and suspicious eyes under fluorescent lights. You need a reason, a project, a grant, a purpose—it's the ultimate existential joke: "Why are you here?" We bury our memories, but we hide our history. My grandparents didn't want their memories anymore, they weren't doing them any good, so why not bag them up, tie a bow around them, and toss them out the window?

My grandparents dance around the edges of all the pictures I've seen. The only film I saw her in was that clip of the Germans walking along the edge of the grave. I found him in a film of Americans opening boxes of medicine; he's standing in a row of five other soldiers and I think they're opening boxes of aspirin. This is the only picture I've seen of him smoking a pipe; I immediately recognized the tall bowl of the pipe my grandmother smoked for decades. It's a black and white picture, but I know that if it was a color shot, the pipe would glow a deep contented rosewood. There is another photograph, of a General touring the crematoria, and there is a GI whose face is blurred with movement, it looks like the GI is holding a pipe to his mouth; that could be him but I'm not sure.

I feel them standing just out of frame. I know they were there, yet they both managed to avoid the cameras and the flashbulbs. Every shoulder on the edge of a photograph, the back of every helmet, a foot stepping out of frame—any one of them, or every one of them, could belong to my grandparents.

They're both dead now, and I'll never know their specific story. All I know are the broad strokes.

When my grandfather's Company returned to the village a few hours later they found families attempting to load their belongings onto donkey-drawn carts. The soldiers threw the clothing, books, photographs, and toys onto the ground and started filling the cart with bread and jugs of water. A few soldiers kicked down the door of the largest house in the village. They were looking for blankets and tools, but they found the Mayor and his wife both swinging from the second-story banister. They had killed themselves hours earlier and their fingers were still entwined.

They grabbed all the carts and trucks in the village and filled them with supplies taken from the houses. The grocer tried to hold on to the few remaining pounds of fresh vegetables, but a soldier broke his nose and took everything he had. A handful of men took the two ten-pound bags of flour from the bakery; they didn't realize until later that night that they didn't know what to do with raw flour. Two men were stationed in the town square with orders to shoot anyone who tried to leave the village.

By that night other Companies had moved in, bringing water, food and doctors. But it still wasn't enough. The horror was quickly replaced by a numb sense of duty. There was a job to do, but the job kept growing. There still weren't enough blankets, there wasn't enough clean water, there weren't enough interpreters, there were fresh bodies every day and mass graves discovered every day and they didn't know what to do with the bodies that had been there before they arrived. The stacks of corpses were left in place for almost a week. They were told to leave the bodies untouched for the news cameras and the Generals to see. But even if they had been told to get rid of them, they wouldn't have known what to do with all of them.

I don't know who first came up with the idea to make the Germans bury the dead. I haven't been able to find a chain of command on this, but the same decision was made at every camp across Europe. A spontaneous burst of practical revenge that instantly spread across all political and national lines.

For the first few days they made the Germans work individually. They had to excavate the mass graves and then dig separate graves for each body: three feet wide, six feet long, five feet deep. Rows of Americans held their rifles and watched the Germans dig; the Americans then silently walked the villagers the two miles back into the camp and watched them collect a corpse to carry to the newly dug grave. Even the body of a person who has been starved to death is heavy. One strong man could dig seven graves and bury seven bodies in twelve hours, a woman could dig five graves and bury five bodies and the children older than twelve but younger than sixteen, who were paired off to dig and bury together, could bury four a day. There were eight wheelbarrows taken from the town and these were given to the oldest men and women to make it easier for them to transport their corpses. The Germans who were sick or had broken bones and other confirmed medical conditions were allowed to work in groups of three.

I've only found a few pictures of the Germans trying to carry the bodies in their outstretched arms; the recently deceased could be slightly folded and cradled like an overgrown child, but decay moved faster than burial and soon the bodies were too stiff and immovable to be carried this way. Instead, they had to pull the bodies up by their arms into a kneeling position and then turn their backs on the corpses; the Germans would then crouch down, reach over their shoulders to grab the dead arms, and then stand up bringing their corpse to a near-stand draped over their backs. They would then stumble forward and hunch down and slowly fall towards the cemetery. The fluids of the corpse slowly leeching into their skin and hair. By the time they made it to the cemetery, occasionally the dead skin and muscle of the upper arms and wrists had crumbled apart under the weight of the dragging hands. I think that the corpses might have been easier to drag once your hands could hang on to the bones of the exposed wrist.

Cold math told the Americans that this was taking too long, and they soon allowed the Germans to work in pairs and then groups of four or more. This sped up the process, but in the end they had to resort to bulldozers to transport bodies. Every person in the village over the age of twelve had to carry and bury at least one of the bodies. I don't know how many bodies my grandmother carried on her back under a May sun and over two miles of dirt road. It's possible she escaped, maybe my grandfather found her and pulled her out of line, maybe he told the rest of the soldiers that she was different and that she was the only one who actually didn't know what was happening. Maybe.

❁ ❁ ❁

After my grandfather died my grandmother was alone almost all the time. She resisted her children's offers to move her into one of their houses and she wouldn't let any of them stay with her. She didn't need anyone to take care of her and eventually her children stopped asking. She would clean her house, walk two miles to the grocery store and back every day, and tend her flowerbeds. I would get her out of the house sometimes, but she was never comfortable; she would quietly sit through a movie and then she would mechanically eat her food when we went to her favorite Chinese restaurant. She had even stopped smoking her pipe.

I think back on the time I spent with her after my grandfather died, and I can't remember what we discussed. She was dead by the time I saw her in the museum and I never asked for more details about the war or how they met; I assumed I knew that story from the old newspaper clippings and 16mm footage.

I never thought she missed him. She never talked about him, she didn't have pictures of him in the house and she didn't celebrate his birthday like my mom sometimes did.

A few months before she died, I came over to the house and found her in the stifling garage moving through old boxes of books and old clothes. Dust billowed up and the heat hit me in the chest as I opened the garage door. I could just see the top of her frazzled gray hair as she moved stacks of boxes to the side. I asked her what she was looking for; she jumped up an inch or so to look at me, "Projector." She was out of breath.

"What?"

She jumped again, "Projector," she said impatiently through the dust.

I made my way towards the back of the garage and pulled her back into the air-conditioning. I spent an hour or so opening boxes before I found the projector. My shirt stuck to me as I carried the heavy green metal projector inside. I set it on the same end table it always sat on during Thanksgiving. She tried to pull the old 16mm footage down off the bookshelf but couldn't reach it; I stretched up and pulled the green canisters off the top shelf.

Neither of us knew how to thread the machine and we kept laughing as the film fell off the spools or I pinched my fingers in the gears. I forgot to turn off the machine as I went to screw in the lamp and was immediately blinded by the heat and the sudden flash. I stood up and tried to blink away the blue and green spots that filled my vision; I couldn't help but smile when I heard her laughing.

The film started to play, and she turned off the lights. I sat next to her on the couch and tried to watch the film through the kaleidoscope my vision had become. There was only about twenty minutes of footage, and it was halfway done before my eyes calmed down. They were standing there just as I still see them in my head. He was wearing his olive green dress uniform, his ribbons and Purple Heart stood out on his chest, and his cap was at a sharp angle over his forehead. He looked tall and steady. Her hair was in curls and hung elegantly over the shoulders of her blue cotton dress with white fringe. Her dress was simple yet she made it look luxurious. They were looking straight ahead and talking to whoever was holding the camera; my grandfather never had the audio track, so he used to make up funny narration, "This is where Irma's telling them about the time I fought back an entire Panzer brigade just in my socks." They were pointing off camera and throwing their heads back in deep laughter. As their laughter tailed off they leaned towards each other and she slipped into the space between his shoulder and his chest. Her marble eyes met his oak eyes and they kept smiling, but whatever they were laughing about now wasn't between them and the cameraman; they settled into the comfortable flirting of lovers at the end of a long day.

The film went white, the test pattern flashed briefly, and the film rolled out. I could hear the gentle ticking of the empty spools spinning in place.

My grandmother had pulled out her pipe and was slowly chewing on it as tears steadily marched down her face. She was staring at the white screen like she could still see the past if she just looked hard enough. Her eyes narrowed as if she was staring into the sun, she pulled the pipe out of her mouth and her tears dried as her eyes slipped back to an old memory. I squeezed her hand and she relaxed her eyes. She came back to the present and she looked at me softly; she stood up and, as she headed into the kitchen, she asked me if I was hungry.

From the collection of the Editor, photograph

The Nazi Officer's Wife

Your name is Greta (Edith) and you are a registered Aryan (Jew).
Your papers are authentic (false) and you have nothing—your family
gone (dead), your ghetto purged (exterminated), your yellow star

crumpled in a dustbin. You must leave Vienna—if you are caught,
they will punish (murder) you. You hide in the park, the museum,
plan your next move. You stare at Germanic art (propaganda).

In the marbles, you hear your relocated (dead) mother's voice. She says
go to Munich. It is 1942. Your name is Greta (Edith). You are
a registered Aryan (Jew). So you go. You plunge (assimilate) into

the Reich, bandage Nazi (enemy) wounded for the Red Cross—
stay away from inspectors (spies). You say nothing about yourself,
just in case something of Edith (you) slips out of your mouth.

A German (Nazi) man falls in love with you (Greta), you cook
and clean for (serve) him. He comes home from the munitions (pistol)
factory, he looks (spies) at you through the keyhole. You stir

a saucepan at the stove (oven), become the perfect Aryan frau (*isha*).
He knows your secret (blood) but ignores it. He is lonely (pathetic)
and you play your part (Greta) so well it is easy for him, he loves Greta

(Edith) so much he forgets. You give him a daughter (Jew) and he is drafted,
marches to the Russian Front. You actually cry real tears (salt)
for him and have become what the internment camp Jews (prisoners)

call a U-Boat—a Jew in Aryan clothing—cold as metal and always
submerged (drowned). You pass (lie). You live (die). Ears and nose
plugged tight as you swim—the sounds of war, muffled underneath

leagues of heavy water. You smell nothing of burning cities, burning
homes, burning clothes, burning skin. After the war, you try to come up
for air—the land, even the sky has changed, turned to powder (ashes).

You wander Nuremburg and search lists of names (survivors),
search masses of faces (survivors). Your family is gone (murdered),
you are the only one left and while they were killed (gassed), you

were in Munich eating chocolate (poison). So you pick up your life —
pocked, ruined; like Munich — bullets, razor wire, your own instinct
to survive (hide) have left it full of holes. You are a U-Boat.

Your periscope (brown eyes) so narrow you cannot even see the horizon —
filled with bombed buildings, bombed cities, all of Europe slumping
like a white skeleton, bones turning to chalk in the smoldering air.

From the collection of the Editor, photograph

Hyacinth

Outside the back door, the world smells like
hyacinth. The thought comes into my head
and I think — I have no idea what hyacinth
smells like, looks like. But I like the way
the word sounds — lush, alive.

Every summer my grandmother, her sisters,
get together and tell stories — farm work,
running the store, barn dances. Never once
do they talk about all the books they've read.
Theirs is a history of doing, of walking dirt roads
and knowing the name of every manner
of green thing.

I watch them at the picnic table, trees' limbs
bending low as if they, too, are listening
to the patter of older days, worn paths.
I imagine them — Margarie, Toby, Katie,
Lyda, and even Jackie — all in gingham:
the prettiest girls, all in a line,
shelling pole beans under pines.
My grandmother puts her work down,
turns to look at me.
She smiles.

She knows hyacinth.
Knows camellias. Bougainvilleas.
Wax Myrtle, Crepe Myrtle and
every azalea that ever bloomed.

Life Saving Lessons

When Bubba died, I saw a man I hadn't seen since the summer Elizabeth and I were twelve, the summer of breasts and love and life saving lessons.

"We must, we must, we must increase our busts," we chanted, arms moving up and down, a Coke bottle clenched in each hand. It was stifling hot in our room with the door closed, but this was a secret pursuit. Nobody except our young aunt Ruby knew about these exercises designed, we prayed, to give us breasts. She didn't put much faith in them.

"Things happen when they happen," she told us. "If you want exercise, you'd be better off swimming."

Elizabeth and I liked to swim, not so much for the activity as for the lifeguards, one in particular, our idea of perfection, just out of high school, going to Fayetteville that fall. For now, he sat on his perch with limbs like a statue's—thick and perfectly formed. When we walked past, we could see pale blond hair on his calves, more on his chest. We dared each other to speak to him.

"Hey, O.T.," Elizabeth drawled. "Hey" was foreign to me, the Yankee cousin from St. Louis. We said "Hi" and so my salute was slightly off.

"Hey, Yankee," O.T. answered. "When you girls signin' up for Life Saving?"

Life Saving. We hadn't dreamed we were eligible. We'd watched him instructing Gwendolyn and Mary Beth for the past week, but they were fourteen. We'd observed with longing the way O.T. towed them across the pool demonstrating rescue, the girls' bodies obediently limp as if half-drowned. The way, after lessons, the girls stepped out of the pool, shedding water, their arms making brisk brush-strokes now against their newly rounded hips. The way O.T. watched their wet ruffling from his reclaimed roost.

Elizabeth and I became brave. Big on Greek gods and goddesses that summer, we'd nicknamed O.T. "Apollo" because his skin was bronze. The sailor cap he wore rolled down to shelter his eyes distracted from the image, but we felt that without it he would look like the Apollo in the encyclopedia at the public library.

This was 1953. You had to go some to see pictures of male bodies, adorned or otherwise, and we had found the Britannica a good source, art books similarly rich in possibility. The librarian had no idea what we were so interested in. Our taste was catholic: it ran to anything explicit, male or female, but there was something furtive about our paging through those books. At any time, the librarian with a slight but definite mustache might loom up silently, "Finding what you want?"

At Uncle Bubba's and Ruby's house, there was yet a better book, a huge coffee table volume of American paintings. Elizabeth and I each had our favorites, and Ruby didn't mind what we looked at. She was not yet thirty that summer, our youngest great-aunt, and for that reason we didn't "Aunt" her. She exclaimed with us as we turned pages. Frequently we made up stories based on the pictures. The ones we liked best had people in them, and one that drew us always was a Thomas Hart Benton, *The Jealous Lover of Lone Green Valley*. A woman in a pink dress clutched her breast. Blood flowed. A farmer stood before her, dagger in hand, hat tilted. In the foreground, an indifferent trio of musicians played fiddles and harmonicas, oblivious to the drama behind them.

"Never," said Ruby, "take up with a jealous man. Look what can happen to a woman, and nobody does a damn thing about it. That girl is going to bleed to death for sure. And over what? She had a generous and loving nature is all I can see." We shook our heads, sad for that poor woman.

"Another thing," said Ruby, who loved an audience, "never take up with a musician. Look at those men," she pointed to the trio. "In a world of their own, is what."

"And Orpheus," one of us would say, sinking into this lovely afternoon litany, "look what he did to poor Euridyce."

"Don't never look back," said Ruby then, "that's what you have to learn from that one."

Here was a man running with a baby in his arms, a ladder against the house behind him. In a hushed voice Ruby told us about the Lindbergh kidnapping. We shivered. We worried. Grandmother's house was low. Our shared room was by the driveway, and sometimes, after dark, men came to the window seeking

Grandfather to come out and deliver babies or sew up wounds. We'd got used to those urgent tappings, but what if, some evening, it wasn't a patient but a kidnapper? Ruby laughed.

"Scream bloody murder," she advised. "It would save your life. Unless of course there's just musicians around. That poor woman." She'd flip the pages back to The Jealous Lover.

Relieved to have us out of the house visiting Ruby, Grandmother wasn't the slightest bit interested in life saving lessons. O.T. had told us his class met every afternoon at 2:00.

"I cannot possibly take you," said Grandmother. "Ask Ruby. She just sits around in that empty house with not a thing to do. No children, and not likely to have them either," she said, pursing her lips. We didn't know what she meant. She was always saying unpleasant things about Ruby even though Bubba was our grandfather's own baby brother. It was as if he and Ruby belonged to someone else's family. Grandmother had said, however, that we could ask.

"I'd be tickled pink," Ruby told us, and then, inspired, she drove us down to Bubba's store to buy new bathing suits. Grandmother and Ruby had completely different taste. Grandmother's ran to plain blue tank suits, whereas Ruby liked color and patterns. She thought we'd look cute in two-piece floral prints with ruffled tops, but they were too juvenile. We elected black sarong-style suits. Ruby smiled and said we could have whatever we wanted, but black absorbed all the heat; we'd be more comfortable in a color.

"If you are ever in a desert," she said, "in a big tent with a handsome sheik offering you something to wear on your camel ride to the next oasis," here she paused and lowered her voice. We bent close to hear, there in the side aisle of Bubba's store. A desert sheik. He would look like Robert Taylor. "Choose white robes," Ruby said urgently. "Remember what I'm telling you. It could save your life out there."

"Grandmother will never go for black," said Elizabeth practically. She didn't plan to travel much and tended to see things how they played in Arkansas. "We'll just catch hell," she sighed. It was hard, very hard, to see the justice in life. Here was Ruby offering us any suit we wanted and Bubba himself echoing her generosity, and there was Grandmother's propriety floating like a huge cobweb from the ceiling of their store.

"You can't take bathing suits back," I told Elizabeth. "There isn't a thing she can do if we take them home."

"Boy, are you dumb," said my cousin. "What kind of underwear are you wearing?"

I shrugged. Elizabeth and I wore sturdy white cotton underwear, Lollipops, because Grandmother had firm ideas about intimate apparel. It should never be anything but clean and sensible. We had been shopping the first week of my visit, Grandmother horrified at my skimpy blue nylon panties with their stretched elastic and straggly lace.

"How could your mother have possibly let you go for a visit with underwear like this? Accidents," she continued. "You have to consider accidents. You never want to be hit by a car in dirty underwear." Elizabeth and I pouted. We didn't plan to be hit; we didn't see how Lollipops were going to save our lives if we were run down. Grandmother told us not to be sassy.

We could imagine what she would say when she saw the sarongs. There was no way we could even think of taking home the ones with the tiger print or leopard spots, yet we tried them on, parading around the back of Bubba's store, dashing behind the gray curtain of his changing room whenever we thought a customer was approaching. We vamped, inspected ourselves in the three-way mirror, and looked carefully for any sign of breasts. We sat on the triangular plywood seat in the dressing room and shared a Coke from their machine.

"For the jungle suits, we really ought to have breasts," said Elizabeth glumly.

"We don't want to look silly," I agreed. We thought about black absorbing the heat. We selected a white sarong for Elizabeth, a turquoise one for me.

Life Saving started on Monday. When we first began the lessons, Ruby's arms were smooth and white, her shoulders freckled. By the time we finished, triumphantly heaving up a burlap sack weighted with ten pounds of coal from the bottom of the pool, Ruby was freckled all over. "Speckled," she laughed, "like an old barnyard hen." She had stretched out during our lessons on a towel with white fleurs-de-lys embossed on it, turning her long full body regularly to get "even."

She wore a tiger-striped suit and had a swimming cap with a rubber spangle of fuchsia she said was a mum. We could spot her anywhere in the large pool, just looking for that cap as she swam steadily back and forth a prescribed number of times. Because she was so tall, her arms were long and she moved through the water as if it were her native element. When she swung up onto the cement and pulled off her cap, shaking her head, her whole body shimmered. The tiger stripes waved as she stamped her feet.

O.T. watched her too with something like longing on his otherwise inscrutable face, but he was respectful, even though she had told him not to "ma'am" her, it made her feel old.

"He's right cute," she told us as we whispered to each other from our own stretched-out towels, and we giggled agreement, picking at the frayed edges of the towels as we sucked in our tummies, trying to puff out our chests. All that summer we strutted in front of O.T., made countless trips to the Coke machine, did laps, practiced our life saving techniques.

"That's right," Ruby assured us, "you learn best by doing. You just keep doin', sugars."

When she took us to the pool, she changed her clothes there in that dressing room so that anyone who wanted could admire her freckled shoulders and hands, her milky white body, which sometimes bore mysterious lavender bruises, either on her shoulder just above her breast or sometimes on her neck. She was a country goddess.

The passion we felt for O.T. was something she understood, knowing about love. She said it scarcely had to do with the lifeguard himself, but she told us it was natural. O.T. was a triangular-shaped fellow with close-cropped hair and broad shoulders, a Noxzema-ed nose wedged onto his face like an afterthought. His sailor cap didn't quite hide the way he watched the older girls, especially Gwendolyn, as she dipped her painted toes into the bleach-water trough you had to walk through to get to the pool from the ladies' dressing room.

It was distasteful as anything, that cloudy white trough, the necessity for it unspoken but ominous. Some people thought going to the pool was the closest thing to heaven, but for me, even though I had begged for lessons, the community pool was full of reminders about how dangerous the universe was.

Beyond the trough, there was the maze of damp benches and dark green lockers past which we had to file. We had put on our bathing suits at home, modestly, but there in the locker room, we saw women dressing and undressing: pubic hair, fat thighs, sagging breasts with great rose nipples. None of this did we see at home where everyone dressed behind closed doors and respected privacy. Here there was none. The universe did not admit of privacy. That was something which existed in Grandmother's prim white house.

There was then a terrifying aspect to those large uncovered female bodies we saw on our way to the swimming pool, their bulk, their odor, their ease, a series of laughing women pushing their hair up into rubber caps, kneading their breasts into the tops of bathing suits, or peeling their suits off, running their large hands down their sides in a caress of relief at being out of the bone-held suits they wore.

Grandmother was slim. Her body encased in simple linen dresses smelled good, did not bulge or sigh for release. These bodies seemed to ache for it, you could tell, in the way a large-boned woman would swing her leg up onto the bench and lather it with Coppertone. We felt daring just to linger there without any excuse for our presence, observing them.

In Ruby's book of American paintings these women leaned over rooftops drying their hair or rested naked against haystacks, while a lecherous farmer peered around a tree, Thomas Hart Benton's *Persephone*. Respectability had its pages too—the girl from Philadelphia all dressed in white, dreamily holding a fan. We described her when Grandmother looked up from her gardening to ask what we'd been doing over at Ruby's all afternoon. And the farm couple by Grant Wood or his group portrait of the Daughters of the Revolution.

These, Ruby told us laughing, must be respectable, so these were what we described, omitting Ruby's gloss on respectability, her stories, our adventures. We had asked the only person we trusted to tell us, the last person Grandmother would have recommended. Ruby was nominally of the older generation because of her marriage to Bubba, yet she seemed caught between.

Elizabeth and I elaborated on our gods and goddesses, Ruby like Persephone, shuttling back and forth between the kingdoms of darkness and light. We and the swimming pool were the light. Bubba's store and all those old people she had to endure, well, they were obviously the dark. But the thing was, travelling back and forth like that, you could learn a lot. Ruby seemed to know everything.

123

"Ruby," we asked, lying on the dank yellow grass by the pool, trying to get warm after our lesson, "what is it like to be in love?"

She lay on her stomach, her chin on her folded hands. She stared past O.T.'s lifeguard stand, past the poplars at the edge of the chain-link fence, seeming to focus on a shadowy place we couldn't discern. What she didn't say was that we would know when it hit us. That we were too young, that it was foolish to ask.

Ruby's hair was auburn, plain red in a certain light, and now, as she stared off into the distance, some of it was almost black from being wet at the nape of her neck. We watched her carefully, eager for what she had to say. We knew about oracles, gypsies, how they told your future, but somehow, even then, we had sense enough to put our money on Ruby.

"It's not like the movies," she said slowly. "It's not really like the books." We knew her for an avid reader. Sometimes she took us to the library where we were enrolled in a Read-a-thon.

"You can tell us," we said confidently. "We won't tell." Meaning we wanted to be initiated into the secret club. We wished to know, really know, what we were in for. The mystery of life. We already knew about babies, we'd seen kittens born under the back steps at Grandmother's only last week. Even so, Grandmother wouldn't let us see *From Here to Eternity* at the Uptown Theatre. We were caught too that summer in a frenzied limbo between worlds we didn't quite inhabit. We wanted now, our first summer of adolescence, to know about love.

"Why isn't it in books?"

"Shut up, Elizabeth," I said. I didn't want to know why. I wanted to know what. It. Was. Like. Love. We had been practicing Dead Man's Float while O.T. ferried us across the pool, his impersonal arm crooked across our shoulders and beneath our chins. He was demonstrating how to save someone but we were, one at a time, separately towed and thrilled. Was what we felt, the water parting around us as O.T. swam, was that rippling, spinning pleasure akin to love?

Ruby rolled over on her back, hitched her bathing suit well up over her full breasts, and closed her eyes. Maybe she'd seen something beyond the poplars and the cyclone fence that kept the colored out, something she knew about love out there in the mown field where preachers set up revival tents and traveling shows set up carnival rides whenever they came to town.

"It is like going on the Ferris wheel," she said, "getting on with someone you think is really nice, and the man operating the Ferris wheel kind of winks as you get in. He slams that bar across the two of you, and you're in it together, however it's going to be. When you lurch forward as it's cranking up, maybe you're a little scared 'cause maybe it's one of those hot nights with the threat of storm, but it isn't raining yet, only a hint of it, thunder clouds off in the distance. Maybe you're shivery because of the county fair, all that activity, those big stuffed animals, the penny-pitching jars, the freaks, canned goods in the tent with bright lights. Well, all of it gathers together and then swims under you as you rise in that little compartment for two people, and it all falls away. There aren't, any more, all those crowds. It's quiet and private and you're turning around and around through the air, just the two of you, looking at each other, not seeing everything below, not seeing anything but one another."

She lay very still then and we waited patiently for her to begin again. Behind us, O.T. took his bullhorn and yelled at some kids on the diving board.

"Falling in love is like being suspended on top of the world in that Ferris wheel when the operator has stopped to let someone else on, but you're at the top so you can't tell, and you don't care whether anyone down there is getting on or off. There's just you and him." She sat up and hugged her knees.

"And what it's like down below where Mrs. Smith is in a swivet because Mrs. Brown's fruit cobbler got a blue ribbon, or some kid's balloon twisted to look like a poodle has popped and she's screaming for another, or a carny's trying to lure the youngsters inside to see the contortionist, or Joe Boy is standing in front of the funny house mirror looking at how he'd look if he didn't look the way he does, what it's like down there with everyone wishing for something they don't have, it doesn't matter at all. You have what you want, and that's what counts."

Elizabeth and I were motionless, our faces serious, eyes fixed on Ruby.

"Love is selfish like that. The whole earth could fall away and you wouldn't give a fig. You can look off into the distance, you're eye-level with the clouds, you could pitch lightning into the middle of the cattle pen and cause such havoc! You could stop the thunder and bottle it up, you feel that powerful. You know a storm might make a liar of your feelings, but you don't care. You are on top of the world," she said slowly, unwinding her arms from around her knees and extending her long legs carefully, as if she were stepping down from a great height. She lay half back, resting on her elbows, studying her painted toenails. She looked at us sitting up expectant and cross-legged at her recital and she smiled.

"You'll see," she said, "you'll see."

"How do you know you're in love?" I asked shyly.

"Well, how do you know you're on top of a Ferris wheel? Doesn't anybody have to tell you that, do they?"

Elizabeth shook her head. "It sure ain't in the books like that."

"Nope, that's a real problem with these books. Still," she said, reaching for her crocheted bag with the wooden handle and pulling out some Dentyne gum, offering it to us before taking a stick herself, "we best be reading anyway."

"Our books aren't due until Friday," I said stoutly, "but I've finished mine." I always carried a book to the pool, for what I had observed during the first week of Red Cross instruction was that O.T., for whom I had the most intense desire, didn't even know my name at week's end. Worse, he called me Yankee, and Elizabeth, Squirt. He paid us no attention at all outside of class. Books offered solace. But now, lying on my towel, chewing gum, I thought not about books but about Ferris wheels. I almost always got dizzy and slightly sick with excitement. Sometimes I was downright scared. I took a deep breath and confessed this.

Elizabeth snorted as if to say she already knew that. Unfortunately she did because I'd thrown up all over the seat when the carnival came to town for the Fourth of July, but Ruby only said that falling in love was kind of like that too.

She stood up then and brushed grass clippings off her legs and looked down at us.

"Nothing in life is a bed of roses," she said. "That Ferris wheel goes up, and it comes down. You got to pay to take the ride."

We stood too, prompted by something in her voice that told us it was time to leave. We shook our towels so as not to get grass on Bubba's backseat when Ruby drove us home, slung the towels around our necks and followed her through the loathsome Clorox foot-bath water, into the locker room where we sat on a bench and waited while Ruby showered. She re-appeared with her towel around her like Dorothy Lamour.

"Your mamas wouldn't be so pleased with all this conversation about Ferris wheels," she said. "You want to take a survey, you ask them what they think love's like, but don't be quoting me, and don't tell me what they say neither." She took her underwear out of the wire basket in which she'd left it, and gravely we watched as she bent to drop her breasts, like pears, into each cup. Her panties were red nylon with black lace around the legs. Instinctively we knew that hers was not the kind of underwear in which to have an accident.

Sometimes we did errands on our way back from the pool. Not infrequently, we stopped at a nearby orchard for a bushel of fruit. Ruby allowed us each to take a peach and to eat it over our towels as she drove. We'd have to wipe the peaches to remove the fuzz and whatever germs might be resident on their soft skin. In the front, driving rapidly now, Ruby would also eat, her own towel spread over her lap. Once in a while she talked absently to herself, but most often she turned on the radio and we listened to Patti Page, Jo Stafford, and Teresa Brewer as we covered the distance home. Collectively we decided to see the pyramids along the Nile together. We would take Bubba along, seeing how Ruby loved him so much.

"You *do* love Bubba," I wanted to say, watching her face rearrange itself at the suggestion. Jo Stafford had just finished singing, and the air in the car was thick with peach scent and dust from the orchard. Instead, I said nothing, slightly uneasy for a reason I couldn't identify.

The idea of falling in love was exciting, but it seemed to happen to people when they were young, and Ruby and Bubba were scarcely that. It was even more difficult to imagine Grandmother or Daddy Doc in love, or our parents. Although these people surely loved one another, it seemed different from falling in love. I began to see too that what Elizabeth and I wanted from O.T. had more to do with recognition than with love. If a god bowed to you, did it make you some kind of a goddess? If he failed to, might you still be divine? I thought about Diana and the hunt, goddesses in disguise. I longed to be translated into another shape. Breasts would have been a terrific help.

Sometimes instead of going to the orchard, we went to the ice house and the man on the platform slid back the heavy wooden door, revealing blocks of ice. From where we stood below the platform, he looked like one of the figures in Ruby's painting book. Like the boxers in the match at Sharkey's, his arms bulged when he took tongs and hefted ice into the trunk of Ruby's car. She always kept newspaper back there, and it was our task to spread the paper quickly before the man brought the slippery ice down from the scales.

Once or twice, we observed another man who seemed to know Ruby. He spoke quietly to her, appearing, it seemed, out of nowhere. The third time we saw him, I noticed that his car had been parked at the ice house when we drove up, as if he were waiting for something, but ice wasn't something you waited around with during the summer in Arkansas.

"Who *is* that?" I asked. Ruby said he was someone she used to know, and now he sold insurance. She spoke in a matter-of-fact, offhand manner, but Elizabeth and I were so full of romance and love and our futile obsession with O.T. that we teased her. "He loves you, doesn't he?"

"He's just sitting here waiting in case you need ice," I added. "I saw him here last time."

"Nonsense," said Ruby sharply. "It's coincidence, is all. John Clay's married with two kids," she said. Her voice rocked a little then. "They got an ice cream maker like I do. Probably their kiddies like peach ice cream just as much as you two." She spun the car away from the ice house so rapidly that gravel rattled beneath her tires. After that, I was sorry I'd said anything, for we never saw the man there again. I remembered he was as tall as she was, rather dark, and much younger than Bubba, closer to Ruby's age. Although he looked nothing like O.T., he too carried himself proud. He had a distinctive chin, sharp and cleft.

❊ ❊ ❊

Years later, when Bubba died, I saw him again, at the funeral. I'd been away myself for close to thirty years, and I'd taken a ride or two on Ferris wheels. When we returned from the cemetery, that same man was at Ruby's house with a woman who must have been his wife. She was looking around like someone burnt-up with curiosity. I saw her finger Ruby's Hummel figures on the mantelpiece, watched her turn over a teacup to see the pattern. All the while, her husband never took his eyes off Ruby, who was receiving friends and neighbors on the sofa. I found Elizabeth in the dining room pouring tea and asked her, since she had lived all her life there in that small town.

"John Clay? One thing I'll say for you, you don't miss much, never did."

"Who *is* he? I think I've seen him, but where?"

"Ruby's friend. She was engaged to him—not really, but in a way—before the War. Then she fell in love and married Bubba."

I took a cup from Elizabeth, looking back into the living room across the china rim, blowing softly on the hot tea before I sipped. I have never needed to haul anyone up from the bottom of a pool nor even tow someone across an expanse of water. All that preparation had been for naught. I have never been even remotely near the scene of a water accident. Of course I have, as everyone has, passed people and ambulances on highways, and because of Grandmother, I almost always hope they have on clean underwear, as if that fact might save them from the consequences of their wrong turns, the slick pavement, whatever in the troubled universe has brought them to that sad moment.

Standing next to Elizabeth and the teacups, I saw John Clay's wife fingering a silver frame with Bubba's picture in it. A small thick woman with fat ankles, she was apparently near-sighted but too vain to wear her glasses, for she brought the picture close to her face. She looked entirely respectable, like one of those women holding a teacup in that Grant Wood painting.

I hadn't thought of that picture book in years, yet here in the house where Elizabeth and I had pored over its pages so many afternoons, the images came back. Ruby, subdued, alone for a moment in the midst of the funeral company, an hour back from the cemetery, laid her head against the sofa and looked around the room. John Clay gazed hungrily at her, like that Thomas Hart Benton farmer peering around the tree at the country goddess who'd stripped off her clothes in the summer heat. Ruby met his gaze. Although her hair had silver strands after all these years, she still looked like Persephone, full of life and just back from the kingdom of the dead.

Photograph of my Father
(The Art of Seeing Things)

I was mesmerized by the skim that poured
into the vats he kept beneath the bench,
the smell of glass ground against a stone
slicked by water. He screwed each lens

into its frame, and I'd listen to the Sox,
turned up to drown out the edger.
Each pair became a stranger seeing a
letter or landscape, eyes forced to chime

by his shop. He tried to show me how
to plot diopters, correct myopias,
coax two corneas out of a Monet
through their weakened muscles.

❊

The myths of Gremlins, and rooftops:
at thirteen he trapped homing pigeons
for bread money in Brooklyn;

he told me stories of fistfights;
I busted my knuckles.

❊

His first day in basic, 1960-something,
he only held the rifle,
looked through the scope.

It was an object of purity.
It had no purpose.

Later, they thought they'd fallen.
He made them fall.

❋

I can see you as a calligrapher
of land-shapes and bodhi
unencrypted by your eye.

I can see an order
divorced from redemption,
an object bloodied by chance,

digits puckered under dew-dripped foliage
so thick it coats like a hauberk

while you wait in your bunk, half asleep,
waiting for the next day's duty.

I can see you
as an object
edged into light,

your hand on my hand
whispering *exhale and squeeze.*

❋

After the bombs went off,
the trees were red
as Christmas.

❋

Intoxicated, sight might produce grackles
behind eyelids, or even-handed furies;

it might produce roads or stones
skipped off the ocean's teeth.

The Buddha lit a flame before Ananda
and asked, "Do you see it?"

You painted, before I was born, two birds
a branch, three forms on a field,

sharp as kanji stroked
by the hand of an arhat.

The Buddha snuffed the flame
and asked, "Do you see it?"
The fire makes us blind.

*

Another story: you told me about a knife
in a village. You watched them
come in and purify the men.

In the dark
you silenced them.

The village was small
and on the way.

*

To unfold you in the light,

to hold a glass of water,
to know water
will change its color,

to know the limit of correspondence

I see you twice.

Ascension

I think of the day the hot air balloons drifted
into our city

and I watched as a purple and red one climbed
behind the house

across the street and I followed my mother's green bicycle
to the river

where the valley opened wide like a mouth.

Fifty-three orbs, their torches and baskets hanging
in the dawn

and my mother's smile repossessing her face.

What was it like for her the year after my father
left us? She said

it was like sleep and it was like God
lifting her up

the way she floated with the balloons, the dark city
beneath her.

Portrait

You wanted to paint me
        wearing my black linen sundress,
my summer freckles.

In Brigantine at night,
        the ocean blew inside,
lamps swayed.

You wanted to paint white wings
        on my back, the moonlight
over the dunes, I ran

alone to the water, stripped,
        and dove right in, the foxes
keeping watch like they did

when you were a girl. The night
        you saw my moon was in Cancer, deep
and watery, porous against

my Sun in Capricorn. You knew
        to leave the light on, tea in the cabinet
for when I couldn't sleep, the dark

then blue dawn. My hands
        would be folded in prayer in my lap,
the train ride home, tunnels

of green through Jersey,
        the wings, my face reflected
in decrepit houses in North

Philadelphia. My head
        would be lowered, like when
you were lowered.

Everything is for a reason,
         a friend said, even moons
in Cancer, my pen

on the paper writing it,
         the wings growing out
from inside.

Jen Hoppa, photograph

The Invitation

When I woke, I was already in her arms.
She was carrying me down the hall to the night
and the glimmering crickets. I knew her.

I had a name and she was speaking it.
I knew my name and she was telling me
it was all right, saying come out

and see the stars the beautiful stars
with her and daddy and little John. Then
we were out in the soft night, on the front step

with the crickets and wet grass all around.
She showed me the stars. I heard their voices.
I sat wrapped in a pink blanket. Johnny danced

on the lawn, held up his arms to my father,
who swung him around on the grass under the stars.
I was waking, waking into something

already in motion, like the soft shaking
of an earthquake, rolling me side to side.
That night they were young, passing

into my arms the possibility of stars,
a sheer vase for the capture of flowers,
the thin and meltable film of memory.

Later there would be other stars. Later
I would rise up, I would run down
that hall to see her upright, raging

against the newest children in the house
who sat frozen and wrapped in their beds,
their faces the brightness of hammered glass.

Later the house would be full of voices as angry
as separate oceans. They would spill out.
I would spill out. I would rise up

and hand back to them their rage, the broken
vase of memory. But the stars still
live there. When I left that house

I carried my name. The way ginger
lights the inside of my mouth,
I carry that night. Johnny still holds

up his arms. Like waves we return,
are thrown every year back to the step
for a photograph. Together we paste

a thin film of happiness over the waves
of ground formed by heavings and erosions,
planted over with living things.

That night's invitation brings me
to the thin moment of a poem, to each word
placed for its brightness. I carry her with me

and when I look at the stars, she looks with me.
When I woke, we were already moving
toward the night, toward the crickets and the stars.

We were both waking, she and I.
She was calling the name she had given me.
I was already in her arms.

The Note He Might Have Left

He might have left
it taped to the back door—
corners clinging
to the glass as the lights
inside pulsed, illuminating
an empty hall. The envelope
might have bulged,
each nervous page
embracing the next.
The ink might have bled,
the thoughts reaching
through the paper
out to our hands that would
later find them
& clutch them fiercely,
as though they were
his feet, just stepping
into the night.

Superstition

They spun our small bodies
in mint-green checked sheets,
slipped us under the hood
of the Moses basket
on their dresser each night.
They wove nests
of cotton & wool blankets
at the foot of their bed when
we had nightmares, fed us
stories until we were safe.
They built a spaceship
out of two-by-fours,
so we could sit in the driveway
steering up & down
the fringe of the sun
without getting burned.
& they called us
their *pig babies*
to fool the gods
into thinking we weren't
worth taking.

Bounty

The basement of my family's house was exotic, as all submerged places are. It was damp and dark and, with each heavy rain, flooded to our knees. Wolf spiders, legs spread to the size of my palm, thrived here, and when I poked under the steps, sometimes I found the tiny skeletons of mice. A shallow cardboard box sat on a three-legged table propped up with a stack of French novels, their covers stained and buckled. The box held African violets, six pots to a row. Grow Lights strung from a ceiling pipe hovered and bathed the plants in a purplish shimmer.

My father owned the plants, and no one, not even my mother, was allowed to touch or move them. They needed the dank environment, he said, and this controlled pink electric light. He experimented with different plant food: Go & Grow, NutriRoot, Green-Grow. My father said if water touched the leaves, the plants would die, so he watered them from underneath, filling the plastic trays from a needle-nosed watering can. The plants would also die if the leaves touched the edge of the plastic pots, so my father pruned the lower leaves with slim Japanese gardening shears.

Sunday nights, I would sit in the middle of the basement and monitor my family's whereabouts by which section of the ceiling creaked. Then I'd listen to the latest episode of Nick Danger on an old cracked radio. After *Radio Mystery Theater*, the creaking ceiling would become ominous, and wanting more of a thrill, I'd run up the stairs and hit the light switch. The basement would go black. Within seconds, pink vapor lifted the dark. When my eyes accustomed to the haze, I'd follow it to the source. The box of violets would be glowing like a radioactive crèche on a December night and I'd look at the flowers with a kind of wonder. According to my father, the plants were tender, delicate, but to me they looked unearthly, waxy, the blooms embalmed. Purple petals, centered with BB-sized yellow pistils, swarmed the leaves. The plants were the most beautiful things I'd seen. I'd blow on them, then wave my hand, worrying that in the morning my father would discover brown spots on the leaves.

One Saturday afternoon in summer, when I was ten, I sat in a corner of the basement working on science projects made from stolen kitchen spices and water, which combined to make pungent-smelling gray paste. I mixed the spices in Petri dishes my father had brought me from his work at an agricultural plant, and within a couple of days the gray would ferment into yellow, brown, and green molds. If you ate the yellow mold you'd fall in love, if the brown even touched your skin you'd die. I hadn't yet settled on the powers of the green, and that gave me options. I made it clear to my family that these experiments were mine. No one was allowed to even look at them. The dishes were stored in a wooden closet with a hair taped across the door. But my family wasn't interested in my secrets.

Now, as I bent over the Petri dishes, my sister, Edie, who had come downstairs to rummage around by the back door, interrupted my concentration. She was sixteen and my father acted as if he despised her, as if he thought her ugly and willful and stupid. He called her Edith, and on his lips the name sounded like spitting. Just the sight of her could make him angry. When he flew into a rage, trying to get at her, she'd run upstairs to her room and I'd hide on the landing, one ear cocked for sounds behind her door, the other straining to hear my mother's pleading words downstairs. If my father had banished her from the dinner table, calling her a pig because she asked for more potatoes, I wanted to sneak food to her. But I was afraid. And maybe she deserved to go hungry.

Sometimes Edie had anger fits and slapped me. My mother had seen this more than once. She'd say, "Be kind, Eliza. She can't help it." Then she'd shrug. "It's just—you know." And so I took it, because I did know. I always got the second helping. But Edie also let me try on her clothes and sometimes fixed my hair. We harmonized to Odetta and Joan Baez albums. She told me things she told no one else, that she was ugly and stupid and fat. When she said this, I thought my father must be right, but I couldn't reconcile his view of her with what I saw: thick, glossy hair, sexy bee-stung lips, curvy calves, and her ferocity. And I'd seen the way men sometimes looked at her on the street.

As I sprinkled paprika into my green mold, I heard the scrape of the back door's rusty dead bolt. My sister was using both hands to slide it free. "What are you doing?" I asked. We never used that door. Edie threw open the bulkhead, and in a blast of sunlight that illuminated every crack in the cement floor, Jarek, her Polish boyfriend from Trenton, rushed in. When my sister let the bulkhead thump back down, he was momentarily swallowed by darkness. Jarek was thin and pale with a slick, dark cap of hair. His accent stretched my name into "Eleeeezza," which sent a shiver down my spine. He was handsome and smelled of tobacco and clay from the ceramics factory where he worked. Edie had met him at the beginning of the summer on a street corner while waiting for the bus. My father called him Trenton trash and said that, at 20, he was too old for my sister. She was forbidden to see him, or any other boy, even those younger than Jarek.

Edie crossed the room and lifted me by my armpits. "Bonnie's looking for you. Go." Bonnie was my best friend.

"I'm working." I tried to sit back down, but she held me up.

"I'll wash your hair tonight," she bribed.

"It's not dirty." I watched Jarek pull a cigarette from his shirt pocket. "Daddy'll smell the smoke. You're going to get it."

"Go on," my sister said, pinching my elbow, "or I'll wring your neck."

"How are you going to get him out of here? Daddy'll be outside soon." From the living room where my father was, strains of opera vibrated the floorboards. After he went outside to tend his garden, the opera would still blare through the house in earsplitting waves of emotion, until none of us, especially my father, would be able to think straight.

Jarek picked up one of my Petri dishes. "Yummy," he said, smelling it. He and Edie smiled over my head. She looked exotic and happy. She wore a white peasant blouse with an elasticized neck and puffy sleeves. Her hair bouffanted off her forehead and fell into curls around the side of her face and in the dim light you couldn't see the eyeliner that rimmed both upper and lower lids, just its effect—luminous, almond-shaped eyes. "If you're a good girl," Jarek said, "you can come back later, and I'll teach you to blow smoke rings." I frowned and looked up at the ceiling and he blew on my cheek. Upstairs, my mother thumped in the kitchen and I thought she must be washing her pots and pans. Sometimes she got lost watching herself in the metal surfaces, and I'd imagine her wide forehead, pale eyes and fleshy lips reflected back, ghostly and curved.

"You'll be trapped," I said to Jarek, "and get even skinnier and die." I thought of my green mold. That could be its power. I could bring him back to life and he'd take me away.

He shrugged. "I'll live under the staircase. You and your sister can feed me." He walked his fingers up my arm. "I'll be your spider." When his hand started to crawl across my collarbone, my sister knocked it off.

"Give this one a couple of years," Jarek said, and my sister punched him in the stomach. Laughing, he doubled over. By the time I walked to the stairs, they were kissing.

Outside, in the brilliant sun, our half-acre of suburbia was studded with small apple and peach trees my father had planted when we moved in. The summer had been hot and already, in mid-August, the apples were red and bent the scrawny branches. The peaches plumped in sherbet tones of orange and pink.

My father, an agricultural chemist, believed in the protective powers of poison. Every night after dinner he retired to the garage where the chemicals were stored. From clear glass jugs, he'd mix the proper proportions into his metal spraying canister, a recipe that killed everything smaller than a field mouse. Dressed in baggy army fatigues with holes in the knees, he'd emerge from the garage at twilight, armed with his spray gun. In the front yard, playing badminton or Wiffle Ball, we could hear the scrinching sound of the pump being primed, and soon the chemical permeated the neighborhood. It stung the inside of our noses. In bed at night, sometimes I'd taste it in the back of my throat.

Now, in the middle of the backyard, I stared at the peaches until the color flattened against the green leaves, and the blue sky filled the spaces between leaf and black branch. The screen door slammed and my father came out onto the porch. He was almost pretty, with deep-set blue eyes, sharp cheekbones, and curving lips. Prewar photographs showed an almost skeletal face, merciless, but at the same time his features looked dainty, as if they could damage easily. A scar ran the length of his long nose, a World War II wound from a fall down icy steps while carrying a box of volatile chemicals. His only war wound, an accident. Last year, at his company's picnic, I'd heard him tell another vet that he'd gotten the wound fighting at the front. But the scar always gave me hope, its puckered length a seam that had been ripped out, relaxing the taut skin of his face in a forgiving way.

Strains of opera followed him down the back porch steps as if he emitted high-frequency Italian turmoil, and I started to worry about what might be going on in the basement. What if Jarek had found the flowers? My sister could be showing them to him, picking up the pots. What if my father went down there to give the violets a tasty treat of Go & Grow? But approaching me, he smiled and I relaxed.

"How's my squeaky, skwunky little girl?" He said, patting me. Once he told me every hair on my head was his until I was eighteen. Out here, in summer, in our lushly poisoned nature museum, that was okay with me. Our yard was the envy of the neighborhood. Or so I wished to believe. He pointed to the peaches on the ground and said, "Pick them all up and cart them to the compost." I ran eagerly to the garage for baskets. I knew how to stay on his good side. Behave, my mother cautioned. That's what she did.

When I returned with the baskets, he was digging in his vegetable garden with a pitchfork, overturning dark soil to widen the squash patch. The hands curled tight around the pitchfork's wooden handle were small and squat. When he was growing up, his mother gave lessons on a grand piano. My father's finger span was too narrow to play, but once, my mother told me, when he was trying, my grandmother brought the cover down hard on his hands.

By the side of the house, the dahlias were in full showy bloom. My father was absorbed in his work, the pitchfork's tines twanging against rock, and so I sneaked under one of the bushes to spy, pressing my nose flat to the basement window. Edie and Jarek were lying on a sleeping bag on the floor. Jarek was on top of her, his hand under her white blouse. Maybe she figured in the gloomy basement he couldn't see the scar that dented one breast from an operation to correct a faulty heart valve when she was two. She protected her deformity with a padded bra and speculated on the size and shape of other girls' breasts, claiming that no man would ever want her. But Jarek didn't seem to care as he pushed her blouse up, whatever he made of the smooth scar beneath his fingers. When Edie and I were alone in her room, she'd sometimes flash me her tit, and I'd see a red line, flesh spilling out on either side. But then she quickly covered it with her bra, as if the bra were a bandage. My mother told her she was being silly, it was nothing. I wanted to study the scar, say I agreed with our mother, but didn't know if I was brave enough to look. It could be worse than I thought, and I might faint or throw up. But Edie was brave, letting Jarek feel her up, touch her place, with our father just above, digging through dirt. My breath fogged the glass and my thighs tingled as if Jarek's spider hand was walking up me. I thought of my molds. What I saw through the window gave me power, something to hold over Edie.

Behind me, twigs crackled, and then I heard my father's voice. "What are you doing?" I flattened, hoping to disappear, and breathed dust. "Get out of there." He tugged my heels and I scooted out from under the bush. Sweat dripped from his chin. His t-shirt was plastered to his chest. "What are you looking for?" He asked.

Wiping my face, I thought hard. "Stormy," I said.

He pointed to our cat lying in the middle of the front lawn, the black fur clearly visible against the green. "I told you to pick up the peaches."

He was suspicious. Dancing around him, I jumped high as if on a Pogo Stick. My feet wouldn't stay on the ground. I cartwheeled, trying to distract him, and looked into the neighbors' yards hoping someone would come over. But the pesticide had driven the neighborhood inside, the lawns empty. He yelled at me to hurry up and moved back towards the garden. I ran after him to the fruit trees where I bombed the baskets with peaches and dragged them across the yard to the compost pile. Things were allowed to live there—worms, bugs—creatures I was interested in. Last week, Edie had plunged my arm into its center, punishment for spying on her in the bathroom. The hot, moist dirt had filled my palm, and towards the cooler, outer edge of the pile, worms nudged along my arm. Later that night Edie gave me a manicure.

I arranged the spoiled peaches on top of the pile, as if creating a still life, and admired the effect. Behind me the garden became too quiet, and when I turned, it was deserted, my father's pitchfork stuck into a mound of black dirt. I dropped the basket and walked towards the house. By the time I reached the patio, I heard yelling. At first I thought it was an aria; sometimes it was difficult to tell. Then the bulkhead erupted and Jarek catapulted into the yard. He ran towards the street, tucking his shirt, and as he passed me, he shook his head ruefully, but a smile was on his lips. He rounded the corner of the house as the back door opened and my sister clattered down the steps, calling his name. My father chased after her with my mother behind him.

In the middle of the yard, Edie stopped and whirled around. The three of them stood apart in a loose circle, as if about to play a game. My mother touched my father's arm with quick, nervous pats. "Let's go inside and discuss this," she said, and I wondered, what did my father see? Edie's blouse pulled up, Jarek's hand between her legs? Something worse? He jerked his arm away, and my mother ran fingertips down her cheeks. Edie's face was flushed, her bright lips parted. Her hair hung in wildly disarrayed curls and her eyes jumped inside their border of black liner. She was out of breath, her chest straining for air beneath her blouse so the outline of her breasts was visible, and I saw her heart pounding. Her whole body seemed to be pulsing. The air was scented with her deep, earthy sweat. She was magnificent, the real thing, and around her, the garden, the grass, the scrawny fruit trees seemed to take heart, and glow with greater abandon. My father moved towards her, then stopped short. He slumped, and seemed to grow smaller, and, for a moment, I thought he might cry. The expression on his face was a mixture of pain and fear and something else. It would be a long time before I could fathom this look, before I could begin to understand the nature of his feelings for her. She was what he feared and yearned for, the wild, lush beauty beyond his control. Her very existence mocked him, her vitality draining his. Despite his efforts, she burst through and thrived.

"What is it?" My mother cried, glancing rapidly between them. She untied her apron and balled it tight, as if that could put an end to things. But the apron fell to the ground.

Staring at Edie, my father's lips began to move silently.

"You want to say something to me?" Edie asked.

My father's face reddened. My mother stretched out her hand to him, and nodded encouragingly. Then my father's lips tightened, he bore down, closed his eyes, but the word tore through. "Whore."

Edie's arms opened wide. "Come and get me," she said, and ran her glistening tongue slowly across her top lip, her chin thrust towards him. Then the yard seemed to split apart as he pounced and grabbed her hair. She twisted wildly, but his hand was buried, snaked through the dark strands so only his knuckles showed, pink and bony. He forced her to her knees. My mother came at them, her arms swinging bonelessly.

"For God's sake!" She yelled. "Oh for God's sake." She swatted at my father and he finally disentangled his hand. Edie began to run and I started towards her, to capture her, or help her escape, I didn't know. She shoved me aside with such force I fell down hard. Then Edie was gone, straight through the garden to the woods beyond.

❊ ❊ ❊

What I recall of that night is this: at dinner, the opera blares from my father's hi-fi so that it blankets the silence among the three of us, and the peas on my plate are so startlingly green and perfectly round I can't eat them. When I glance sideways, my father's hands shake and I think, good. If she never comes back, everything will get better. But my father's hands look as if they need something solid to hit to make them stay still, and my own hands begin to tremble.

After dinner, he leaves the house to spray the backyard, and I go down to the basement. The sun hasn't yet set, the light a gray veil. The opera, still playing upstairs, is muffled down here as if the singers have been rolled in carpet. I try to work on my science projects, but the idea that the molds hold power seems childish, of no use. I'm about to throw the dishes away, I can't stand to look at them any longer, when I hear my name being whispered. Circling the room, I find Edie stooped under the basement steps.

"Edie?" She doesn't answer, just looks at me. The elastic neck of her blouse is pulled down, revealing her shoulders, and in the grainy light her skin appears to be moving. Our father's hand has tangled her hair so it falls over her eyes. She is as still and stunted as a figure in a wax museum. I say her name again, and she brings a finger to her lips. "Shhhh," she whispers, and picks up a can of NutriRoot. She scoots out from under the stairs and I follow her to the violets where she unscrews the top of the can.

"Don't," I say. The liquid has to be diluted first.

"Don't?" She mimics, her voice rising as if she's about to have an anger fit. "They need some attention, the pitiful little things. This makes them beautiful and strong." She pours onto the first plant. "Don't you want that?" The liquid is golden honey.

It pools on top of the soil, and then slowly disappears. I can almost feel the roots sucking up the stinging liquid, and I start to cry. Above the plants, my sister's face twists in concentration, her eye makeup smudged, her lips swollen, distorted. My father is right. She's a monstrous girl. I squat down, hide my face between my knees, the thick odor of the fertilizer still in my nose.

"Stand up." She nudges me and I curl tighter into myself. She pulls me up and pinches my chin. "Listen." Her voice is determined. "Don't be a sissy. There's no future in being a sissy. Do you really think it'll be any different for you?" She clicks her teeth and pushes the can towards me. "Just wait."

I shake my head, but her words make me feel sick. What if she's right? I try to remember if there was ever a time when he didn't despise her, when he smiled and patted her, and called her his girl. Vague memories start to float through my head, but I was too young, and it's like trying to see something at twilight when the world begins to fade and comes undone.

"Give them a shot," she says, and wraps my fingers around the handle.

The heavy can starts to slip. By morning, the plants might be gigantic, with twice the blooms, the leaves cracking the ceiling with their hard wax-green, the BBs at the center of each violet grown to the size of cannonballs, exploding through the floor of the living room, splintering the roof, turning us into orphans, and I see my sister again, outside and brilliant under the sun, and see the strange way my father looked at her, *in awe, as if he were afraid of her.* I squeeze my hand tight around the handle, and without waiting for Edie's signal, I pour until nothing is left.

Cotton-Picker

I

The hair on his temple is pulled back more
from the scar, white against the clay
color of his skin. Sometimes, out here
I believe the story he is half Osage,
making me an eighth. He kneels
among the tall prairie grasses, finds one
tufted with white, seedy down, and his fingers
close around one of the thorny cotton heads
as if it were a baseball. He shows me
the grip for a southpaw's sidearm curve. Dizzy
Dean, he says, he could make the hard ball
sing three up three down like a national
anthem just for pitchers. He limbers up, then
heads back across the outer field
to the house where I lived until I was nine. Fired
orange by the light at sundown, his coloring
makes the Osage Indian story
more than an old man's tale.

II

He pitches a burlap sack
into a corner. It collapses
like a lung, the cotton-balls
spilling out onto the dirt floor
like water, but dry, as dry as his mouth
the morning after he killed
a pint of Thunderbird.
He knows I've come back
from someplace where they tell me

to say as little possible. Neither of us needs
to speak, breath hard after
a lesson in his fields. Later
in his rocker he will fall asleep, drowning
in the dream of pitching
in the majors, and not wake up
until after dark, when I have gone
again, back to the school
of fewer words, unsure what day it is.

M. J. Flanagan, pencil

Mirrored Text

Set your fragments deep
where they will do the most good;
square in the beholder's eye.
Set them deep before the focus
shifts and you become elsewhere
and other, a shadow's edge.

Blood and bone and flesh
in a skein of senses,
mise en abyme,
reflected whole where the gaze
will not note and dismiss them in an instant.

If you would be here,
if you would be
more than a handful of words
trailing down a sheet of paper.

When the Sun Stood Still

I took a leaf from Joshua and stopped the sun.
Things had been getting out of hand
what with decay everywhere,
encroaching ruins, signs
that the trick of matter to reflect itself,
to sing to itself of love and terror,
was growing old.

I held it still in a blue-black sky,
the earth too pausing.
And the moment turned clear and pathless,
without a trace of past or future.
Free of regrets, dreams, vanities,
it lay stark in me,
open to a random drift of being.

The blood in its narrow channel quickened,
carrying in its flow fresh moments
unbound by who I was.
I knew the shape of what vanishes,
what re-emerges. I knew the living pulse.
Then a thought set the sun in motion again.
I resumed my name, edged closer to night.

To the Invisible

You're facing the bay. You see the boat.
The boat itself portal, an entering.
And then
to navigate.
The way light falls on only half the boat. You see now
on the water
a feather—
myth of beauty no longer myth. The feather,
the wetness, the porous you.

Jen Hoppa, photograph

kind woman lives here tell a pitiful story

begin with the baby's death

call her elizabeth

recall the night
the animals ate one another
the wind that ripped holes in the sky

tell her about the fire
the voice you heard
inside of the flames

scare her
make her thankful
for all of the terrible things

there is no good
there is no ill
there is only the truth

changing from day to day

These two poems employ hobo signs and symbols used between 1920–1950. The poems themselves are meditations on the transient lives of the hobos and the unsettled nature of our own society.

good place for a handout

if this is written in chalk
come alone
come sober
do not meet their gaze
use your christian name
talk of your people with respect
leave a different way than you came

＊

if this is written in coal
come at night
wait for a sign
a window propped open with a jar
an apron tied to a broom
if the food is rotten
take it anyway
show them you've been there

＊

if this is scratched into wood
wait by the barn
a man will come to feed the animals
say nothing
animals show thanks
with obedience
you are an animal

All the Evil in the Animal Kingdom

In the heat the glue has melted away and nothing will remain fastened.

Sometimes I still wish it would all suddenly and gently end.

We perhaps could have seen these things coming, if we had looked close enough.

This body huddling in the corner. This body playing chess, still. This body glued to the television. Also preserved.

Simultaneously in four continents there is a mass hallucination of a giant skeletal hand in the night sky.

The bones can no longer hold the skin.

I've been showing a lot of legitimate moments of weakness lately. A lot of people I know would call that growth.

In nature, a cornered scorpion will sting itself to death, refusing its enemies the glory of the kill.

So what of repentance.

Love as tree choked in vines. Love as infinite Russian doll. One is broken in two, and inside there is another. Love as the wrong bottle from the medicine cabinet.

A pan to catch the blood.

Please call and tell me the story of how everything went wrong again.

In the sixteenth century, a blood-red comet appeared in the night sky that many thought resembled a figure holding a giant sword for the attack.

Some blades when heated to almost the point of melting can leave a wound that nothing will heal, not science, not our best mystics, the skin all burned and white, and the bone burned too.

Any notch for any hook will do. Exposed skin. The cheek. The belly.
Furies, oh Furies.

I am still here.

If you look to the night sky, your gaze touches nothing for a million miles.
A dog tumbles into a bottomless pit and starves to death.

There's a real connection here, babe. But I should warn you that I don't
know what a real connection is.

Manly Johnson, photograph

Destroyer

I know I lost my girlfriend
to your quick pluck and charm a year ago, and soon
you two were married (married
for God's sake!), but now
I understand all of that. I don't wish

the worst highway death and skid of blood on you
anymore. These days I'm impressed
when a new weapon is unveiled, as I am when I see
the guy on the talk show who spins
a hundred plates on sticks. Sometimes, one breaks,
and they all soon follow.

And I'm done with asking the Lord to spare us from
our place in Hell. There is a careful record of the movements made
in our collected name —
this penny means a child starves; this penny means a bullet

passes through a soldier's chest; this penny saves
a village from machete-wielding rebels. Our pendulum, our pit,
our precious mayhem. A boy finds a fallen nest of robin eggs

and chooses not to smash them into a red mess.
A poor young mother can suffocate
her newborn child. Our destroyers wander the ocean.

There are scenarios designed in which their missiles
can be pointed at any city, from Shanghai to Paris
to Lexington, Kentucky. Sometimes,

one plate falls, and it doesn't break.
Maybe it is caught at the last second to a great musical
flourish.

None of us think we are evil. Even after
we kick the dog for eating our favorite book, we know justice
is done. And you,
you did what was best for you and the girl. Which is all
any of us should be expected to do.

CHRISTINE E. BLACK

Prayer for Andrea Yates

And I will gather them
like eggs in a basket,
run to a clear field,
a close barn,
dim and cool
and away
from godthefather,
the minister —
where I cannot
be found.
I settle them to sleep
on the ground,
smell the animals,
summer flowers.
As I watch
their quiet breaths
and feel my own
return, I believe *them*,
my children,
believe their lives
made from my body,
like the body
of the earth,
full and good.

What Remains

There has to be something —
Painted barntops. The rusty skeleton of a tower that
once held a beacon. Marks on the land, now plowed and harvested
for nearly eighty years. But if they are here, I cannot find them.

The altimeter in this little Cessna 152, tail number Five Three
Two Nine Bravo, says I am two thousand, five hundred feet above
sea level, and over this part of the North Dakota prairie that means
one thousand, six hundred feet above the ground. Yet it's a beautiful spring day and I can see to every horizon. The wind is from
the north at only three knots. The sun is shining. There was some
ground fog earlier, but now there is just a haze in the air — some
showers on the radar, off to the west and north, but they are light.
The rain may not even reach the ground.

It has been almost a year since I sat in a pilot's seat, and the
feel of this small airplane in my hands and feet is a reintroduced
joy and grace. Last night, going over the calculations for weight
and balance, the need for fuel, planning my route, looking at the
weather, I smiled at how easily the mind can switch from one set
of borders to another. Last night, early, I was thinking about
small repairs I need to make around the house, about the thousand chores that need to be done. My world was limited, scarcely
larger than the three-mile walk I take with our collie. But when I
retrieved my flight bag from a bookshelf and unfolded a sectional
map, the world became a much larger place. Instantly, the definition of *here* included magnetic deviations and airspace rules, winds
aloft at three thousand and six thousand feet, reported from a thousand different locations. *Here* was everything within about three
hundred miles of where I sat. All of it present. All of it necessary.
Here, whatever that space is in the brain, suddenly included the
curve of the earth.

And today, what I am wondering is if *here*, which is nearly the
same word as *now*, can include decades of time, time long passed.
I have been wondering about the first pilots in this region, the old
airmail pilots, and how they saw the land. How they found their
way from one place to another. I have GPS and radio navigation.
I would have to work to get lost. They had neither, and getting
lost was not only possible, it could very well be fatal. Follow the

land, the rivers and the roads. Beware of haze, of mist, of clouds—anything that could send you off course.

In the old days, I have learned, there were barntops painted with arrows pointing to airports. There were flashing beacons every fifteen miles for navigation at night. There were intermediate landing fields too, just pastureland made available for emergencies. And all through this past winter, every cold and windy night slamming itself against the windows and siding of my house, I have been wondering if any of those first things have survived. Is there a barn, old and gray and leaning tremendously to one side or another, with a faded arrow on its roof? Is there a plowed shape in the ground that would tell me this place was once a landing field? You would see these things only from the air. Every time I laced up my winter boots, I knew a little more deeply that I would have to find out.

What I am looking for, of course, is evidence, some small piece of the *then* that has made it through to the *now*. And I am looking for that moment of encounter.

What I am looking for is the connection between history and self—hard and physical and real in a way that notes from an index in some corner of a library will never be—the very same thing that people look for when they retrace the route of Lewis and Clark or Marco Polo, when they stand on the stone of the Coliseum or in the grass at Gettysburg, when they find themselves in Jerusalem or Delhi or Machu Picchu or Auschwitz or the Olduvai Gorge. How would I have measured up? Who would I have been? The time between then and now is very large, and my life is very short. I need to know.

* * *

Start with 1918—

World War I is four years old. The Russian Constituent Assembly is dissolved by the Bolsheviks, Czar Nicholas II and his family are executed, and the Germans bomb Paris. The Allies begin a new offensive on the Western Front. The U.S. Post Office burns magazine selections of James Joyce's *Ulysses*, H.L. Mencken publishes *In Defense of Women*, and there are new books by Aldous Huxley, D.H. Lawrence, Bertrand Russell, and H.G. Wells. Paul Klee is at work, as are Freud and Jung. Claude Debussy dies and

Leonard Bernstein is born. The Dada movement begins. There is new music by Béla Bártok, Irving Berlin, Jerome Kern, and Igor Stravinsky, and Max Planck wins the Nobel Prize in physics for introducing quantum theory. Vilhjlmur Stefansson returns from five years exploring north of the Arctic Circle. A horse named Exterminator wins the Kentucky Derby and Knute Rockne is named head football coach at Notre Dame. Missouri is the last state to ratify the compulsory school attendance law. Daylight Savings Time begins. Billy Graham is born. Jack Dempsey knocks out Carl Morris in 14 seconds. Eight-and-a-half million people have died in the war. Twenty-one million have been wounded. An outbreak of influenza begins, which turns into a worldwide pandemic that kills nearly twenty-two million.

It is a difficult year, and a tremendous year as well. Disaster and the work of creation. Chaos, and then a renewed sense of purpose. Perhaps a desire to make things better after they have gone so terribly wrong.

On April 21, 1918, Manfred von Richthofen, the Red Baron, the most successful ace of World War I, is shot down and killed. Chasing one Sopwith Camel and being chased by another, he takes a bullet through his heart and lungs, and still manages to land his Fokker without damage. Although there is some question, it's most likely the bullet comes from the ground. He is buried with full military honors by his enemies, the British and Australians, and a British pilot flies over German territory to drop the news.

Not even one month later, on the other side of the planet, another era starts. Less dramatically, awkwardly but insistently, airmail begins in the United States. This too will change the planet.

Airmail. Like our visions of the Pony Express, the very *idea* of airmail fills our heads with images of daring pilots on noble missions. Fast news from the outside, delivered selflessly and at great risk, regularly and on time. The fighter pilots of World War I were heroes, battling an enemy, finding victory because of better skill, better equipment, better luck. But the airmail pilots were extraordinary. You couldn't outwit a thunderstorm. You couldn't surprise a blizzard or shoot down the fog. You made it through, or didn't, only by what seemed like the grace of God. Charles Lindbergh was an airmail pilot, and even he had to bail out twice and float to earth under a parachute because of weather.

In the Introduction to a book called *Pilots' Directions*, William Leary writes: "The country's first regularly scheduled airmail service opened with great fanfare on May 15, 1918. Even President Woodrow Wilson took time off from his demanding wartime responsibilities to attend the inaugural. At 11:46 a.m., Lt. George L. Boyle departed Washington's Polo Field with 140 pounds of mail for Philadelphia and New York. Unfortunately, the young pilot became lost en route when he followed the wrong railroad tracks out of Washington. Attempting to land to get directions, Boyle managed to nose over, flipping the Jenny on its back. To [Assistant Postmaster] Praeger's great chagrin, the mail went by train."

Not the best beginning. And not only did Boyle follow the wrong tracks, three days later, he was given a bit of advice he followed exactly. Keep Chesapeake Bay on your right, he was told. But then the north end of Chesapeake Bay showed up and he followed the other side, always keeping the water of the bay on his right, until he landed in Cape Charles, out of gas and out of land, in completely the wrong place. But it was a start nonetheless. Other flights followed, and a little later that same year, the first New York to Chicago route was opened. Flying time: 10 hours and five minutes.

❖ ❖ ❖

If I were driving this route, the names of towns would come to me in order: Fargo, Harwood, Argusville, Gardner, Grandin. Places and people I know, events that can be marked in the soil. Flying, however, means a different perspective. Even just a couple thousand feet up the world needs to be rethought. Altitude brings the surface together. Pilots still mark waypoints, towns and structures and physical earth identifiable from the air, and they mark the time it takes to fly between them to make sure the plane is on course. Before takeoff, with a check of the winds and some fast calculations on a computer or a type of circular slide rule called an E6B, a pilot knows, for example, it should take 18 minutes to fly from Town A to Town B. If Town B shows up too early or too late, or on the wrong side of the airplane, or does not show up at all, the pilot can keep track of where the plane's shadow falls, and correct what needs to be fixed.

But to be honest, from the air the towns do not seem so separate, their buildings and their stories more mingled than apart. The Red River, old and meandering, cuts back and loops and winds. Smaller rivers, usually invisible to the roadways, join the Red from both sides. In 1997, there was a flood here that made world news. The land is flat, the bottom of the Pleistocene Lake Agassiz, the largest inland sea in the Earth's history, and this river is the remainder of its drainage. When seven blizzards and more than one hundred inches of snow fell that winter, the spring melt became a problem. The Red flows north and when the southern end thaws the northern end is still ice-locked. The water has nowhere to go, so it spreads over the prairie. Following a river is one of the earliest forms of airplane navigation. At altitude, to follow a river with history is to see the connections and to feel afresh a sense of humility.

I have been away from flying long enough that I want someone with me, to make sure I remember what I think I remember, and so Joanna, an instructor from the Fargo Jet Center, sits in the right seat today. We take off, the plane a light dance in my hands as the wheels leave the ground and we make the short jog over to the river. If you had to follow something to Pembina, to mark your route, the river would be the first best choice. Because I am flying, Joanna gets to do something rare for a flight instructor—she gets to look around. She knows what we're looking for and she's eager to find something. We call out to each other what we see.

"That's a pretty farmstead," I say.

"Look at that wooden bridge!" she says.

"It's all *new* barns and Quonset huts," I say. "I don't see a single old barn."

This is early May and the fields are all brown. There is still snow and ice hiding in the shadowed spots. We see farmers out tilling the land, plowing and planting.

❊ ❊ ❊

Now imagine 1921—

Warren Harding is inaugurated as the 29th President of the United States. Hitler's storm troopers begin a program of terror. Enrico Caruso dies. Sacco and Vanzetti are found guilty of murder. The first radio broadcast of a baseball game is heard from the Polo Grounds in New York. The KKK is openly violent. Charlie Chaplin stars in *The Kid*.

In just three years, airmail has grown from one local route toward the opening of a breathtaking transcontinental airway. New

York to San Francisco via Cleveland, Chicago, Omaha, Cheyenne, Salt Lake City, Elko, and Reno. Just like the Pony Express with their horses, an airmail pilot would fly one leg, land, and a relief pilot would hurry into the cockpit, ready to fly the next stage, to keep the mail going. And just like the Pony Express, many pilots die working out the routes, fighting their machines, dodging the weather. The *New York Sun* runs an editorial that calls the route "homicidal insanity." Yet the biggest problem is night. Pilots cannot find their way over the mountains at night, so the mail is transferred from airplane to train and then back, and the total time savings turns out to be not very much at all.

But night is only a problem to be solved. And the solution is the prairie. Begin in the morning on either coast and you cross the mountains in daylight. To fly the nighttime prairie, it seems, all you need is a good sense of direction. And between Cheyenne and Chicago, the Post Office has built 616 flashing beacons, one every three miles, to light the way. So on February 22, 1921, four airmail planes are sent out to demonstrate the night-flying abilities of the new transcontinental airway, to ensure the speed of delivery the idea has promised. Two leave New York, bound for San Francisco. Only one makes it to Chicago, where the continuation is cancelled because of bad weather. Two leave San Francisco, bound for New York. One crashes in Nevada and the pilot, William Lewis, is killed.

But one plane makes it through. As evening falls, a pilot named Frank Yeager takes over the controls of the deHavilland DH-4 biplane in Salt Lake City and flies via Cheyenne to North Platte, Nebraska. In North Platte, he gives the airplane to a man named James "Jack" Knight, and at 10:44 p.m. Knight leaves the ground, heading for Omaha.

What happens next is the stuff that creates a legend. People on the ground know the flight is coming, and somehow know the route. They certainly know the weather. And suddenly there are bonfires lit along the way to guide the pilot! No signal more ancient, no signal more welcome, no history book says how this was planned. No text explains what it must have been like, standing outside in midwinter, tending a fire, listening for the sound of one small airplane in the sky.

In Omaha, the replacement pilot either fails to appear or refuses to fly. The weather is cold, below zero, and turning nasty

with snowfall and fog. For whatever reason, Knight decides to
fly on. His takeoff time is 1:59 a.m. The plan is to stop in Des
Moines, but deep snow prevents a landing. He flies on to the
emergency field in Iowa City, where the night watchman lights
railroad flares to aid the landing. Across Iowa and then Illinois,
through bad weather slowly turning better, he finds Chicago's
Checkerboard Field, and a crowd of people who have turned out
to see him land. A hero's welcome at 8:40 a.m. In the history
books, the scholars say this one flight kept airmail alive.

❉ ❉ ❉

On my desk I have a small book, a reproduction in part of
a book published in 1921, called *Pilots' Directions: New York — San
Francisco Route*. The book is exactly that: directions for pilots flying
the first transcontinental airmail route. But instead of radio beam
or GPS, these directions are all ground-based. The first section,
New York to Bellefonte, begins this way:

Miles.
0. Hazelhurst Field, Long Island. — Follow the tracks of the Long
Island Railroad past Belmont Park race track, keeping Jamaica on
the left. Cross New York over the lower end of Central Park.
25. Newark, N.J. — Heller Field is located in Newark and may
be identified as follows: The field is 1 ¼ miles west of the Passaic
River and lies in the V formed by the Greenwood Lake Division
and Orange branch of the New York, Lake Erie & Western Railroad. The Morris Canal bounds the western edge of the field. The
roof of the large steel hangar is painted an orange color.
30. Orange Mountains. — Cross the Orange Mountains over
a small round lake or pond. Slightly to the right will be seen the
polo field and golf course of Essex Country Club. About 8 miles to
the north is Mountain Lake, easily seen after crossing the Orange
Mountains.

No maps. No sectional charts. No radio beacons. No VOR
or ADF. Just a pocket-sized book of directions. Fly from this
river to those railroad tracks, turn south, follow the tracks until
you see the city, turn west, there should be a notch in the mountains. Cross the whole country this way. Good luck.

✿ ✿ ✿

In a light brown field, wide dark paths mark where a tractor has been, pulling disks or plows. But the paths loop and curl and cut back on each other, ramble all over the section like a drunk's wandering after too long at the bar. Farmers checking their land, wondering if the fields are dry enough to plant, turning to earth to look just under the surface.

Joanna spots a beautiful green house, with porches and decks and a rounded turret room too. She finds bridges then drainage pipes in ditches. She spots bright green tanks that could hold water or feed for livestock. The river is nothing but bends and twists, riparian trees shading the banks. We talk about the trees that make the ruler-straight shelterbelts for farmers, and about the evergreens that appear in the incongruous cemeteries, about how only the burr oak is native to this part of the prairie. Looking out her side window, she finds a point on the river where the grasses have been burned, black earth with some gray ash mounds still smoking.

But no painted barn tops. No beacons. No signs in the earth. My own eyes are fixed over the nose of the plane, looking for what might appear in the distance, looking for what type of aid or invitation there might be.

The winds have come up, 17 knots of headwind against the plane. Looking at the Interstate highway, I watch a semi-truck pass us heading north. We have to land in Grand Forks for gas, to have enough to get us to Pembina and back, so we call Grand Forks approach and let them know we're coming in. I ask for a route that lets us stay over the river for as long as possible. The request is approved, but still there is nothing.

✿ ✿ ✿

Sometimes it's tough to get a handle on things.

On the web, from an official North Dakota government site, I read, "1928: An air mail service between the Twin Cities and Winnipeg through North Dakota was inaugurated, and Carl Ben Eielson of Hatton [North Dakota] became the first person to fly nonstop over the arctic."

1928. The year Amelia Earhart becomes the first woman to fly across the Atlantic. New music includes Gershwin's *An Ameri-*

can in Paris and Ravel's *Bolero*. The first Mickey Mouse films appear. D.H. Lawrence publishes *Lady Chatterley's Lover*.

But also on the web, there is an envelope for sale. Theodore Wolke, of Prospect Avenue in New York, sends a letter to Peggy Wolke of the same address. The letter is dated February 2, 1931, and the postmark is Fargo, North Dakota, at 11:00 a.m. The postage stamp costs five cents. Above Peggy's address, "Via Air Mail" is typed in all capital letters. Above Theodore's return address, neatly printed on the stationery, "Chicago–St. Paul Route. A.M. #9" is also typed. Most striking, though, is the large mark below the return address. A circle that fills nearly half the envelope, the outer ring reads "First Flight * Twin Cities-Pembina Extension * Route AM 9 * P.O.D. * Air Mail." Inside the ring there's a picture of a small airplane flying over the trees and fields and buildings of what is labeled as the State Agricultural College, under the banner of "Fargo, N.Dak., Feb. 2 1931."

1931. The year Al Capone is jailed for income tax evasion, the north face of the Matterhorn is climbed, and Knute Rockne dies in an airplane crash. Salvador Dali paints *The Persistence of Memory* and Boris Karloff stars in *Frankenstein*. The Empire State Building is finished and the building of Rockefeller Center begins. Pilots Clyde Pangborn and Hugh Herndon fly nonstop from Japan to Washington state in forty-one hours.

Clearly this was an important day, a cause for celebration and remembrance. But how can there be a first flight in 1928 and another first flight in 1931?

On the phone with the staff and volunteers at the Northwest Airlines History Office, I hear a story too good to be true, and perfectly believable. On February 1, 1928, Northwest became an international airline by starting weekly service to Winnipeg, Manitoba. Three months later, however, the service was stopped because of opposition from the Canadian government. Then on February 2, 1931, the service was resumed. A compromise had been worked out to satisfy both countries. Northwest would fly the cargo and passengers from Minneapolis to Fargo, then Grand Forks, then north to the border town of Pembina, North Dakota, where they would be met by a plane from Western Canada Airways, which would take them the remaining few miles.

But February 2, 1931, was Groundhog Day, and the groundhog did not see his shadow. The fog was dense and everywhere on the prairie. Joe Ohrbeck, the pilot for Northwest, made it only as far as Osakis, Minnesota, before he had to land the plane. He didn't even make it to Fargo. The Canadian pilots never left the ground. The 18,000 letters in the cargo hold of Ohrbeck's plane had to wait until the next day to reach Canada.

What news did Theodore send to Peggy, I wonder? In Fargo, that letter waited, stamped in celebration, for an airplane that would not arrive until the weather cleared.

❊ ❊ ❊

The stop in Grand Forks is fast and pleasant. Hot coffee in the flight support office, some candy from a little dish at the desk. We add only four gallons of gas, but that's nearly an hour of flying time. Once back in the air, we angle toward the river and keep watching.

"How easy," I ask, "do you think it would have been to get lost?"

At one level, we are flying over Thomas Jefferson's dream. Section roads run straight north/south and straight east/west. There are small turns and burps where the earth refused to give way or some creek made a mess of things, but mainly the world looks like an ordered grid, easy to measure. You can count off the miles to infinity. It would be possible to follow one road for a very long time. But in haze, or punching through just one cloud, you couldn't be sure the road you're following now is the road you began to follow earlier. If you let your attention wander, even just a little, you could be lost over a land that is perfectly ordered, and thus perfectly unknowable.

"You have the river," Joanna says. "I could never be lost here."

"Yes, but what if you got away from it?"

"I would never do that. If I had to fly here in those days, I would lock this river right out my window and never lose sight of it."

She is right, of course. Navigation, to a pilot, is one of the basics, like having a propeller. And unlike the parts of the machine that takes you into the air, navigation speaks to the pilot's understanding of the three-dimensional world, to the pilot's skill and artistry. If you get lost, you can't pull over and ask directions. If you run out of gas, you can't just pull to the side and make a telephone call.

If I were flying in the early days, I would be focused on the flying. I would make sure my cargo of letters and packages made it safely to wherever it was destined to go. I would hear the echo of the Post Office motto "Neither rain, nor snow, nor. . ." and it would keep me on task with its noble promise. But I can be easily distracted. There is a farm in the distance, a farmer working the fields, white tanks of anhydrous ammonia parked at fieldside. I cannot see if he is just turning the earth, or if he is pulling planters as well, and there is a part of me that wants to go look.

"Look at this!" Joanna cries out.

In the field below us, it looks like large letter Vs have been cut at the fencerow, angling toward the middle. It looks like an arrow, or a pointer, cut into the ground. We both wonder out loud if this could have been an intermediate field, safe haven for a sudden worry, marked for the aerial view. We make a steep turn to the right, circling over the site. But then we see another field, close by, with the same markings. Then another. In a few days, my friend Jake Gust will tell me that this what a field looks like from the air when a farmer works his land by driving the perimeter, then the next inside circuit, then the next, instead of back and forth across the length or breadth. From the air, a rectangular field looks like the back of an envelope with the flap sealed down, or like the slopes of the roof of a house.

And even a few days later, I will discover that Joanna and I aren't even looking at the same thing. In an email she will write: "You didn't see what I was looking at because what you referred to was the arrows that the tractors leave in the fields and I saw that too, but more interesting, what I saw was three, long, green strips of grass located directly in the backyard of a house, I described them as miniature runways, or runways for model airplanes. But the shape they formed was very distinctive and the three lines all came into a peak that looked like an arrow pointing north, northwest. Perhaps they were strips for model airplanes or just a design the family wanted in their backyard, but it seemed to me the only thing that could have or may have possibly been from the old mail route. Do you know what I am talking about?"

Today, though, 1500 feet above the ground, Joanna and I wonder if this could be that thing which remains, even though we are seeing different things. Hope fills the little airplane. Then sadly, we turn the airplane north again. We are almost to Pembina.

❄ ❄ ❄

On my desk is a photocopied section from a 1920 publication called *Municipal Landing Fields and Air Ports*, sent to me by a historian at the National Air and Space Museum Library. The directory lists eighteen airports in North Dakota. Bismarck and Fort Lincoln are listed as Government Fields, under the control of the federal government. The remaining sixteen — Dickinson, Eagles Nest, Eldridge, Fargo, Glen Ullin, Grand Forks, Hobart, Jamestown, Judson, Mandan, Sedalia, Sims, Sunny, Sweet Briar, Valley City, and Williston — are listed as Emergency Fields, "at which landings have been made but where no facilities exist for obtaining supplies."

Also on my desk, also photocopied and also from Air and Space Museum, a 1939 directory, *Airports: Established Landing Fields and Seaplane Bases in the United States*, that includes a map of the now thirty-nine airports in North Dakota. Following the airmail route, I see that Fargo has become a Municipal Field, the highest ranking. Valley City is a Department of Commerce Intermediate Field. Jamestown is Municipal. Medina is Auxiliary. Dawson is Intermediate. Steele is Auxiliary. Bismarck is Municipal. Just to the south of the route, there is an Auxiliary Field in Streeter, then a Municipal Field in Deisem. Just to the north, Auxiliary fields in Erie and Carrington.

In my hands, though, is the current edition of the U.S. Government Airport Facility Directory, which lists more than one hundred landing fields in North Dakota. But the landing field at Medina is gone, as are Dawson, Steele, Streeter, Deisem, and Erie.

❄ ❄ ❄

What I am looking for, in truth, is stories.

The guys at the Northwest Airlines History Office give me a phone number, a pilot named Joe Kimm, who joined Northwest in 1929 as a flight steward, running cabin service inside a twelve-passenger Ford Tri-Motor airplane when he was seventeen years old. Two days later, we are on the phone with each other.

"I had been building model airplanes since I was ten years old," Joe tells me, "and then a pilot for Northwest Airways named Walter Bullock wrote an article about the Ford Tri-Motor model for *Popular Mechanics* and suddenly found himself making parts and kits in his basement."

Ninety-six years old, his voice and mind as strong as ever, Joe is telling me how his flying career began.

"I won the indoor competition of a citywide model airplane contest in Minneapolis in 1928, in December, about a month before I graduated from high school in January 1929. There were about fifteen or twenty of us in a model airplane club we formed, and one of them knew Walter Bullock. Walter was about 27 years old, had begun flying in 1915, worked for Northwest since 1927. Walter came to the first club meeting and said he needed help. I had just quit a job that paid me $12 a week. Walter said he'd pay me $12 a week to help with the kits. It was through Walter that I learned about flight stewards, and I said if he'd let me do that I'd work on my days off for nothing.

"In June, Northwest lost its first airplane. It crashed on the bluff in St. Paul. The pilot was killed, but the flight steward, Bob Johnson, was only mildly injured. So three days after the accident Walter tells me I can fly with him to Chicago as a flight steward if I got my parents' permission.

"I went to Mother, and I said Mom, I'm all excited. Walter says I can go with him to Chicago tomorrow morning if I get your permission. And she said, Oh, son, you better ask your father. So I went to Dad and I said, Dad, Walter says I can go with him to Chicago tomorrow if I get your permission. And he looked at me and said, Oh son, you better ask your mother." And that was it. I decided they weren't objecting, so I got up in the morning and went out to the airport to take my first flight. Incidentally, I had gone to the hospital the night before to pick up Bobby Johnson's uniform. I needed a uniform to wear, and he was about the same tall gangly kid I was and his uniform fit me fine.

"I got to the airport and they gave me a box of money and tickets, because there was no ticket counter out there, they only sold tickets downtown, and I had to sell tickets if anyone came to the airport and needed one. I never did sell a ticket. The next thing they did was instruct me that I had to wear a pistol. So they gave me a .38 revolver with a holster and belt and told me to put that around my waist and wear it. I had to wear this because I was handling registered mail and it was a requirement of the Post Office that everyone handling registered mail had to be armed. I had never fired a gun before, and they didn't even tell me how to load it or fire it! They just handed me the gun. There's been a lot of controversy in recent years about arming pilots, but back then they had no problem giving a gun to a seventeen-year-old kid. I carried that same gun for twelve years and turned it in when I went into the service. But I had decided that if anyone wanted the airmail, all they had to do was tell me where to put it and I'd take it there for them."

I tell Joe I can't imagine going to the hospital to pick up the uniform of a man who had been in an airplane crash so I could fly in his place, or carrying a gun to protect the mail, and he laughs. "That's just the way it was back then," he says.

"Along about the beginning of 1930," he continues, "I decided I had the wrong job. I was busier than hell, doing all the work for $78 a month, and the pilot, all he did was sit up front and he got $700 dollars. So I decided I had to learn to fly. In 1930 there wasn't any money. The crash in October of '29 had really put the country in the kibosh. Nobody had any money. I was making $78 a month, which was pretty good money, but I was paying room and board, and payments on a 1929 Model A Ford Coupe I had bought with my brother for $725. $30 to my Dad and $35 for the car—that left me $13 a month squander on myself. So I was broke.

"I wanted to learn how to fly but I didn't have any money, so I had to figure out how to get to fly, because I really wanted to be a pilot. I ended up going to the company—I got my nerve up, keep in mind I was a very shy kid, I wasn't one of these outgoing individuals who went out and made life for themselves, but when the chips were down I guess my stubborn streak would come out—so I ended up going in to the company and said, You've got a couple of Waco 10's out there you're not using, can I borrow one? They looked at me kinda funny and thought about it for a second or two and said, Well you'd have to pay for the gas and oil. I said Well, okay, I can do that. Gasoline was only nine cents a gallon. So I had an airplane. I ended up going to one of the captains, Chad

Smith, and I said, Chad, I got an airplane, would you teach me to
fly? And then he looked at me kinda funny and said, Sure, Joe,
I'll do that. So he soloed me. Took me 6½ hours to solo. I had a
lot of airtime in the Ford. In the six to eight months I was a flight
steward I got to sit up front with the captain every once in a while.
They didn't have any autopilot, so he welcomed the opportunity
to have someone spell him off. And they taught me how to fly the
airplane in flight. Well, I got my license and soloed in September
of 1930, and I built up my time and got my limited commercial
license in November. Just about a month after I got my license,
the Department of Commerce, which regulated aircraft in those
days, came out with a new ruling requiring two pilots in aircraft
weighing 12,500 pounds or more. That was just fit for the Ford
Tri-Motor. So I just automatically became a co-pilot. Same job,
same pay, but now I'm a pilot. This is unbelievable, but this is how
aviation was in those days.

"I ended up flying a Hamilton and a Travel Air. I flew a
couple flights when I was 22 years old as captain. Then the government came out with a new ruling that you had to be 23 years old
and have an air transport rating, which required 1,200 hours of flying time. I wasn't going to be 23 for about a month, until August,
but after my birthday I went to Chicago and qualified and got my
rating, came back at the end of the month and then the company
told me I was going to be flying as captain from Fargo to Grand
Forks to Pembina.

"You can imagine the thrill of going out and being on your
own and being captain and flying your first captain flight, in a
single-engine Hamilton. They had another captain up there, and
between the two of us we covered everything. We were station
manager in Fargo on one day and the next day we were flying captain to Pembina and back, so we alternated that way. There was
always one of us operating the station and one of us always flying.
It was interesting because there was no radio aids or any of that
kind of help. Clarence Bates was the name of the other pilot, and
he happened to be a ham radio operator, and he had a ham station
at home. And for some reason or other there was a radio in the
Hamilton, so we used Clarence's home radio to keep in contact. If
I were out for a flight, Clarence would call me and tell me what the
weather was doing down in Fargo, and give me any information he
thought I might need. I lived right next door to his home, so when

he was flying up to Pembina I would go over to his house and give him a report on his radio."

On my end of the telephone, I tell Joe I am amazed. "Compared to today," I tell him, "This was the glory days of flying."

"It really was," he says. "You know, nobody knew anything about flying. There wasn't a single experienced pilot in the whole country. These guys that were flying were guys that after WWI bought surplus airplanes from the government for $400 and taught themselves to fly. And then to build up experience they would go around to small towns and give passenger rides, or they would go to the state fair and perform stunts like aerobatics or wing-walking, even parachute jumping, anything to make a living. It was a carnival atmosphere. Nobody really had any experience, nobody really knew what they were doing. We had to learn as we went along."

"It's a wonder you guys didn't get lost!" I say.

"We got to know our routes," Joe says. "Every farm, every barn, every windmill. We could fly that way until the weather got down to about 200 feet above the ground, and about a quarter of a mile visibility. When it got down to that we were not able to fly any more, so wherever we were we would find a farmer's field, circle it to make sure there wasn't a haystack in the middle, and then land."

"What did your passengers think of that?" I ask.

"I'm sure they weren't very happy about being landed in the middle of a farmer's field, but that's the way it was. And you need to remember that the people who were flying were hardy people also. They were daring. They had as much courage as the pilot just to get into an airplane in those days. We would take them to town and put them on a train, and we would take the mail and put it on the train, and then we'd send a Western Union message back to St. Paul to let them know where we were. And we would stay there until the weather was good enough to fly again. Sometimes we would be there for two days!"

I ask if there are any stories that stick out in his mind more than others.

"You can't fly all the time I flew without having some episodes that are a little bit on the dicey side," he says. "I remember this one flight that was supposed to go to Chicago. The pilot was a man named Fred Livermore, who was a dapper young man. A natural born pilot. When he sat in an airplane, that airplane became a part of him. He did amazing things with that Ford. He was also a daring type of individual. And remember we had to fly with visual reference to the ground at all times. Anyway, we got down to Winona, Minnesota, on the Mississippi River and the weather popped down to practically nothing. We couldn't get any farther, so we turned around and decided to go back to Red Wing. When we got to Red Wing, we figured we'd go across the country and go down through Rochester, so we were coming in northwest of Rochester when the weather got really close. And for some reason or other he thought he could get out on top. He started climbing, and remember there were only a few instruments, and we climbed up through the overcast. When we got up to about 5000 feet, what happened was the Venturi tube on the outside of the aircraft iced up, so we lost our turn indicator. Then we stalled out. And when we stalled out we went into a dive and the engines would really hum, and then we'd pull back and the engines would get softer, but we'd stall out again. We finally broke out about 200 feet above the ground and headed right for the trees, and he pulled that thing back as hard as he could. When we got back to St. Paul, they picked branches out of the landing gear."

"That's a great story," I tell him.

"You're never going to forget anything like that!" he says.

"How long did you fly?" I ask.

"42 years, 1 month and 17 days. About 36,000 hours."

There are more stories. Joe tells me about flying a way through the mountains with Amelia Earhart as a passenger, and about his last flight, coming back from Tokyo, flying a Boeing 707-320, how the tower operators in Seattle let his wife into the tower to give him final clearance to land. But I am thinking about 36,000 hours of flying and what the turns of the planet must look like from that deep altitude.

❉ ❉ ❉

At Pembina, North Dakota, the highway and the river are not very far apart. And as we follow the river, the airport simply appears in the distance, right under the nose of the airplane. It would be impossible not to see it. We're already lined up for a long final approach. We haven't found a thing. Not one barn top. No painted arrows or lights. But we have flown the route and looked.

We have a story now, and that's worth everything.

When I land the Cessna, Joanna looks over at me.

"You have something against flaring?" she asks, smiling.

Ever the instructor, she points out that I've just made my second three-point landing in a tricycle gear airplane. Just a little bit off, and that would be a good way to collapse the nose gear. It's been a year, and even though the plane feels familiar and good in my hands, there are things to remember and things to improve.

The runway pavement is broken and uneven. We taxi to the hangar and office and find the airport deserted. There are no planes on the ramp. No people in the office. The server is down for the computer that provides flight planning and weather information. Weeds grow around the metal rings in the ground for tie-downs. But the buildings are new; this whole place was underwater in 1997. A weathervane in the shape of a P-51 Mustang with a whirling propeller buzzes near the driveway. And just beyond it, a sight too good to be true.

An old metal light tower, exactly the type from the 1930s, rusted but upright, stands in the grass. An old beacon remains on top. It is not spinning, and I have no idea how long it's been dark. But there it is. At the end of the route, the light to welcome you home.

Sources

Historical facts are taken from the wonderful *Timetables of History*, by Bernard Grun, Touchstone Books, New York, 1982.

Bonfires to Beacons: Federal Civil Aviation Policy under the Air Commerce Act 1926-1938, by Nick A. Komons. U.S. Department of Transportation, Washington DC, 1978.

Pilot's Directions: The Transcontinental Airway and its History, edited by William M. Leary; preface by Wayne Franklin, University of Iowa Press, Iowa City, 1990. *Pilot's Directions* was originally published by the Government Printing Office in 1921.

Western Area Update, newsletter, Vol. 6, no. 3, March 2007, U.S. Postal Service.

Safer Skyways: Federal Control of Aviation, 1926-1966, by Donald R. Whitnah, Iowa State University Press, Ames, 1966.

Aviation's Golden Age: Portraits from the 1920s and 1930s, edited by William M. Leary, University of Iowa Press, Iowa City, 1989.

North Dakota State Historical Society. http://www.nd.gov/hist/chrono/htm#1932

Airlines of the United States Since 1914, by R.E.G. Davies, Smithsonian Institution Press, Washington DC, 1972.

Bob Johnson, Bruce Kitt, and Dave Olson, staff at the Northwest Airlines History Office. Multiple phone calls.

Joe Kimm, telephone interview, 8/24/2007.

W. Scott Olsen, photograph

Nature's Own

as the great blades of
a helicopter

circle you in shadow, a song
of your spine rising inside

undisquieted now
with sudden remembrance of the present

as immense feathers stir
the idle air's accompaniment
as from a visible line above

as the solidarity of ravens
play replaces the murder
of your ignorant struggle

you

feel this is you

hummingbird here to inspect you
dragonfly drops to apprise

as bells, baby birds
constant, arrhythmic

nature's own metronome
the tune of each dream

What the Owl Knows

The owl sings in loud shadows.
Its wings wrapped around its body
like an old oriental rug, its voice
revolving in hypnotic circles.

The owl sings of blood, rapture
staring down the world with its
black magnet eyes, directing the lost
and translating the darkness.

His song forms smoke rings
through the mist, vowels drifting
past the dunes that turn to gold
under the moon, where he sits
perched at the edge of the cliffs
watching the shoreline lift itself
into the night sky like a silver tongue.

He sits frozen and expectant,
knows the shadowy speech of the earth

by heart, knows how the wind changes
direction or how the unthinkable wanders
into thought when no one is watching.

He knows the ocean too well.
Its belly sinking and rising, the world
breathing its deep sleep, while he
is awake always searching
for signs of something
other than his own voice,
at that awkward moment
when the morning is born
and finds itself alone in the dark.

Humpadori 41 (Cell-Friend)

Call me Little Scarab.
My heart has tendrils, segmented with a tongue's thin friction.

I'm a gem. I have wing-pieces.
My heart is slick

with losers—unwashed, that's my preference.
Consider yourself one of mine: since

you'll always live in my personal
Book of the Dead. Here

there are many ways of knowing oneself, many bits and combinations, even though
the smells sometimes run together, the skeins,

the elevated ridges of one

crenulated strip creeping into
the posterior harp of another, articulated here and there with a claw.

Let me replay your voice again because isn't that just
how I feel right now? My heart, all scratched and punctured

with minute cracks, all loving digits
an entire storm can flow through—

That storm is human. That storm is you.

Red Bird in Winter

If we say it
we grow feathers or disappear,
so we try not to say it,
a name, a belief, a death.
We write and paint,
searching, not wanting.
We disappear into the details,
heavy frost silences the grass,
leaves click like fingers,
one word waits
the way the cardinal waits
on the edge of the oak.
The bird, pertinacious, sits,
Fat-bellied but silent,
while trees renounce their leaves,
every street becomes river,
the humped back of the river
rages at what comes next,
love, its negligence laid bare.
We wait to be what we will be,
the dark stirrings of one word,
a cardinal perched
on the edge of the soul.

The Heart in Its Cage of Bone

A winter wind blasts from the Mississippi
past caves and oil tanks, over train tracks
then down West Seventh where it batters
the girl who walks with iced-lined scarf
bruising her mouth. Under her uniform skirt,
ski pants that her mother makes her wear.
These she removes and hides carefully
in the bushes behind the bowling alley.

She passes Nedved's florist then the bar.
Down the road Schmidt's brewery sign flashes
a staccato that stays in her striding bones,
her always cold, wrapped in layers, hiding bones.

Her mind churns with voices. Her mother warns:
Stay away from the river; it's dangerous for girls.
Get in the car and help me find Highland Park,
the man says. Voices of nuns push her feet
as she runs from him, *stay pure stay pure,*
runs with guilt in her frightened, Irish bones.

She runs through the stacks of the library.
From the tall clerestory window where the sun
is always going down, she reads the ice-
encased river snaking southward,
the dwindling light, spare, unforgiving, is her own.
Frozen there, the chinks in her heart stuffed
with feathers, she imagines a Fra Angelico lazuli,
feels eternity in her bones.

Her thin shoulders hunch, where once were,
and maybe some day again will be, wings.

Private Balconies and Wrap-Around Sky

My grandmother's language was a language of illusion. Vivid and thrilling, it was nonetheless an idiom of smoke and mirrors; a predominantly dark-eyed dialect of cryptic coloration camouflage spoken almost exclusively by wanderers, mystics and thieves, a large family of aerial acrobats, daredevils and goat lovers and a couple of world-class musicians. My grandmother's language was born in a fit of speechlessness. When words failed, my grandmother's language stepped in and bridged the gulf between seeing and believing. It sounded like children playing. It was a Gypsy serenade, a sing-song rendition of life almost impossible to speak without showing your teeth and opening your mouth in what resembled a very large smile. In my grandmother's language there were twenty-seven different words for "sky" and not one word for "trash." If you wanted to throw something away, of course, you could; you simply couldn't talk about it. My grandmother's language traveled light to begin with and, once assimilated, an entity or a concept was pretty much locked in for life. My grandmother's language recycled everything. It took the unwanted object and, with a flourish or a stress switch or a gender crunch, turned it into something else. It added endings to the nouns and adjectives, declining them into graphic but effortlessly rhyming complexities that rolled right off the tongue and depicted not only the physical characteristics (size, color, shape, weight, depth, and artistic appeal) of the person, place or thing they represented, but the potential mobility (can you pick it up and carry it?), the emotional responsiveness (does it hurt when I do this? can you stand it?) and the spiritual essence (the invisible truth of the thing, be it animate, inanimate or elusive as the fog; a widely theorized, highly speculative and totally subjective linguistic can of worms) as well, and it did all this with such precision and diversionary detail it fulfilled the requirements of skillful storytellers, perpetual liars and determined lovers roughly since the world began; yet it made no verbal distinction among the past, the present and the future. My grandmother's language was a language of timelessness. It descended directly from music and was originally spoken by the very wise and colorful birds who at one time ruled the earth.

At least that's what my grandmother told me. But then, my grandmother told me a lot of things. She told me, "Vone day you veel steek out you tongue and eet gonnu fall rrrright off. Then, vile peeg he come walking down zee road and eat eeet up and you neverrrr gonnu see you tongue no more," and she told me, "Don't you go een der overrr you head or that rrrip tide gonnu suck you out to Sidi Ifni", and of course, "Eat you Spaghetti-O's or I gonnu haftu call zee Deputy Dawg."

Even though the adult children from his first marriage hired a lawyer and took my grandmother to court, she still got the Cadillac, the motel in Florida, all the furniture and the family dog—the entire estate of her third dead husband. So, when my mother bailed out of her marriage to my sperm father, she took me and my two favorite teddy bears, 250 dollars in cold cash (which she actually let me hold for about two seconds), her fur coat, her jewelry box, and the latest issue of *Vogue* magazine and we rode Amtrak all day and all night down to Sanford, Florida. From there we took a Greyhound bus over to Melbourne where my grandmother met us at the bus station in the pink Cadillac with tail fins. I moved in with my grandmother at the Sea Horse Beach Motel on State Road A1A between The Casino and The Shark Pit. My mother stayed just long enough to get a suntan, then she headed up to New York City.

The plan was: my mother was going to The Big Apple to find me a new father. If she became a famous fashion designer while she was up there, so much the better, but the most important part of the plan was the new dad. My mother and her best friend Darla "Dee Vee" Varrelle, who had lived in Manhattan since two days after graduating high school with my mother, had it all figured out. My mom would move in with Darla, sleep on the sofa-bed, get a job downtown and meet a gazillion people. Then, one evening in the not too distant future, at a gallery opening on Fifth Avenue, at a cocktail party held in the private home of some close friends in the Hamptons, or maybe at a coffee house in Greenwich Village, it would happen: my mother would run into Mister Right. She would recognize him immediately. He would be tall, dark, and professional; a man with a plan, as handsome as Gregory Peck, with a good education and absolutely a man who adored children. My mother and Mister Right would fall madly and instantly in love, get married, set up housekeeping in a penthouse apartment overlooking the park and then, in a frenzy of fanfare and ticker tape, confetti and hot air balloons, they would send for me. In the meantime, to pay the bills and to keep me in Gummi Bears and Sno-Cones, my mother took a job at Macy's as a salesgirl. She worked in Lady's Apparel, right up the escalator from Dee Vee in Fine Jewelry. The clincher of the deal for me was, at Macy's my mother received an employee's discount, which, she assured me long distance, also worked in the Toy Department.

At night, in a flurry of feather-weight fabric and sensational color, my mother sat at her sewing machine and created her own line of "Out and About Evening Dresses" and that's exactly where she wore them every chance she got. Still early in her career-girl adventure, my mother hooked up with Walter, a shy but wild-eyed photographer in The Village, where she landed a couple of jobs modeling swimsuits and lingerie and underwear on the QT. Wherever that was, it sounded extremely glamorous to me so I immediately told all the neighbors about it. My mother also sold Avon products to her ever-expanding network of girlfriends and anyone who would open the door within a two-block radius of my mother's and Darla's apartment building. All those jobs, however, took a backseat to my mother's primary mission of finding us a man.

I missed her. My mother was beautiful. My mother read me stories. Every night for as long as I could remember my mother read me the story of *The Twelve Dancing Princesses*. My mother's long fingers traced swirls across the illustrations of the princesses dressed in their vibrant chiffon fluff and feathers and floating organza ballgowns as nightly they slipped in and out of the castle through a super-secret chink in the rocks. We invented our own names for each of the princesses. We named them after nuts. My mother loved nuts. My mother's love for nuts was third only to her love for me and for Dairy Queen Double Dipped Ice Cream Cones, which explains how the princesses ended up with names like Paula Peanut, Connie Cashew, Annabelle Almond, Chelsea Chestnut, Wendy Walnut ,and my mother dubbed me Princess Mimi Marie Macadamia Nut even though she, better than anyone, knew my actual dumb name was Elizabeth.

My mother taught me to dance the Bossa Nova, the Cha Cha Cha, and the one-two-three, one-two-three like Anna in *The King And I*. "Shall we DANCE brrrrum bum bum," my mother sang as we held hands and leaped and twirled across the Sea Horse Beach at low tide. My mother told me not to worry. She said very soon my baby fat would melt away and I would be even more beautiful than the twelfth dancing princess (Penelope Pistachio) and all the boys would beat each other up to get one dance with me. "Take it to the bank," she said and I believed her. My mother could make me believe anything, even that she didn't really want to go.

She left on the 6:35 a.m. Greyhound and I was as wretched as a beach without an ocean. Life without my mother was a lonely pail of sand. I cried for months. I cried until snot became my new middle name and I finally got sick of it. I looked around one day and realized I had a pretty good thing going on. Granted, I didn't have a mother, but I did have everything else. I had the Atlantic Ocean and the Indian River, a new red bicycle and a trailer park down the road full of loud-mouthed shrieking children who came with their own swing set, jungle gym and above-ground swimming pool.

At my grandmother's motel I had it made in the shade. I had my own bungalow with a private bath and a bathtub full of bubbles all the way up to the ceiling any time I wanted them and I had my own personal baby-blue Princess telephone. I had Malibu Barbie with her own Barbie jeep and a huge Barbie doll house that took up half my room. I also had enough Barbie doll clothes to choke a horse.

The horse being the only thing I couldn't talk my grandmother into buying me or my mother into sending me. But I did have a big wiry-haired dog named Go Buzz who dug the moats for all my sand castles ,where Barbie successively beat out Midge and Talking Julia in the International Screaming Cat Fight Competitions for Queen of the World. I had goggles, snorkels, flippers, pails and shovels and my very own raft. I had the ocean crashing in my dreams and by the time I started first grade I had twenty-seven different ways to say "sky".

Eventually, I even got the new father. He was just like Superman. When he came home from work and took off his glasses he was a real hunk. He was worth the wait. Not only that, he was an honest to God, totally professional, 100% rocket scientist and he was going to take me up to the jetties and let me watch the rockets blast off from up close. My mother said it was ironic. She said she spent a whole year in New York City looking for Mr. Right when, wouldn't you know it, there he was 10 miles north of Nana's

Sea Horse Beach Motel living in a bachelor apartment, eating TV dinners, watching *77 Sunset Strip* just waiting for my mom to come home that Christmas and meet her girlfriends at the Mouse Trap Lounge for a quick round of fishbowl martinis so he could stare across the dance floor until he finally got up the nerve to walk over to their table, look into my mother's dark, dreamy eyes and say, "Hello. My name is Mark Richardson and I was wondering—do you have any real, solid plans for the rest of your life?"

My mom never went back to New York. She had Darla turn in her timecard for her, pack up the rest of her clothes, her sewing machine, and her Barbra Streisand record collection and send everything to Florida. My mom and my new dad got married in a matter of months. They bought a four-bedroom, 2 1/2 bath, swimming pool home on Neptune Drive, where I had another room all my own. The plan was: as soon as school was out I was to pack up Barbie and move into the Neptune Drive house with them. Then, in the fall, I would make a smooth transition to my new school. By fall my mother was pregnant with twins and sick as a dog and the last thing she needed was me to worry about. So I stayed with Nana. Sometimes I spent the weekends with my mom and my new dad. Sometimes I didn't. There weren't any real clear lines between households. There was a huge overlap of telephones ringing and cars roaring up and down the road. My mother lost the twins. She also lost touch with reality and the outside world in general for the better (or worse) part of a year. She was depressed. She was medicated. She stayed in the house and read novels, enormous novels. She was still beautiful but she didn't comb her hair any more. Sometimes she let me do it. While my grandmother unloaded bags and bags of groceries in the kitchen, I combed and teased and sprayed my mother's hair. My mother was still my mother. We still had long conversations about Barbie fashion and stuff I did at school, but she no longer left the house, combed her hair or wore real clothes. My mother wore slips. She looked like Elizabeth Taylor in a movie that might never end.

Then one day she snapped out of it. It was right before Christmas. My mother got up, flushed the pills down the toilet, made a fresh pot of coffee, took a shower, got dressed and then drove over to JoAnn's Fabrics and bought five-and-a-half yards of gold lamé. She made herself a gold lamé cocktail dress with a deeply scooped neckline and spaghetti straps. She planned a

New Year's Eve pool party for fifty guests, with tiki torches and mountains and mountains of shrimp and crab legs and her famous, secret-ingredient cocktail sauce. I wore my new gold lamé hot pants and Barbie wore her gold lamé, slit-up-the-side sheath dress. Within months my mother was pregnant and the next year she was pregnant again. I had a brand-new brother and a little sister almost overnight and my mother never wore another slip again.

Which is how I ended up the only kid I ever knew who grew up with three bedrooms of her very own. That is, if you counted the one with the balcony at the sperm father's house, which, until he remarried to the broomstick witch, resembled more of a shrine to my mother than a child's bedroom. The room was tiny to begin with but was further diminished by the massive painting of my mother that hung over the cherrywood dresser and stared me in the face immediately upon entering the room. In the portrait my mother wore a white gossamer fairy dress. I imagined it was her wedding dress. It was difficult to say for sure since my mother was suspended amazingly in mid-air and surrounded by ropes of wisteria. My mother looked like a dark-haired free-falling angel. She wore a crown of hearts and stars with a long white veil billowing in the background. The painting gave me the creeps. It looked like my mother was falling through the sky but the expression on her face gave no indication whether or not she was enjoying the ride. My mother was wearing her poker face. In my experience that spelled trouble. The same poker face stared back at me from an assortment of photographs that graced every flat surface of the room—the writing desk, the bedside table, the dresser, the bookshelf. Everywhere I looked there she was—my mother in her not-all-there face. Each photograph stood like a gold-framed testimonial to my mother's past life, her face frozen in a mysterious sadness, which could only be explained by the fact that I wasn't there yet. In every photograph my mother faced the camera alone: my mother in a red velvet dress without me, my mother horseback riding without me, my mother carrying a picnic basket without me, my mother under an enormous sombrero in front of a "Bienvenidos a Mexico" sign, holding up a bottle of beer and obviously trying to smile but still very much without me.

But I didn't count that bedroom. That bedroom was another story and had nothing to do with my real life in Florida. Once I did my six weeks with the sperm father, I left it behind me. I never mentioned anything that happened there. I might have told my mother once about the balcony and about my secret passage to The City In The Stars where everyone wore red velvet and spoke in my grandmother's language and the fact that I could go there any time I wanted and nobody could ever touch me because I had extremely large muscles and super-human powers like invisibility and the ability to leap like a cat from building to building without making any noise. Other than that, I never said anything. Not to anyone. Not for decades. I was under a series of threats. The most compelling was probably the dismemberment threat. The sperm father threatened to chop off my fingers with a hatchet. He said he'd have to do it if I told. Even though I never saw the hatchet, I didn't push my luck. I had other concerns. He also said if anyone ever found out what we did together they would all hate me, absolutely everyone including my mother, because everybody in the world hated a nasty little girl like me. So, he explained, if they ever found out, I would have nowhere to live. I would be an orphan. And he said that nobody would ever want to marry me and I would wind up an old maid. Which was the thing that really scared the shit out of me. I knew the deal about that. I'd seen the playing cards. I'd gotten stuck holding the old maid more than once and I couldn't even bluff my way out of it. I definitely knew I didn't want to end up like that. The old maid was not only old, she was ugly as dirt.

The sperm father also told me, "Nobody would believe you anyhow. So don't waste your breath. They'd all just think you were a big, fat liar and they'd hate you even more."

Since I was already experiencing an almost insurmountable credibility problem at the Neptune Drive house, I was inclined to believe my sperm father. Other points I considered that summer when they asked me where I *really* wanted to live included: at my grandmother's motel I had a dog and my best friend, Amanda, lived right across the road. At my grandmother's I never had to wear shoes, go to bed, get my hair out of my face or stop running, *and* I could eat and watch TV at the same time. Which probably explains why I packed up the Barbie mansion and moved back to the Sea Horse Beach Motel where I lived with my grandmother until the day she died, years later, out on the sundeck lying on a lounge chair staring up at the sky. She died with a waffle pattern on the back of her ancient little thighs, a fact that I'm sure would have given her a big chuckle. She also would have been delighted that I spent an hour and a half with a corpse—a deeply tanned, highly henna-ed dead woman—deliberately ignoring her because I thought she was playing another one of her freaky Gypsy tricks. Now *that*, I know, would have caused her to laugh until she fell out of the goddamn lounge chair. But I do know, in my heart, she would have appreciated that it was me, that we were out there together under a lapis lazuli blue sky while the waves crashed louder "zan zee haird ob tondering vile eleephant." The Sea Horse Beach Motel was our home.

As many times as I tried to move into the Neptune Drive house with my mom and dad and my little brother and sister, it didn't work for me. I couldn't sleep. I couldn't hear what was going on outside. The air conditioning suffocated me. I couldn't breathe. I knew I wasn't getting enough oxygen in that house. I opened my windows, stood up on my bed, mashed my face against the screen and tried to catch some real air and suck it into my lungs. I felt a warm rush. I heard the low hum of a night breeze coursing through the dangling needles of the Australian Sea Pines. I heard crickets, maybe frogs, maybe alligators. It didn't matter specifically what I heard. It was something. It was life. Then they knocked. Those were the rules. Always knock. They knocked and knocked. They told me to close the windows. They had some way of knowing when I opened them. I never figured it out. It could have been closed-circuit television, although I never found the cameras. It could have been some kind of thermo-nuclear device my new dad brought home with him from the Cape. It didn't matter. Open windows were against the rules. They told me I was letting all the cool air out and costing them a fortune. They told me not to be ridiculous. They told me I didn't *need* to hear what was going on outside. They told me don't be stupid. There was plenty of oxygen in there. They told me good-night, for God's sake, go to sleep, then they walked down the hall and told each other, Jesus Christ, what a weird kid I was turning into.

But seriously, if a kid couldn't breathe a kid couldn't breathe. That's all there was to it. It's not something I had a lot of control over. They told me I could make the adjustment. They told me I wasn't trying hard enough. I didn't really see where trying came into the picture but I did it anyway. I tried the snorkel. My thought was, trapped in there real tight, up close, between the screen and the glass panels of the jalousie windows, there might be just enough air to sustain life. All I had to do was get to it. It was a little theory I had worked out while watching the fish in the aquarium at the Eau Gallie Public Library. I noticed those fish kept swimming to the top of the tank like they were looking for something. I decided they were probably looking for air. It was a pretty exciting moment for me and it looked like an idea I might be able to apply in my own bedroom on Neptune Drive.

That night, kneeling on my Neptune Drive bed, I stabbed a hole in the screen with my Goofy scissors. I jammed the top of the snorkel through the hole, wiggled it around, then I put the snorkel in my mouth and began breathing. It was hard to remember to breathe only out of my mouth. I found myself, time and again, breathing through my nose, which defeated the whole point of the snorkel. I decided I needed my face mask. I left the snorkel dangling from the hole in the screen and sneaked out of my room and down the hall through the kitchen and out to the garage where they made me keep my beach toys in a plastic baby pool so I wouldn't drag sand into the house. My mom hated sand in the house. I don't think she was too happy about sand in the garage. Actually, she wasn't happy about sand anywhere. She called it "dirty." I tried to explain the deal to her. I told her sand wasn't dirty. I told her that sand was sandy. *Dirt* was dirty. I told her that was the way it worked. Her eyes narrowed. Her jaw shifted. She stood her ground as if deliberating. "What?" I asked. My mother didn't reply. She really didn't need to. I knew I didn't want her out in the garage now looking at me, not like that, so I quickly rummaged through the toys in the baby pool feeling for the familiar contours of my face mask.

It was dark in the garage. I could only see outlines and forms. It was also hot. The air in the garage hung like dead bats on a clothesline. I could tell there was even less oxygen in the garage than there was in the house. I knew I didn't have a lot of time. I worked as fast as I could. Finally, I found my face mask. I slipped the strap on the back of my head and adjusted the mask so it sat on top of my head. Then I dashed out of the garage, raced through the house, down the hall, back to my bedroom where I closed the door behind me as quietly as I could in the middle of a dead run. I dived on the bed and grabbed for my snorkel. I groped in the dark. I couldn't find it. I was becoming hypoxic. I started to choke. Suddenly the overhead light flashed on. I screamed.

It was them: the mom and dad. Obviously, it was an ambush. They had been standing there waiting for me to come tearing back into the room. I don't know how long they had been there or how long I screamed but I do know it was loud and it woke my brother and my sister. Within seconds they were screaming too.

My mom grimaced like she had been struck by a bolt of tempestuous pain. She grabbed her head and raked her hands through her hair. She began pacing the floor. She wore her periwinkle blue baby-doll nightgown and blue satin slippers with white balls of fluff on top. Her toenails were painted Pandemonium Pink Frost and they peeked out the open toes of her slippers. Even my mother's feet were beautiful. I watched the white fluff and my mother's toes as she turned and paced the other way, back across the terrazzo floor of my bedroom. My brother and sister started screaming louder. My mother pulled her hair, gazed up at God and announced in a desperate voice, "I can't take another minute of this shit." She exited my bedroom, still pulling her hair, and walked down the hall to my brother's or my sister's room.

I don't know whose room she went to first. I wasn't paying much attention to that. I was too stupefied by the realization she had left me all alone with my new dad who really wasn't so new any more but he was, I was pretty sure, truly angry. Something about his mouth. He looked very much like a dog snarling. He was also wearing his black horn-rimmed glasses which looked quite odd with the boxer shorts and the MIT t-shirt he was also wearing and only added to the gravity of the situation. If he needed to see anything that well in the middle of the night, it couldn't be good news. The dead giveaway, though, was the fact he was holding my snorkel. That pretty much explained everything. I had no idea what would happen next.

"Do you know what you're doing to your mother?" he asked.

"No," I answered quite seriously. I really wanted to know. "What?"

"Well, just look at her. You're old enough to know better. Your mother is fragile. You know that. She's very delicately balanced and your behavior has put her on the brink of another breakdown. Do you understand what I'm saying? Your mother is on the edge, the very edge, and I want to know what you think we should do about this."

The misunderstanding occurred because, when my new dad asked me what I thought we should do about this, he was holding my snorkel and using it like a pointer and, as such, it quickly became the focus of my attention. It was my snorkel, after all, an object very familiar to me, which had become the cause of so much turmoil and midnight drama in our Neptune Drive household that I was anxious to get it out of everyone's sight and hoped they would magically forget about it. So, when my not-so-new dad asked me what I thought we should do about this, I assumed he meant the stupid snorkel which he was using at that precise moment to tap holes in the air like adding punctuation marks to his speech. Not for one quick minute did I even consider that he might be referring to my mother's precarious mental health.

So, when he asked me what I thought we should do about this, I didn't even have to think about it. I replied with enthusiasm, dying to get my hands on it, "Here. Give me that goddamned thing and I'll put it back in the baby pool in the morning."

Which was the wrong answer.

My not-so-new dad reeled backwards. He trembled and shook as if the impact of my statement threatened to knock him over. But he rebounded. Then he seemed to shoot out of his skin. He threw up his arms, waved my snorkel in the air and railed, "Don't you *ever* talk like that! Why you selfish little brat! Is that all you ever think about? Your toys? Don't you even care what happens to your mother?"

"What? What?" I screeched.

But it was too late for explanations. It was too late for the UN. The Reverend Jesse Jackson, Jr., could not have extricated my not so new dad and me from the mire of misunderstanding we had waded into.

While I screamed and pleaded, "Wait a minute! Wait a minute!" my not-so-new dad chased me around my Neptune Drive bedroom with my very own snorkel. demanding, "Don't you dare run away from me! Get back over here!"

My mother reappeared in the doorway. She looked stunned. Then she looked frightened. My brother and sister soon joined her. My little sister, Reena, toddled and screamed and grabbed at my mother's beautiful knees, while my brother, James, at that point in time known primarily as Jimbo, wide-eyed and silent and wearing his turquoise and orange number 22 Miami Dolphins football jersey, jumped up in the air as if he were taking a foul shot, then draped himself around the door jamb for his own 50-yard-line view of the action.

I continued to dodge my snorkel-wielding, not-so-new dad by running around the room in circles, ducking behind the Barbie mansion, and by jumping on and off the bed screaming, "I didn't do anything! I didn't do anything!"

"You didn't do anything?" my new dad demanded as he took a swipe at me with the snorkel. "Well, maybe that's the problem. You never do anything around here to help your mother. All you ever think about is yourself and your toys. How can you say you didn't do anything?" He took another swat, missed, and then swatted again. "Just look at the mess you made."

His timing was getting better. He was getting closer. I felt a breeze blow by my legs. "I'll fix the screen. I'll sew it up. I promise."

"You can't sew up the mess I'm talking about! You can't make tonight go away!" That time he connected. The snorkel landed on my butt. It didn't hurt but I screamed anyway. "You can't repair any of this! Look at your brother and sister." He got me again, that time on the back of my legs. I kept screaming and running around the room and my not-so-new dad kept swatting and yelling, "Look at them! Who can know the damage this may cause their little psyches? Goddamn it. Quit running away from me! Isn't it bad enough that this night has caused your mother so much anguish? Isn't it bad enough that you have probably contaminated your brother and sister for the rest of their lives? Is that what you want?"

My mother, evidently taking her cue, said in a high-pitched voice, "Quickly, children! Into the master bedroom! Quickly!"

I tried to bolt through the bedroom door but my not-so-new dad grabbed me by the collar of my Tinker Bell lounging pajamas. "Not you," he said.

"*Mom!*" I screamed but she was gone, carrying my sister on her hip and dragging my brother by the hand down the hallway.

I kicked. I stood in the doorway holding on with all the strength I had while my not-so-new dad tried to pry my fingers loose from the door frame.

"Help!" I screamed. "Owwww!" I screamed louder and louder, even though I don't remember anything hurting. I screamed, "You're not my real father! I don't have to do what you say! Help! Help! Let go! You're killing me! You don't know anything! You don't know what I do around here. I do a lot of stuff but you can't see anything because you're so ugly in your stupid glasses! Nobody wears glasses like that any more. Bonita's dad is a fireman and he wears aviator glasses. No wonder you don't see any of the stuff I do because you're ugly and you're blind in your stupid ugly glasses. That's why!"

I don't think any of those observations went far in my favor when my not-so-new dad finally pried my fingers loose from the door frame and put me over his knee. However, if my memory serves me correctly, all he did was tap me on the butt three times. It was a joke. It was a day at the beach. I was still wearing my face mask like a party hat. I screamed my head off anyhow.

The next morning, surprisingly, the sun came up and once again we sat around the breakfast table in the kitchen. The specific day of the week must have been Saturday, Sunday or a Federal holiday because my not-so-new dad was in charge of the cereal. Reena sat in her highchair smearing soggy, mushed-up cornflakes in her hair. Jimbo rested his head on the table while he scooted plastic army men around the placemats, up the side of the juice glass and across the wooden tabletop. My not-so-new dad was slurping coffee and reading the *Orlando Sentinel*, which he had folded in half next to his cup and saucer with the bottom of the paper hanging over the edge of the table. He focused on an article at the top of the page as he shoveled cornflake mush into my sister Reena's little baby-toothed mouth.

My mother was absent. She had not yet emerged from the master bedroom. Evidently she was still sleeping off the anguish which I had perpetrated the night before. Her absence was not a point of concern. It was not unusual. It didn't become unusual or a point of concern until about noon. If she didn't come out by then, it was time to worry. In the meantime, we were to play quietly, eat cereal out of the boxes and not make a mess. Unless, of course, it was Saturday, Sunday or a Federal holiday when my not-so-new dad was in charge of the cereal. Since he was quite capable of getting the bowls out of the cupboard without smashing them to smithereens and since he was also quite capable of maneuvering the milk out of the refrigerator and pouring it into the bowls on top of the cereal without causing a flood or an avalanche or a national disaster, on Saturday, Sunday and Federal holidays we got cereal with milk. Sugar, however, was tricky. Not one of us sitting at the breakfast table that morning was truly qualified with the sugar. Sugar was a lot like sand, only worse. Much worse. Believe me, you never saw a real mess until you saw a sugar mess. It was best to stick with the Smacks or the Fruit Loops.

"I want a chocolate donut," I said.

Nobody said anything.

"I *said*, 'I want a chocolate donut', " I repeated.

"We heard you," my not-so-new dad said. "But as you can see, there are no chocolate donuts."

"Well, you could go get in your car and drive down to Food Town and buy some chocolate donuts, couldn't you?" I asked.

"I certainly could, but I'm not going to. So, forget about it and eat your Fruit Loops."

"I hate Fruit Loops. How come there's never anything good to eat around here?"

"And I suppose you categorize chocolate donuts as something good to eat?" he asked me.

"A lot better than Fruit Loops. Did you ever read the back of the box? Did you? Did you ever see all the different kinds of poison they put in there?" I grabbed a cereal box and started reading out loud, "Tria...., something, something, sugar, sugar sugar and BHT!"

"Those aren't poisons," he pointed out. "Those are preservatives. There's a big difference."

"There's no difference at all," I said. "Amanda's mom says that the parents are poisoning the children by making them eat Fruit Loops. She says that Fruit Loops and Coco Puffs and Smacks are so full of poison that it makes the children go crazy."

"So, what does Amanda's mom feed her children, chocolate donuts?"

"Oatmeal," I told him. "Amanda's mom gets up in the morning and makes oatmeal. She even cooks it. She stands at the stove and cooks it and then she sprinkles raisins on top."

"Well, when you grow up and have your own stove you can cook oatmeal too," he told me.

"I don't *want* oatmeal," I said. "I told you, I want chocolate donuts! How many times do I have to say it?"

"Me too," Jimbo said, "I want chocolate donuts."

"No you don't," my not so new dad told my brother. "And get those army men out of your cereal." Then he turned back to me. "Is that the kind of junk you eat over at your grandmother's?

Chocolate donuts? I am not surprised. What else? Chocolate donuts and Gummi Bears for breakfast? Well, you're not getting any chocolate donuts and Gummi Bears in this house, I can tell you that, so you might as well forget about it and you better watch your tone of voice when you're talking to me, young lady."

"You can't *watch* your tone of voice for Christ's sake. Everybody knows that. Everybody knows your tone of voice is invisible unless you're in the comics. Unless you're Batman for Christ's sake. Unless you're . . ."

"What did you say? Don't you dare say that again. Don't you dare use that language. Don't you ever talk like that around your brother and sister again."

"Why not? You say it all the time. For Christ sake, Jesus Christ, Goddamn it. Who cares? Nana says Jesus Christ isn't really the son of God anyhow. Nana says it was all a big trick Nixon made up to get the people to pay more taxes and send Sasha's brother Nick over to Viet Nam to kill babies."

"Your grandmother never said anything like that and you know it. Your grandmother couldn't put that many words together in the English language if her life depended on it. And you better knock off all this lying before you find yourself in big trouble."

"It's not a lie!" I screamed. "I'll prove it to you! Call my Nana on the phone and ask her if you don't believe me. Ask her if she said it. For the main reason, she didn't say it in the English language, *mister smarty pants*, she said it in *her* language!"

"Okay, that does it." My not-so-new dad dropped the baby spoon in the Quack Quack Duckie cereal bowl. The spoon clanged. The milk splashed.

"Get up!" he yelled at me. "*Get up!*"

My not-so-new dad shot up so quickly the legs of his chair screeched across the tile floor like the scream of a mortally wounded animal. Jimbo looked up, jarred from The Battle of the Edge of the Placemat. His eyebrows arched. His eyes were wide open. He held one army man in mid-air suspended over his very full glass of orange juice.

"Jimbo, I thought I told you to get those army men out of your cereal," the new dad pronounced every syllable of every word; slowly, calmly, but firmly, in an apparent attempt to downplay the theatrics of the screeching chair, to get his point across, but at the same time, prevent his anger at me from spilling over and contaminating the innocent bystanders.

"His army men aren't in his cereal," I remarked.

I'm sure I knew it was the wrong thing to say. But I said it anyway. I felt compelled to set the record straight, to point out the fact that my not-so-new dad, in all his eloquence, had misspoken. I seriously doubt that I was sticking up for my brother. Jimbo didn't need sticking up for. It hadn't come to that. At that juncture, the lines were not yet drawn in the sand. That would come later. On that particular morning, I think all I wanted to do was make it perfectly clear, let it go down in history, that there were absolutely none, zero, zippo, open up your eyes, go ahead and count them, there was not one army man in the cereal bowl. There wasn't. Except for a tiny puddle of milk at the very bottom, the cereal bowl was empty. All the army men were bivouacked around the milk carton with the exception of the lone kamikaze juice diver, the army man my brother still held by the grenade launcher and dangled over his orange juice.

"*Get up* and get over here!" my new dad yelled at me.

Which was my signal to immediately shape-shift, turn into a jet-propelled, slithering iguana and slide out of my chair, under the table, onto the kitchen floor while my brother gave the command, "Dive! Dive!" And the kamikaze juice diver dropped feet first into the orange juice —*plop, splash* and squeals of delight as Reena pounded her little hands in the cornflake mush and mashed everything in her hair.

Except I got stuck. My body was getting too big. I had miscalculated. My shoulders and my back were wedged between the seat of the chair and the underneath side of the tabletop. I was trapped. The chair wouldn't budge. I couldn't breathe. I was no longer a slithering iguana. I was a little girl held prisoner in a chair with my shoulders stuck, my body writhing under the table and my head sticking up tabletop level like Anne Boleyn in the Bloody Tower. It was unbearable. I flailed. I screamed like I had never screamed before. I saw my not not-so-new dad coming at me and I screamed louder. I screamed like my life depended on it. I screamed bloody murder.

I kind of remember my not-so-new dad pulling the chair out and lifting me out of there. I think he may have carried me down the hall to my bedroom. I don't remember that part exactly. I don't know for sure how I got there, but I do remember lying on my Neptune Drive bed gasping and choking and finally able to breathe. I remember how quiet everything had become, as if the only thing left in the world was one breath of air after another. I remember my mother standing in the doorway and I remember my dad said to me, "You're okay. Take it easy."

I nodded my head. I stared up at the ceiling and I tried to imagine sky—a deep dark, Superman blue one with giant white puffs of elephant clouds.

My dad got up and joined my mother in the doorway. He ran his fingers through his wavy brown hair and he shook his head. Then he placed one arm around my mother's shoulder. She nuzzled into his side.

"Jesus Christ," I heard him say as they walked together down the hall.

The Axioms of Love

I.

From Roger and Weber's Book of Math, chapter 12: Axioms.

Step 1: *Use topographical maps, a basic rubric, historical wind speed data, and the formulas at the end of this chapter to create an algorithm.*

You've figured out the first seven steps but get stuck once one lover
     moves thousands of miles from the other. You need that eighth
     algorithm to discover the distance love can travel.

II.

She writes: *I saw two herons. I thought of you.*

III.

Step 2: *Figure out your variables.*

     x = the heron of the river [2].
     n = their rooks in the sycamores [2].
     b = the mileage between you and her [2,561].
     c = the way, when you asked if you could kiss her, she gasped,
     Yes.
And A, yes, A must = how she said, *You threw a rock in my river,*
     now I am all ripply.
     Or are you wrong about this, and does A = how she said,
     I like you.
     How she whispered, *I like you a lot.*

IV.

Step 3: *Using your variables and the formulas from page 412, find your axiom.*

Trying the Expansion of a Sum $[(1 + x)^n = 1 + \frac{nx}{1!} + \frac{n(n-1)x^2}{2!}]$, is this
     your axiom:

     There are two herons. Sometimes they are alone.
     Sometimes they are a pair [2] at the confluence.

Trying the Area of a Circle [$A = \pi r^2$], is this your axiom:

> She and you were in the cabin. It had 3 rooms.
> You only used 2.

Trying the Quadratic Formula[$x = \frac{-b \pm \sqrt{b^2 - 4ac}}{2a}$], is this your axiom:

> She and you were in bed.
> Her white shoulders sang above you.

V.

The math no longer makes sense so you throw your scribbling
and equations to the floor, clear your desk of everything
[everything]. You think of smoking a Marlboro Light
[to clear your mind] though you've never smoked before.

Using butcher paper, a dirty protractor, and a No. 2 pencil,
you draw slowly expanding concentric circles from her
eastern Pennsylvania cornfields to Idaho — a Venn diagram
all the way to your cramped and cluttered office.
Circles as beautiful as clouds.

VI.

She mails you a letter: *I liked kissing your sleeping back.*

Chapter 12 shows you must respond in 1 of 2 ways:

1. There is love. There is distance. They are inverse functions.
Or:
2. If math were love and love were herons, your axiom
would be the pinions of a bird breaking
the surface of the river.

VII.

Step 4: *When you run into problems, check the variables, the lemma, and the formulas used.*

The deeper into the chapter you get, the more the math gets confusing.
Intercepts with a locus. Quotients and equivalent fractions.
The associative properties of multiplication.

You double check your lemma.   It's got to be the lemma.
Can it be the lemma?

VIII.

Step 5: *Measure the diameter of each concentric circle. Divide that diameter by z.*

Z, you figure, must = the times she kissed you while you slept [6].

IX.

Pacing your Idaho streets, you search the sky low and you search the sky
        high but there are only ravens [3 in a tree] and vultures
        [5 circling above what death, you don't know].
        You cling to a final memory of herons [2] taking flight [at dusk].

Are you and she their wings?

X.

Step 6 shows that the concentric circles are just disjointed sets,
        empty sets. If even one was a superset.

XI.

She calls and says, The rains are coming. The cabin is empty.

XII.

If you better understood Roger and Weber, any of it, you'd create
        new models [using new equations] that required banks
        of computers [36] toiling for days [112] until they melted
        [1 by 1]. Then you'd take your work and return to scribbling
        on paper while chewing those No. 2s almost in half.
        Using the stubs [whatever remains], you'd erase
        every mistake you ever made.

The Blue Planet

We allege color,
the calculus of science
toned to mood.
Thus, in describing Earth,
an astronomer may see
grief born of brevity.
Blue as might sorrow
the music of the spheres,
blind the universe
to its billion beacons of light,
In fact, it is *blue* the color
of water, water so finely
atomized and riven with sunlight that the very veil
of air around the earth
becomes *blue*. Yes, we reason,
tears of light, the sadness
we live and breathe.

Orange

An orange pasture crosses my dream
like a wide Fauve river. For what is color
but attribution: a road cone, metal primer,
hunting vest and, in the extreme, Agent Orange.
Keep out, it says, falling rock, wet
paint, chemical spill, a crime zone.
At times, this is how I see things happen.
The orange river crossing my sleep
pretends a pasture where cows are purple,
sheep are green and my imagination runs wild.
After all, what is color but radiance.
It is the dawn's DayGlo, quiver of a monarch's
wing tip, the clock ticking and then its alarm.
And suddenly, river and pasture turn
pastel and out of the morning mist churns
a tanker upstream big and brown and black.
And from the television comes news
of a foreign war, its flames orange,
orange that crosses my mind on impact of a fist,
orange the Fauve ghost hanging over me,
the warning I carry like a lunchbox to work.

Afghanistan

There is only this stain
only this growing fist
of poppies, only these birds that gain
the cliffs of winter, these avenues that hang
beside a well. Somewhere a stag
dies on a plain, then dies again.
Summer's air suffers with the tang
of the lost faith
of children. This is the gist
of all the songs we sang.
This is all that we began. This.

At the Door

He kneels to God
on a pile of broken dishes
where light pours
onto the white floor.
An old man, his radio fades
as he moves farther and farther
from town. He remembers
storms lit by stars, bluebonnets
in the back yard, tomatoes
warm from the sun.
The clock in the corner
tolls three. Soon,
they will dismantle
this place
and carry him away.

The Censor

1.

The new rules on kissing are, it's allowed if it's done Indian-style—lips breathing close, behind smoke and mirrors, or more often hazy bushes. But no American kissing. Couples can approach, entangle, embrace, depending on where their hands rest during the peak moment. Hands must be off, so to speak. Definitely European shamelessness is still out. But I wonder. There are times when eroticism becomes so flat, so predictable, it becomes the kind of safe thing a capitalist might pursue in leisure time, not a driving obsession. So shouldn't we be disallowing discreet snuggles, the sneakings and maneuverings of our own dainty heroines, as posing far the greater danger? I wonder, I wonder. Not a word of these doubts to my superiors.

2.

Yesterday afternoon, at the awards ceremony, on Islamabad's most pristinely boring boulevard, surrounded on both sides by castles of bureaucratic rectitude, my supervisor's supervisor is bestowed a medal of honor by the Culture Minister: "In these times of global strife and misunderstanding, you do an invaluable service in removing the distractions diluting the pure cultural artifact. Without your intervention, what we would get is enhancement of conflict, not its lessening." Everyone, politely dressed in seventies safari suits, open at the collar despite the wintry chill, claps, looking glassy-eyed. A waiter, balancing a huge tray of comestibles, nearly trips on the microphone wires, to collective applause when he corrects himself at the last second, like an experienced ballet dancer. I suppose he is gay. Half the population in the city is gay—that is, the permanent part of it. The transients tend to be more correct in their sexual preferences. It has been a long time since the openly gay people have bothered to storm the ministers at their lavish soirées. The cheering in the auditorium suddenly escalates. A midget-sized man is raising his hands in the air, like the Shi'a at prayer, appraising the acclaim. The holy month of Ramadan is just around the corner. It will interfere with the diet, ruin many delicate constitutions which will not be able to handle the rigors of abstention.

3.

"Khan sahib, do you remember when we were at the Sorbonne, and those long-haired students asked our delegation why it was that the Bengalis were thriving after letting go of the western part of the country, and that was in the middle of one of their worst famines ever? When they were the basketcase of the world? Thriving, they said, in French, I forget the phrase they used, but certainly that was the meaning. What is the purpose of such bias, do you think?" I have survived every regime, democratic, pseudo-democratic, dictatorial, fascist, virtual, and yet I can keep every ruler's face distinct from the others', as though I had gone to school with them, had helped them cheat on exams, and was obligated to protect them because we played cricket on the same field.

4.

One's colleagues, one regrets to report, are often so enamored of the dead past, valuable for the perceived common mudslinging that came one's way, that one had rather not face mornings at all. Anyway, it is a satisfyingly cold day, and I suspect that the fruit stalls in the evening will be open later than usual. The wind blows as though straight from the other side of the border, from the height of the Karakorams, bringing in its wake the smell of cashews and pistachios, and of women whose unveiled face no man has ever seen.

5.

It is an old American classic, a Jimmy Stewart movie, and I doubt there can be anything worth excising here, but I am obligated to go through with the motions. "Cut," I tell myself, making the snip-snip gesture honored by mimes, "Cut, this is a piece of shit, this will ruin our young minds." I read somewhere that nearly a quarter of the university-educated have access to high-speed Internet. Yet my job persists, in fact becomes more tenured than ever, more secure by the day, like the guards at the Quaid's mausoleum, protecting the honor of the founder with their waxed faces and immobile bodies, looking past the ticking hour, past paupers and princes alike. "Unity, faith, and discipline," the Quaid's motto holds, and I suspect my late bachelorhood has something to do with getting bogged down in its mechanics. Each part contradicts the other. You cannot even have two of the elements at the same time, let alone three.

6.

The new rules say we can show the Taliban's faces, instead
of blurring them. Individually they are no longer terrorist threats.
However, talk of Russian influence in the border areas is still
forbidden. The mullahs in Karachi have made a new deal, so we no
longer need to pretend the urban madrassas don't exist. The price
of wheat is going to skyrocket this year, so it is all right to mention
travel to India (if you don't see the connection, well . . .). This need
to hold many contradictory thoughts in my head at the same time is
the price I have to pay for versatility. Colleagues who have stuck to
one genre, movies, say, or television documentaries, have smaller
guts, more hair, whiter teeth.

7.

There is an explosion at ten in the morning, and the lights
go out. We are prevented from leaving the building by the guard,
"for our own security." There is no window in my office, a "security measure" from the time the building was inaugurated. I don't
know what is happening outside. Many hours go by, during which
I ponder why the movie *Network* is so objectionable that despite my
work on it, it is still considered an affront to the country's sensibil-
ity. It is a relic of the past, laughable in its pretensions—yet *All the
President's Men* is okay, because relations with America are cooler,
now that our ruler is paying the price at the polls. Also, it is time
to take another look at *One Flew Over the Cuckoo's Nest*, and *The
Deer Hunter*, and *Julia*. They tell me someone blew himself up in a
suicide truck not far away, but what is curious is that he didn't aim
for any structure at all—it was purely suicide. So suicide bombers
are now committing only individual suicide, and leaving the public
alone. This must be some new stage of the dialectic.

8.

After all my education, my foreign hopes and diversionary
dreams, this! It's all because I couldn't lose my shyness around
white women. Or at least not until it was too late, and I found myself back in the country, through no fault of mine, hypnotized by
the train wreck, the streaking vehicle of failure on which was loaded all the artistic dreck of the century, heading for utter collapse.
They say Hitler was a failed artist in prewar Vienna. I understand
how small frustrations multiply into world-altering resentments.
People everywhere are bitter, secret poets, mystics at the breakfast
table. There is a steep ravine behind my house, ending in utter

murk. Our very own Grand Canyon. Sometimes the moon tramps so slow over the horizon that we feel it pausing over Islamabad, for a special blessing. "O ye failed romantics, exude not too much faith, in the land of the pure, because the centuries are relativistic anyway." The rising price of flour and sugar, the proverbial insult against the common man, is insinuated in this independently produced movie I have been screening now for possible lapses this entire last week, only to conclude that its realism is so banal, it's the most threatening thing to come across my desk in years. I make a special note of the director's name, a young man who claims to have learned his art in Canada. I can do him no favors, his fate is sealed.

9.

A woman who claims to have known me as a soldier on the Wah front in the 1965 war calls me out of the blue. She has a notice-able North Indian accent. "I'm sorry, I was never a soldier in my life." She won't accept my version of the past, and insists on her nar-rative. It is too sophisticated to be a prank, and besides I no longer keep up with such frisky people. "No, this is how it happened, you can't tell me otherwise," she says, hanging up in disgust.

10.

The new rules about political speech have come out. It is okay to say "terrorists" now. For years we have been saying extremists, or fanatics, or militants. But now the word of choice is terrorists. Only the president used to be able to say terrorists. But now all must be encouraged to say terrorists. It is the new honesty. I notice, at the proverbial water-cooler, my colleagues throwing out the word at the slightest opportunity. "The chowkidar is a bloody terrorist, he wants to open the trunk of my car to inspect it. Imagine, I have been com-ing to work here for ten years, he sees my bloody face every day, and he wants to know what's in the trunk of my little Daihatsu?" Another says, "My mother-in-law is a terrorist, she wants us to spend the entire holidays at her ancestral home in Abbotabad." There is a cold-ness in my walk back to my office that I cannot explain to myself.

11.

Imagine having a daughter. Imagine having to explain the facts of life to her. I would have lied. I would never have been able to imagine her grown up. One has children only to keep them childlike, forever, despite the harm to them. Yes, that is the most benign pa-rental impulse, and cultures that don't allow children to be children suffer in the long run. I speak like a retrograde fossil, but in return for my silence, I am entitled to have my opinions.

12.

There is a state funeral for a former prime minister, a figure-head who had served under one of those pseudo-dictatorial presidents long ago. I had no idea he was alive still. He must have been over a hundred. There is disagreement over how to present this news to the country. It evokes memories of when we were entangled in the fine print of constitution-making, to the extent that we never got a workable one. His legacy is beyond reach. It is at such moments of uncertainty, when the definition of the truth becomes a question of priorities in flux, that those much higher up than me, dealing with such subjects as Olympics preparedness and tamping down the blasphemy lawsuits, suddenly start acknowledging me in the hallways and parking lots. I too inflate to monster-like proportions during certain times of the day when my services are in such acute need. Of course, the independent satellite channels are officially beyond our reach, as is the vast expanse of the Internet, a universe unto itself (we can try blocking and jamming, as we do from time to time, even if this is something I've never approved of, this kind of underhanded tactic), but they do not speak for the government, so this is not how we judge ourselves. I would say that our minority status in a world of proliferating media is what gives us endless vigor, to fight on and on, and I would say that this is what keeps me youthful, at least in spirit.

13.

What is the fight all about? Who knows. I recall a Beckett play in which nothing happens. Every morning at seven a veg-etable-wallah rolls his cart past my house. His specialty is bright green cucumbers, fresh as though washed in the sea, a thousand miles to the south. I stretch on my lawn, or sometimes on my roof, in clear sight of the Margallas, mountains for the bourgeois, unlike those other mountains for the Taliban, which rise like infallible towers for the icon-busters. I idolize my physical and spiritual remains, in the best sense of the word. One side of my body is a little shorter than the other, without having been a problem. A callus that threatened to erupt on the back of my hand has receded spontaneously. "Sahibji, shall I wash the car?" my driver interrupts me, and I let him. "Of course, wash it thoroughly, leave not a scratch mark, not a spot of dust. If I see so much as a speck . . ." I have teased him like this for years, and yet he has never got the joke.

Bread Crumbs

*Hansel and Gretel believed the bread crumbs were a mistake
because they didn't help them find their way back home.*

Swedish fish and gummy bears
planted or slipping untended
through sleepy fingers to the ground
call to the unfortunate children
who follow, forbidden to fingerhook
the fruit animals dotting the sidewalk.
I imagine birds puzzled
by the chewy bright crumbs—

❁   ❁   ❁

We call it serendipity when it turns out well, tragic when it doesn't.

Balancing zwieback and brie on my wrist while
at a poetry reception at Radcliffe, in an elegant,
carpeted room, white walls heavy with portraits.
Everyone else seems so comfortable here,
all I want is a parent who attended college
and reads the *New York Times*. Then, a woman
comes up and introduces herself—as we talk
she remarks that her siblings and parents
are all Radcliffe and Harvard grads. So, I ask,
how about you? She is a Wellesley dropout.
A grandmother now, she'll always
be the one who dropped out, especially here.

❁   ❁   ❁

Tracing the dropping to the picking up is largely speculative.

I bought a ring at the consignment shop
mostly because I was told its former owner was Middle
Eastern and my country was at war with Iraq.
Two days later a stone fell out of it,
leaving a tiny hole in the wall of the ring.

And I bought earrings there—also because of a story.
Their design, the shopkeeper explained, began
as a lover's gift; amulets and beads paired to win
a woman's love. Old metal and stone carrying
old blessings and protections, joined with new silver.
And then people who didn't even know him—like me—
were charmed and wanted to buy them. But, I want to know
—did it work? Does she love him?
Does he still love her?

         ❄   ❄   ❄

We begin one place trying to do one thing.

Hansel and Gretel, you tried to ensure your safe passage home
and used what you had—it's just the bread crumbs
were too tempting for others. But, still, didn't the lives of the birds
lessen the hell of the witch's candied kingdom?
God scattered people to the winds—seeds and ashes alike.
Even God can't always play god.

Sometimes, I find myself thinking a stray comment
is foreshadowing. For instance, my seven-year-old son
asks what would happen if a skier tried to go down
a perpendicular slope. He doesn't use the word "perpendicular"
but illustrates the straight up and down with his hand
—fingers forming an L with the top of the table.
I shudder. His dad, whom I love, is skiing, alone, today,
and as I reassure him that Daddy is careful and skilled
(is this even what he's talking about?)
I remind myself that life is not art.

Except— it's true—we can look back
as through photographs of our younger selves
and see, more or less, how we got here,
where we are today.

Beneath The Weeping Beech

The low branches make us reverent;
nearly kneeling, heads bowed,
we enter its upside-down world.
Hanging strings of gold-drop leaves
make the most of November sun
against the black of Norway pines
in near winter shadows.
Within the airy curtain
of sun-caught leaves
my child takes my hand.
If we could build a house
beneath this tree he says
and in the morning walk out
into this —

Manly Johnson, photograph

A. J. COLLINS

Clothes Hung on a Line

In the splotchy midday light next door,
they're the river-dipped hand my face
tightens against and welcomes, ghostly,
inviting me to lean on the chainlink and breathe.

Once I grew tall enough to touch the line,
I had to pin up the socks and tank-tops I usually let
sit too long plastered to the washer's spun walls.
I walked with a basket of cool damp cotton through the sun.

In the fields behind the house a tobacco harvester
stalled at the end of a row for a water break.
Dust silted over and down, my hands and the sheets
dinged in the way you can see only once it's smeared.

Standing between two white sheets in the wind-
blown moments before a downpour, an astonished
gauntlet. I thought that was what church should be.
In the comfort of a reverie, all throttle and demand.

Upon Cutting My Thumb While Reading Ariel

A jagged ice-chip of glass,
once the curved side

of a perfect bowl, slices
through flesh, tendon, and artery

as easily as a fin
through clear water.

Raw tissue blooms
first pearl-white then peony,

until blood wells and floods
this unsealed canyon,

spilling over to defile
a white-tiled floor

with glittering bloodspots
like oil-paint on marble.

Stunned nerves quiver,
strain to reach for severed mates,

sizzle in electrified panic
at their premature parting. Now

hear the wailing, the wailing! —
A thumb in its refusal to clot?

Or my crimson-lipped mouth
that has waited years for an excuse?

The Hiding Place

At last, April. We drive past the forest preserve,
treetops simmering green. I roll down the window
and press my palm to the wind.

I've read that in spring, young girls are driven
to places like these, forced to huddle under damp logs.
Some are thirteen, some are ten, some are six,
shivering in stilettos and halter tops.
They draw daisies in the dirt with sticks
as they wait for the men to appear at twilight.

The girls teach themselves to float away,
drifting to the canopy of branches.
One girl becomes a wisp of cloud;
one becomes a squirrel. One becomes a sparrow,
flitting among the open spaces
until she alights on a bud. She perches there
and refuses to move. When the wind tosses
the branch, she dips and sails with it, oblivious
to the whimpers below, the sudden pops
of raindrops, the rush of passing cars.

Dea Abscondita

—for Lucille Clifton

Hattie lived in a shotgun house
in West Town, its walls adorned with quilts.
She raised me, my first word, her name.
I think of her on alfalfa-scented mornings,
when earth exudes dark fragrance after rain.
I do not remember her lullabies, but their rhythm
beats within, and I am driven to live a passionate life,
because once she rocked me in the soul of Abraham.
Her spice enveloped me. I thrived at the edge of her hem.

When I was alone with my own pale child,
Ruby cared for him while I finished school.
She gave him expressed milk, bathed him,
made sure our clothes were clean and pressed.
Sometimes we'd watch her stories on TV,
talk about the characters as if they were neighbors,
praise the baby to each other, laugh.
My sorrow healed as we spoke
the familiar singing cadence.

The Black Madonna of Montserrat
offers me gifts in dreams. Burnished
by fire, seared by the numinous,
patron saint of childbirth and the abandoned
who've learned to use their wounds,
guardian of the child that was, that is, that will be,
she calls me home to play on the brick streets
of warm cicada nights, and when she says,
"You are willing not to know," she names me.

The Legend of Maude

It was Teddy who said it. Three weeks before our wedding. He looked up from the *Journal* and said simply, kindly, as if he was thinking to throw some money at starving Angolans, "We ought to invite Maude."

"Hm," I said.

You'll think, when I'm done, that I should have said more. But when Teddy says we ought to do something, it means he's going to do it. The "we" is just politeness, the "ought" cautious. That evening he was dialing information for the whole Tri-State region. This was before the Internet, when finding a person took some time. But Maude turned out to be easy. She was close by, in St. Charles. She did technical writing for a software company. She'd be happy to attend the wedding. Did Evie want to have lunch?

Evie—that's me—did not want to have lunch. Evie did not want to think about the weirdness of this. Evie was having enough trouble with Teddy's parents, who had taken over paying for the wedding. Evie wanted to marry Teddy and move to Chicago, and she didn't see why the Legend of Maude should stalk her days. Call her selfish if you like, but allow that she had asked for none of the package excepting Teddy, and Teddy was the innocent one.

When people hear that Teddy and I both grew up in St. Louis, they assume we were an item since childhood. Not so. It was as if I couldn't even see Teddy, much less fall in love with him, until I'd had about a million other relationships. Still, I tell these people we met when he was ten and I was nine. "He was trying to give me a quarter," I report, and Teddy rolls his eyes and shakes his head.

❀ ❀ ❀

When I was nine we lived in one of the townhouses they'd built off Pike Road, behind the health club. They sprang up everywhere in the Seventies. Sets of four and eight, prefab vinyl siding, windows at front and back even on the end units. My mother had been impressed by the street signs. "Camelot," the development was named. Guinevere Drive intersected Lancelot Lane, which dead-ended into Mordred Manor. The playground at the back, soon littered with broken bottles of Bud, sported a brown plastic castle and two shaky bridges across a foul-smelling trench that we dubbed the Moat. Around this space walked sallow mothers, their cigarettes dangling like a sixth digit from the hand with which they steered their frayed strollers. My brother Frank and I chased each other down to the drainage pipe; we devised kickball games; we challenged the other Camelot children—retarded, in our view, victims of radiated water in some other, worse development—to endless, excruciating games of Capture the Flag at twilight when the mosquitoes took over.

Then Frank won a full scholarship to St. Louis Country Day School and everything took a turn for the desperate. Against all reason, our mother insisted not just that he go to the place (the bus, not yellow but robin's egg blue, stopped by the entrance to Camelot and Frank slouched on), but also that he bring someone home. A friend. One of the boys, she pleaded, just for the afternoon. After all, he'd gone to their Tudor homes, a couple of birthday parties already. After a few weeks of resisting, Frank shrugged his shoulders at dinner, said, "You'll see," and went to the phone to call Teddy Castlebaum.

Why Teddy, I can't tell you. Maybe he was the richest, so the humiliation would be greatest. Or maybe, Teddy having no friends, the humiliation would be contained. I've never asked either Frank or Teddy. However chosen, he came. He was pudgy and pale and bored by our TV, our back lawn, the Moat. That evening he took me aside in the common vestibule of our building, told me I was the most beautiful girl he'd ever seen, and offered me a quarter.

My mother made me give it back. "Girls don't accept money from boys," she said crisply. Though she sold paintbrushes for a living, she never forgot what she called the aesthetics of life. My heart was doing cannonballs from throat to chest. In tears, just as Teddy's alarmed mother drew up in the shared parking lot, I returned the quarter. I couldn't look into his pale green eyes.

That spring, my mother sent me to take a test. Then she dressed in the suit she wore to funerals and presented herself to the financial aid office at Mary Institute. Next thing I knew I was weeping goodbyes to my public-school friends as if I were being carted off to labor camp. Only girls populated my new school, and at first I took a different bus than Frank, a kelly-green van. But the two campuses adjoined, and when Frank saved up his grease-monkey money for an old Pontiac, he gave me rides.

We were smart poor kids, and not the only ones. Maude Millerton was the smartest, for instance, and if she wasn't poorer, she was at least more of a card-carrying Scholarship Girl than the rest of us. She actually wore the clothes her relatives sent her, knee-length skirts in olive and orange, brought in at the waist and topped by short-sleeved, pilled acrylic sweaters. Her mother cut her hair in a pageboy, and rolled the ends in foam curlers at night. In addition to starring at chemistry and math, she had a peculiar expertise in A.A. Milne and was given to quoting Pooh in awkward circumstances, like the time Arlette knocked down a hive from the hockey goal and we all started running while Maude said calmly, "The only reason for being a bee that I know of is making honey." I kept my distance from her, as one did from any toxic substance. She lived on a farm, and caught the bus every morning at six, the first on; the other girls who rode from that direction said they could smell the pig slop on her.

My mother said she looked like Katharine Hepburn.

Maude had spent the night in our house after the school choir, to which we both belonged, had sung in the downtown St. Louis Cathedral late on a Wednesday. We were in ninth grade by then, not high school but Upper School, young ladies sharing their Easter harmonies with the city folk. It being planting season, the Millertons were too busy on their farm to fetch Maude home. Over the phone my mother assured Mrs. Millerton that we had a fine pull-out couch, and next thing you knew there was Maude at our breakfast table, finishing her history homework. "I will never live this down," I said that day when I'd ridden the bus home from school.

"It was a favor I did her mother," said my mother. "Nothing to do with you. You can tell the girls that, if you have to."

"She smelled like pig slop. Even after she showered. And that history homework was for tomorrow."

"She's going to be a smart, beautiful woman, that girl," said my mother. "It's the bone structure that does it. Like Katharine Hepburn. You wait and see."

It wasn't true. I sneaked peeks at Maude for weeks afterward. She looked nothing like Katharine Hepburn. She had a pimple on her chin, and her eyes were too small. They both had sharp noses was all, and hair that had gone out of fashion.

For myself, I had done what any self-respecting unbeautiful poor girl did at a country club school: I had made myself the class clown. It was my idea to place potatoes around the school. On the clock in the chapel, on teachers' desks, on the black lacquered armchairs that sat in the entrance hall, on lintels, on the volley-ball posts. No occasion, no punchline, I explained to my cohorts. "Just, you know. Potatoes."

We were seniors by then. We rolled on the floor in the senior room. Potatoes! A girl named Abby picked us up before dawn the next morning in her station wagon, a bushel of Idahos in the back, and we crawled through the unlocked window in the art room. "Potatoes," said my mother that night, when the call came. "No one understands what's funny about this prank, Evie."

"Isn't it great?" I said.

And so I was asked to write the class skit, which would, in the finest joke of all, star Maude Millerton in the role of a Mary Institute girl making her way through the Hundred-Acre Wood. We brought the plan to Maude in the girls' room. "You don't have to sing or anything," we told her.

She eyed us one by one. She was not stupid. A thin smile came over her face. "I don't mind singing," she said. Her voice was slightly nasal, and seemed to run out of breath before the end of a sentence. "But I can't stay late at rehearsals. I live out in the country."

"Oh, you don't have to stay late," we assured her. And ran off, hands over our mouths.

Were we going to spoof Maude, in our skit? No. Like the potatoes, she was, herself, the spoof. But if we had wanted, we could have done plenty. Maude had written her script. First, she had developed a crush on Mr. Lilly. Second, she had had the gall that year to start dating, and none other than my ten-year-old knight in armor, Teddy Castlebaum.

❀ ❀ ❀

Mr. Lilly was the history teacher. He was just over thirty, measured five-foot-five in lifts, wore his dark hair slicked back with Vitalis, and spoke in a slurred British accent intended to impress the headmaster who was a genuine import. He had a habit of staring at our bare knees in class. Arlette liked to sit in the front row and spread her legs apart just to make him stare and then avert his eyes. One day I was wearing a halter dress I'd knocked off, on my mom's sewing machine, from a Gunne Sax design; no one could tell the difference. "You ah looking shplendid today, Mish Jenshen," he had said to me. To tamp down any thrill, I ran to report Mr. Lilly to the other girls.

Mr. Lilly's young wife had died in a car crash, we knew, and he lived with his sick mother. Either his doctorate from Yale had somehow failed him or, we speculated, the Vitalis had done him in. In any case, he was ours. We called him the Waterlily, and all fall Maude had doted on him. That summer her grandmother had left her a wood-paneled Ford Fairlane, and she drove early to school to sit in the Waterlily's office and talk about the Hundred Years' War, which I claimed she had mixed up with the Hundred-Acre Wood.

Then it seemed Mr. Lilly had rejected her. He no longer called on her first in class, and the little pre-school conferences ceased. But did she cry in her chemistry set, our Maude? Not she. How she managed to snag Teddy—how she managed to cross *paths* with Teddy—we never learned, but there they were. At movies, no less. With his grandparents, I was told, at the St. Louis Country Club. Holding hands. Maude Millerton and Teddy Castlebaum.

I was pleased. Maude was doing something I'd never do. Teddy Castlebaum had grown from a pudgy boy into a tall, soft-featured young man, with a voice that had changed late and clothes that belonged on an undertaker's assistant. He wore his hair short as a banker's, his class ring on a plump, damp finger.

Meanwhile I had kept my head above the tide for five years. For clothes, I had the sewing machine and the sale rack. My mom was actually great at cutting hair. And being class clown exempted me from accessories like cool vacation destinations or the ability to host a party. I don't know why I thought it exempted me from college, exactly. Higher education, after all, had been the whole point of the private schools. Frank by then was at Tulane. The counselor at Mary Institute kept telling me I was smart enough to get a scholarship, and certainly all the other girls were applying to some institution or other. I just heard the word, "scholarship," and couldn't get myself to do it. Not yet, was what I said.

Driving Frank's old Pontiac to school, that last Mary Institute spring, I made up the lyrics to skit songs depicting, say, Mr.

Briggs the computer teacher as Eeyore floating down the creek. I
sprinkled in numbers from *The Music Man* and *Chicago*. At night
we rehearsed in the Chapel, with Mr. Lilly as the appointed faculty
censor, sitting quietly in the back row, thumbs propping his chin.
After he left, we practiced our Canon of the Censor, for which we
all slicked our hair back. Maude, who went through her motions
with calm good humor, was gone by then as well, back to the farm
and the sleeping piggies.

There were four of us, after rehearsals — Muffy who did the
props, Arlette who played the piano, Lisa who could get anyone to
do anything, and me. Sometimes Lisa brought a bottle of Boone's
Farm, Arlette brought half a lid she'd bought from her brother, and
we sat backstage drinking sweet wine, toking, and talking boys.
Arlette, whose father owned part of the Cardinals baseball team,
had gone all the way with the Newton boy and didn't like the mess.
Muffy was going to have a dozen lovers before she got married.
Lisa was taking her horse with her to Sweet Briar College. I was
poor still, and always, but I'd been forgiven by the other girls long
ago. With their approval I had gone to second base with a boy
named Bruce Jefferson who had, according to Lisa, cute eyelashes.
I had beaten the odds. I saw the other scholarship girls and knew
that mine was no small accomplishment. I cherished Frank's loan
of the Pontiac, not because I was ashamed for the girls to drop me
at Camelot, but because the night ended happiest with each of us
getting into her set of wheels and calling out, "Bye, you bad girls!"
"Bye, Sugar Booger!" I chomped mints all the way home.

The night I forgot my purse was the second-to-last rehearsal.
June had burst forth, sultry and overgrown. On our way to the
parking lot, Muffy pointed. "Isn't that Maude's car?" she said.

I shrugged. "It's a Fairlane. They all look the same."

"She went home already," said Arlette.

"Maybe her car wouldn't start," said Lisa. "Maybe she got a
ride with someone."

"Maybe Teddy picked her up," said Muffy, "and they're making the beast with two backs on the hockey field."

"Ooh!" we cried. We loved that expression. I imagined
sharp blades of grass sticking into my back, hard knobs of dried
mud. "Bye, Tiggers," I called to the others.

When they'd wheeled off, I headed back to fetch my purse.
The art room window still hadn't been fixed, even after the potato

episode. The art room lay just underneath the chapel. The stairs there rose into pitch darkness, but the corridor around to the main staircase was lit with exit signs. I tiptoed over linoleum. I was a little high; my throat burned. My mind was on Arlette, whose graduation present from her grandparents was a summer vacation in London. London! She'd told me I could crash at her flat if I could find the money for a plane ticket. Where did you get money like that? I was thinking. You married it, came the answer.

I felt my way down the hall. I knew exactly where my pocketbook lay, in the back of the chapel where I'd sat to listen to the whole class belt out my parody of "Seventy-six Trombones" in which they declared themselves "Seventy-six Virgins" and Mr. Lilly winced. I would pluck the bag by the strap and bang out the doors to the humid night. I was thinking about the way Lisa stuck out her big rear end when they sang, "And a hundred and ten horny boys close behind." Having a big butt never bothered girls like Lisa, who knew that no matter what happened they would always have a two-car garage with a red Volvo inside. They didn't even have to be smart, girls like Lisa. They just had to be willing to make the beast with two backs with some guy whose best feature probably was his back. I was thinking about Muffy, who'd said she would skip out of Vassar to go pub-crawling with Arlette next fall. And then I passed Mr. Lilly's office.

He was giving it to her, right there on the desk. That was the phrase that came to me: *giving it to her*. Because that was what he looked to be doing, he with his short natty body and she lying the length of the veneered surface, and he feeding and feeding and feeding her in the open jaw of her legs. The hazy moon shone in his window and lit not only their bodies but the white cotton bra flung over the back of his chair. Maude was making swallowing sounds. Mr. Lilly's dark hand reached for her breast; I think his thumb and forefinger pinched her nipple, but I can't be sure. By the time I was ready for that level of detail, my feet had glided away down the hall, toward the chapel. I got my bag off the back of the chair and the next thing I knew I was on the dewy hill that led around the school down to the parking lot. I can't tell you how I exited the building.

I drove. I burned rubber out of the parking lot: right on Ladue Road, right again on Lindbergh Boulevard and north. I drove out as far as Florissant, where Lindbergh turned into a highway near the airport. The ground got hilly there, and the billboards vanished. I drove until my foot could finally let off the gas pedal. Then I turned around and drove home, to Camelot. I parked the car in our assigned space next to Building D, but I didn't go inside, not right away. I walked down the long slope to the backside of the set of units that mirrored our own. Some of the units were one-level, and their bedrooms looked out onto the grass. I stood on tiptoe and peeked into windows—one, two, three, a dozen maybe.

No one was doing it. They read, or drank, or quarreled. There was nothing to drive that image of Maude and Mr. Lilly, humping on the desk, out of my mind.

Teddy Castlebaum, I thought.

He had been a front, a dupe, a cat's paw. Oh, the clever, clever Maude. *Get yourself a boyfriend*, slurry Mr. Lilly had whispered in her ear, and she had polished up her geeky smile and gone out to snare a stooge. Heartless! Meanwhile no more early-morning coffees, only late-night screws. The thought made me dizzy, made me want to tear my hair out, made me kick at the vinyl siding of the moonlit units. How could Maude Millerton be up to something like this? How could Maude Millerton be up to *anything*?

If I had known Teddy Castlebaum's phone number, if I had exchanged as much as two words with him that whole year, I would have picked up the phone in our kitchen and given him the news. As it was I stumbled home, made myself a hot fudge sundae complete with cherry, and threw the cat across the room when she jumped up onto the table for a lick. The ice cream pressed against the roof of my mouth.

By the time I crawled into my narrow bed in my narrow room across from my brother's closed door, though, I knew I possessed a marketable secret. That thought focused me, like an explorer who's finally got a map in front of her. I didn't sleep but lay on the bed—becalmed, waiting for wind, Maude tied fast in my hold.

❊   ❊   ❊

I love the way Teddy looks at me, even today. He thinks I don't notice when he noodles me with his eyes, but I do. His eyes travel over me the way his fingers travel the piano keys when he's playing John Coltrane, which he does late at night. Contrary to appearances, Teddy is not a gentle man — he trades bonds, after all — but he knows when a light stroke is required. Apparently he started playing jazz in high school and kept it up all the way through college. By the time I moved into his apartment in the West End, he had a baby grand set up in the corner.

He was finishing a Coltrane piece the night he asked me to marry him. I don't remember his exact words. Only that I was watering his plants with Miracle-Gro and the piano notes were dying out. I turned around, steady with the can and asked, "Are you saying what I think you're saying?"

And he said, "What else would I be saying?"

He told me later that I yipped. I don't recall yipping, though it's possible. I dropped the watering can, which, though plastic, cracked. It leaked blue water onto the Persian rug.

❀ ❀ ❀

I turned Maude down for lunch, but a week before my wedding she showed up at our place. "I was on my way downtown," she said, "and I didn't trust UPS to deliver this intact."

It was a fluted crystal vase with a single china rose in it. The rose was just for looks, Maude explained. We could take it out and put in fresh flowers.

"It's lovely," I said. I put it on the table in the bay window, where it would catch the light, and told Maude I'd just made coffee.

She was taller than I was, which shouldn't have surprised me, but she wore heeled sandals, which did. "Beautiful apartment," she said as we made our way to the kitchen.

"Well, you know," I said. "Teddy."

"It's still a great place," she said.

"It's sold, though. We're moving to Chicago."

"Good choice." She nodded a couple of times; when she smiled, her eyes narrowed the same way they had in the senior skit. The Charlie Chan look, I'd called it then. She did not look like Katharine Hepburn — I doubt that anyone after 1976 could look like Katharine Hepburn — but there was something of the movie star in her studied plainness. Two gold barrettes held back her straight hair. "You'll like Chicago," she said.

"You've been there?"

"I lived three years on Lakeshore Drive."

"After—?"

"After Brian died, yes."

She took the porcelain mug from my hand with the same satisfied smile any caffeine lover would sport at the smell of hefty Costa Rican brew. I offered cream and sugar, which she declined. "Were you doing the same work in Chicago?" I tried. "Technical writing?"

"No. I was finishing my degree."

"Oh, right. Of course."

                          ✧ ✧ ✧

You're expecting me next to say Maude's life took a new track because I told Lisa, or Arlette or Muffy, about her dalliance with Brian Lilly. Let me surprise you. I said nothing. The day after I saw them, I had Mr. Lilly for history. I noticed the way his mouth moved, the lower lip pinching and pushing the words, the upper lip controlling the tip of the nose. We were discussing the Spanish Armada. When Cissy Desjardins fell asleep, he came to stand right in front of her desk and he said, "So when Sodonia came within sight of the Dover cliffs, the first thing he saw was a great billboard advertising the Ford Pinto. Isn't that right, Miss Desjardins?" and she lifted her blonde head and said, "Oh yes, Mr. Lilly," and we all had a good laugh. On the way out Muffy remarked that the Waterlily wasn't so bad for a suck-up, and I said he was all right. Maude wore her blue shirtwaist that day, the one her aunt had sewn. It copied the tiny pleats on the models at Honeybee, but missed the print entirely. I noticed how freckled her forearms were, how her hands looked like a farmwoman's. *Such shtrong hands, Miss Millerton,* Mr. Lilly would say, kissing her fingers one by one. Two nights later we had skit practice, and Maude managed to hide her car so it looked as though she'd left.

"If only you'd applied to Radcliffe," my mom said. "I hear they're throwing money at girls with high SAT's. You're not pregnant, are you?" she asked, looking doubtfully at my flat belly.

"It'll be all right, Mom," I said.

"I hear that Maude Millerton," she said, "got a full ride to Wellesley College."

Still I said nothing.

And then, three days later, the janitor caught them at it. On a Saturday morning, in broad daylight. *In flagrante delicto*. And he told.

❄ ❄ ❄

She could still have gone to Wellesley, of course. Everyone thought she would. For graduation we wore long white dresses—mine another knockoff, Maude's a fussy thing she'd found at Montgomery Ward. She walked, head held high, to the podium, where she made a valedictory speech quoting Piglet at length and getting laughs from the adults. That night, while the rest of us were burning brain cells with rum and Cokes, Maude slipped in her dungarees out the back window of her house while her father watched the front with his shotgun on his lap. Then she ran through the woods to where her terminated history teacher sat waiting, in his beat-up Mustang, to take her away to Kansas City and make an honest woman of her.

That was the legend, anyway, and practically the last I heard of Maude before Teddy and I started making wedding plans. Of Mr. Lilly I knew the postscript only because my mother had begun a modest business in portrait painting, and one day a small white-haired woman with grief stamped on her face asked her to paint her son from a photo taken the year before. He had struck his head, she told my mother, her finger tracing the white border of the snapshot, on the concrete floor of his garage. Struck it very hard, yes, and in just the wrong place. It was the drink, really, Mrs. Lilly had said, her accent not British but countrified, *drink* and *drank* the same. "He never stopped dranking once they fired him."

"He's a handsome young man," my mother said. "Did he leave a wife?"

My mother failed to learn what had happened to Maude, who had found Brian the next morning, blood pooling under his ear. That was Mrs. Lilly's version. I heard another while I was in East Texas volunteering for VISTA, a little interlude that sent me running back to college and scholarship money like a circus clown shot from a cannon. The version I heard was that Maude had left Mr. Lilly when the drinking started. She was working as a waitress in Kansas City, picking up classes at the state university.

Now, breaking out the biscotti and watching Maude dunk one in her black coffee, I imagined violence. I pictured Maude in a drunken rage, clocking Mr. Lilly on the head with a brick and then dragging his body to the garage.

"What will you do in Chicago?" she asked me.

"Teddy's joining a big arbitrage group," I said. "I'm joining a little flower-arranging group."

"Always the comedienne." She smiled, narrowing her eyes, and waited. I didn't want to tell her. I put sugar in my coffee, though I never take sugar, and stirred.

"I'm getting an MSW," I finally said. "See how much fun I can have with the flotsam of society."

"You're a good person, Evie."

"No, I'm not," I said. I opened my mouth then, and shut it.

❂ ❂ ❂

That was the closest I came to telling Maude Millerton what I'd seen by moonlight, in Mr. Lilly's office. And it was only the thought of Teddy, of not hurting Teddy, that stopped me. "Though I don't know why you've invited her," I complained to him later. "Given what she did to you."

This was a week before the wedding, in our bedroom. I was pacing. Teddy was propped up in bed, reading the latest Clancy. "You're just nervous," he said.

"Oh, really? And without cause, I suppose."

He knew I had cause. His parents were moving the reception again, this time to the Adams Mark Hotel. The guest list stretched back to Reconstruction. Every time Mrs. Castlebaum ran her eyes over me, I sprouted sweat stains under my arms. "Relax," Teddy said. "You're beautiful."

"So is Maude, these days."

"She hasn't got your legs."

"She set you up." He shrugged, turned a page. "You were her alibi. She wanted to draw the veil tight, and she used you to do it."

He put the book down. "Well, I wasn't exactly the catch of the century in high school," he said.

"For which I thank my stars."

"Why do you thank stars for my adolescent disgrace?"

"You'd have got snatched up by Cissy Desjardins. You'd be teaching a pair of pug-nosed towheads how to putt."

"And you?"

"I'd be a nun. Chastity, poverty, obedience."

I'd come to perch on the side of the bed. He lifted off my tank top and ran his fingers over my breasts. It was a warm June.

"Good luck on the third," he said. He pulled me to him. "And the first."

We stopped talking for a while then. Sex with Teddy was always intense, even athletic. He was the only man to whom I'd ever made love without thinking at some point in the proceedings about another man. With Teddy I thought only about the almond plush of his skin, the hollow under his shoulder.

But then later, lying face up on the sheets, I thought again of Mr. Lilly, his Vitalis and his nervous lisp. "She did use you," I said. "They both did."

"Hush." His arm lay under my neck; he curled his hand around to touch my forehead. "Nobody used me. My eyes were open."

"What do you mean?"

"I knew Maude Millerton was having an affair with her history teacher. She needed someone to pick her up sometimes, someone to drop her off. I didn't mind. We were friends."

"Friends?" I pushed up on my elbow. "You were friends?"

"Well, she didn't have very many."

Our bed was next to the window, and a bright moon streamed in. I could see Teddy's eyes, which didn't blink.

"I noticed her at those dances they had, those mixers," he went on. "Mary Institute and Country Day. You rich girls picked on her, you set her up. I saw a girl put a spoonful of red jello on her seat, so when she sat and then got up again, it looked like a menstrual stain. I started talking to her. The first time I asked her out, it was for real."

"Don't tell me you were attracted to her."

"I just told you. I was shy, but I asked her out. When I made a pass, she told me about Brian Lilly. At first I thought, jeez, here's another old man taking advantage of this poor girl. But that wasn't it, at all. They just loved each other. If that school hadn't fired him—" Here his voice trailed off. "It might have worked out for them," he said finally.

"I am not rich," I said.

"What's that got to do with it?"

"You said, 'You rich girls picked on her.' I wasn't rich."

He smiled; with his index finger he traced my lips. "Maude Millerton had a shot at something, is all I'm saying, Evie, and I was glad to help her."

"You think there's just one kind of poor, don't you?" I said. "You think it comes in gaunt and brainy and ill-fitting, and needs you to fix it. Well, my mom clipped coupons. Frank and I sat on the fence at the drive-in."

"You were never going to stay that way."

"Because I had some gumption!" I was sitting up by then, on the edge of the bed. The moonlight felt hot. Teddy wasn't saying anything, but I could smell his deep, post-coital scent, a sweet must. Slowly I turned to look at him. "When you gave me that quarter," I said, "it wasn't because you thought I was the most beautiful girl you'd ever seen, was it?"

"What quarter?"

"The quarter, the quarter. When you were ten. You came to our house."

"Okay." A little smile. "I remember this."

"It was because you felt sorry for me. You wanted to bestow charity."

I stood up. I could have wrecked it, right then. The marriage, I mean, and all the love that would come of it, our very lives. I paced and paced, while Teddy sat there and watched me. Finally he swung his legs over the side of the bed, found his glasses, pulled on his boxers, and went out to the living room. He started playing something soft, Brubeck I think. After he'd played a long while I let the steam out of my head and came to stand behind him and let my hands settle on his neck. "That's a complicated piece," I said.

"It's all complicated," he said.

The next thing I had to say would take me years, and even then I never really said it. This was after we'd brought Maude back into the wider margin of our lives, and met the man who would become her new husband, whom neither of us liked much, and then we lost track of them. Some occasion arose for old photos—Frank was visiting? Or Arlette?—and there was the class skit, Maude wandering through a wood of girls dressed as cardboard trees. "Did she hurt you very badly?" I asked my husband after the guests had left.

His eyes were glued to the picture. "Who?"

"Maude."

That quick intake, his jaw tight, was a truth I could taste. The legend of Maude—her white legs in the air, the sounds in her throat—was a thing he had owned, long ago, in his secret dreams.

"Maude, Maude, Maude," I teased him.

I have told you Teddy was not a gentle man. But though he stirred, though the cords in his neck flexed, he would not rise to the bait. "Stop that, Evie," he said.

I stopped. I stopped and I went to him. I have not said her name since. Because I love him. And I keep my head above the tide.

John Milisenda, photograph

The Enemy of Good Is Better

You've gone back and forth dozens of times
trying to make her understand
but it only gets worse.
The air is blue with words.
In her mind it's enough to say
I'm sorry that first time.

But you persist to sharpen the argument
as if peeling the skin off a grape —
(it will bruise before it bursts)
or doing an aneurysm in a valley of the patient's brain,
your operating hand more eager to grab
its neck in a clip than your own brain
thinking you'll sharpen its edges just a bit,
make everything as straight as an autopsy
and it will all be better.

But enough was enough before it got angry
and a bright burst of blood filled the valley
with regret; you wish you had stopped sooner:
what was good enough to cure is gone
and what is better has left you a ruin.

Before Homer

Across the river Jordan, God kissed Moses
on his lips and took his soul to heaven.

This was not the same as the ascent
of Elijah, his body alive in a chariot of flame

going up to the sky. God took only the best,
that which was beyond the body

and Moses was all spirit, not a territory
but a name. He was beyond the bees

making honey in the jawbone of an ass,
beyond the vast seas withdrawing

from the skies, the light from the dark.
He was a thought, like black letters of flame

on white pages of fire. He spoke
with stones in his mouth —

the first poet — and we too modern to pray
fear to be the last.

Marriage

There might be a thousand leaves
On this massive gingko tree,
Each shaped like a small fan
That would cool her on
This sultry summer day,
Just as in winter when she shivers
He warms her with each
Essential part of him.

The Wife of Narcissus

They make love in the room without answers,
which is more than enough for the man:
he has returned to the pond of his dreams,
she watches him glide over the sunken moon
as if he could travel the impossibility of her.

In the breathtakingly cold air she is:
the mother of his many children,
the nail he hangs his skin on at night,
the one who finds him shivering in the morning,
faceup beneath the ice.

Night from Above

Madison, WI

On the other side of winter, my sister is the endless knot of scarves
drawn and drawn from a sleeve, believing
hers is the trick of voluminousness.

I am in flight, circling an unsprawled city. Light's tight multiplication
on the corseted isthmus. Black lakes inching in.

All night, far from here, she is wakeful, unfed; she is spit-thinned
thread passing through the eye of a needle, the stitch
darting cloth. Taking in and in.

I too have wished to be dazzling. I have wished my skin to hold
an astonishing density of light.

Bright city, model city, capacious as a sleeve, how can you be boundless
and also bounded? Sister, no slighter body
can make you more miraculous.

Snowmelt

after Andrew Wyeth's "Spring," 1977

Now the black mud, the alien ungreen
and memory-stripped hills.

The rawboned man who lay down buried in snow
stares into a not-blue sky and tries to believe
he is bright-cheeked, long-haired.

Beneath, time does not stop. The acres of ice
you lay down by are no longer the lake you remember.

Wake in the crosshatch grass. Unweave
winter's long sleep. Let the white sun be erasure,
let me not come across bones on what used to be shore.

Volatile Crab
XXV

This could be the day of rotting meat. It's noon and the flies aren't even buzzing. But there's definitely something rotting unseen in the sun. It might be these things here I'm thinking and I don't know why. It's 9:42 on a late October evening and something is possibly rotting in the trashcan nearby. Well, I guess it's not noon but there is the muffled somber sound of an adagio rendered on lonely strings coming from somewhere nearby. Inside the trashcan there is nothing but a road-killed wildebeest and a splintered balalaika. Farther up the road a black reindeer crosses between the drifts of oleanders. There's a fist of bees roiling in the dark frost up there along the way, any old way. But as we come closer, it's not a fist of bees but a clump of condensed voices all attempting to tell the same story but in so many different ways they're corporeal. There're so many facets, so many fluxes and coagulations, inseminations, conceptions, concretions, fissions, fusions, complexes and amalgamations, so many chelations they take this physical form. It's a story about love and still water. It's the story of the burnt-down church on the edge of town which is a temple for iguanas. It's a story of random intentions and sweetness, about vinegar fermenting in cherry wood, about albatrosses caught in the clothesline, about rooftops burning with doves (they're always on fire somewhere in a poem). It's a story about nine varieties of festive dread, the dread that makes the rat run the wheel, that dread that hoards orchids, that dread of alembics and distillations, that dread that roasts almonds, that dread that's buried in the holly with chameleons. The story's an epic full of lazy eyes and tongues of glass like greenhouses overgrown with the ivy of the moon and black ice floes formed by all the mental regions explored by sound. It's a story of whiskey and wood ducks.

It's not the story of meat rotting in the midday sun you might have come to expect, unless it's an ancient song of lovers who feed each other to sharks, lovers devoured by the rising sun. But there're no more songs anymore. All that's left are the husks of songs, the shells, the chaff of songs like dry gaping wells, like chants composed of withered fruits, like the residue of a wine of an unknown color. All there's left is a temple of lizards, a temple of meat and a busted balalaika, a temple of earthen blood. It's the Priorat of dreams, the Vacqueyras of dreams singing with little worms, a whorl of little black worms straight from God. We'll never know what unanswered prayer they crawled from. Who needs songs when you have the maggots of prayers?

The mass of stories congeals, fumes and bubbles as if in a crucible or an alchemist's retort. After a while a form begins to appear. A form is all that can be said of it, as otherwise it defies description. It being composed of the raw condensed shit of whatever might make a human being desire to create something for no good reason other than to kill a few moments on this boulder spiraling through emptiness.

Manly Johnson, photograph

Harvest Moon

The spider's pincers are geometrically
enhanced, web of the exact square
for the late summer's catch, appetite
swollen with itself every corner

of the farm, myself against straw,
imaginary lovers by the season down
the hay chute and into my lap.
Harvest like cream rises to the top

with its highly allegorical silos,
overflow of allusion, rose cider
thick as apple skin. Everything
is preening, curling. There I am,

back in the shed, sealing flavors
with raw smoke. My cousin smiles
at me, her lips red in beet
juice, homemade swirls of lace,

our clothing cotton and woolen,
granaries spilling over with touch,
that lease against winter. The drunken
farm tilts, staggers at us

with its arms full. We lie
watching the cracks of the shed
gloss the spider, evening light
gloss our futures, ripe and sticky.

Love Story

The kitchen door opens onto dirt
and the second half of the country
all the way to the Pacific. Rusted
prairie trains out of the tall weeds
elbow the last century aside, rumble
from every direction towards Chicago.

My great-grandfather, who would be
150 years old today, put on his one
tall hat and took the big trip
to Omaha for my great-grandma
with the family ring on his vest
and winter wheat lying wait in seed.

He gave her all the miles he had
and she gave him the future I walk
around in every day. The mountains
were too far west to count so they
doubled back over the land and century
and the real weather kept coming from them.

Window Kills

After we had gone through the closet, winnowing
all but the finest of clothes (suitable to be buried in
was our unspoken thought), and allowed the bills
to arrive in a bolus at month's end until unforeseen
debts could no longer slap us in the face; after
we had pieced together an address book of sorts
out of old envelopes and paper scraps tucked in the desk;
and after we'd come to believe we had tidied up
our mother's life, we opened the freezer.

In the frosty dark we found a dozen bird cadavers,
songbirds that had dropped x number of stories
to the street, only feathers to cushion their crash landing.
When Icarus fell there was at least a sense that balance
had been restored, hubris given its due comeuppance.
Not so these fallen creatures. The worst this purple finch
had done was mistake its reflection for another bird,
and lost that game of flinch. Hardly a capital offense,
to be misled, but office towers scarcely care.

She cared. Though taxidermy is a feeble hope
it was a hope she held. We thought of her lifting
lifeless birds off the sidewalk, tucking them into
her purse with her lipstick, her compact, her keys.
Dickinson was right: Hope *is* the thing with feathers.
She kept her wished-for restoration frozen,
stacked like ears of sweetcorn. Kept a rock-hard
fire-orange oriole. Kept woodpeckers that once could drill
through hundred-year-old oaks, found dead
after one sick thud. Kept a bead-emerald hummingbird
now like a sausage encrusted with freezer burn.
And a redstart that must have been skipping through air
one crystal morning when it simply, suddenly, stopped.

Pain Management

One day, in your forties or fifties,
you will start to think that life is turning
into a long string of small extinctions.
You will feel the word *gone* rise inside you
and might even say it aloud, quietly, the way
you would say it if the house had been robbed
and, months later, you reached for an item
you never knew was missing, thought had been
in a drawer the whole time: *Gone*. Add these
to the workaday wrong turns you half-knew
were coming from the start—you know: the shy
girl with trusting eyes with whom
you did not sleep, the dad who let you down—
and you will begin to think that if you started
crying now, you might never be able to stop.
But that doesn't happen.
What happens instead is you make a cup of tea.
You sit on the front porch, and there you look
at spindly asters on a September afternoon:
flowers with ragged edges that are barely petals,
a color from somewhere down the spectrum
after blue—the same blue of cold skies
in early winter. And behind them,
the deep green of bloomless morning glories.

VIDHU AGGARWAL's poems and photo-text works have appeared or are forthcoming in *Bint El Nas*, *Harpur Palate*, *Interlope*, *Limestone*, and Norton's *Language for a New Century: Contemporary Poetry from the Middle East, Asia, and Beyond*, among other publications. She is currently completing a poetry manuscript called *Playback Singer*.

ERINN BATYKEFER is the Stadler Poetry Fellow at Bucknell University where she serves as the Stadler Associate Editor of *West Branch* magazine. Her collection, *Allegheny, Monongahela*, was the winner of the 2008 Benjamin Saltman Prize and is forthcoming from Red Hen Press. She was a semi-finalist for *Nimrod*'s 2008 Pablo Neruda Prize for Poetry.

RUTH BAVETTA, a lifelong Californian, has an M.F.A. in painting from Claremont Graduate School, has exhibited widely, and has taught drawing and art history at the college level. Her poetry has appeared or is forthcoming in *ONTHEBUS*, *Rattle*, *Poetry New Zealand*, *Nimrod*, and elsewhere, and is included in the book *Twelve Los Angeles Poets*.

NAN BECKER, a 2008 semi-finalist for the Pablo Neruda Poetry Prize, studied at the Philadelphia College of Art and Sarah Lawrence College and earned her M.F.A. at Yale.

JOELLE BIELE is the author of *White Summer*, winner of the Crab Orchard Series in Poetry First Book Award. New poems are appearing in *Harvard Review*, *The Iowa Review*, *Poetry Northwest*, and *Prairie Schooner*.

CHRISTINE E. BLACK has published work in *A Gallery of Writing*, *Mississippi Valley Review*, *Analecta*, *Antietam Review*, where her poem was nominated for a Pushcart Prize, *13th Moon*, *Margie*, *New Millennium Writings*, and other publications. She was a semi-finalist for *Nimrod*'s 2008 Pablo Neruda Prize for Poetry. She lives in Charlottesville, Virginia.

TERRY BLACKHAWK is the author of *Body & Field*, *The Dropped Hand*, and *Escape Artist*, as well as two chapbooks. Her work has appeared in many anthologies and in journals such as *Marlboro Review*, *Michigan Quarterly Review*, *Florida Review*, and *Borderlands*. She is the founding director of Detroit's InsideOut Literary Arts Project and serves on the Board of AWP.

MARY BUCHINGER's poems have appeared in *AGNI Online*, *RUNES*, *The Massachusetts Review*, *Versal*, and other journals. She was the recipient of New England Poetry Club's Daniel Varoujan Award. Her collection, *Roomful of Sparrows* (2008), was a semi-finalist in the New Women's Voices Series. She teaches writing at the Massachusetts College of Pharmacy and Health Sciences in Boston.

ALICIA CASE is an M.F.A. candidate in poetry at American University and works as a content writer and web administrator for the Carnegie Institution of Washington's Department of Terrestrial Magnetism. Her poems are forthcoming in *Poet Lore*.

A. J. COLLINS recently completed his first manuscript of poems, supported by the International Institute for Modern Letters. He is currently working on community-development projects in KaMhlushwa, in South Africa, with the Peace Corps.

WILLIAM DELMAN's poetry has appeared in *The Literary Review*, *The Massachusetts Review*, *Salamander*, *CT Review*, *The Briar Cliff Review*, *Rhino*, *Disquieting Muses Quarterly*, and other publications. He is currently a fiction editor for *AGNI Magazine* and the director of The Bay State Underground.

FOX DEMOISEY, who attended the M.F.A. program at Colorado State University, has worked as a teacher in Colorado and now in the San Francisco Bay Area. His work has appeared or is forthcoming in *Tulane Review*, *Talking River Review*, *Reed Magazine*, *Nimrod*, and other journals. He was a semi-finalist for *Nimrod*'s 2008 Pablo Neruda Prize for Poetry.

ANNA CARSON DEWITT has an M.F.A. from American University. She currently splits her time among Washington, DC, Durham, North Carolina, and El Mochito, Honduras.

NATALIE DIAZ was born and raised on the Fort Mojave Indian Reservation in Needles, California. She completed her M.F.A. at Old Dominion University in 2007. She has been awarded both the 2007 *Nimrod* Pablo Neruda Prize for Poetry and the 2007 Tobias Wolff Fiction Prize. Her work can be found in *North American Review*, *Pearl Magazine*, and *Touchstone*.

JAMES DOYLE's latest book, *Bending Under the Yellow Police Tapes*, was published by Steel Toe Books in 2007. He has poems coming out in *The Grove Review*, *Chiron Review*, *The Briar Cliff Review*, *Cimarron Review*, *Illuminations*, and *The Paterson Literary Review*.

LEILA FARJAMI was born in Tehran, Iran. As a child, she immigrated to the United States with her family during the Iran-Iraq war. She has published two books of poetry in Persian, *Seven Seas, One Dew Drop* (2001) and *The Confession Letters* (2008). Her work has been published in notable Iranian literary journals such as *Karnameh*, *Kelk*, *Nafeh*, *Goharan*, and *Baran*; she plans to publish a book of poetry in English this year.

LUCY FERRISS is the author of eight books, most recently the memoir *Unveiling the Prophet: The Misadventures of a Reluctant Debutante* (2005) and *Nerves of the Heart*, a novel (2002). Her story collection *Leaving the Neighborhood and Other Stories* was the 2000 winner of the Mid-List First Series Award. Other short fiction and essays have appeared in *Shenandoah*, *Michigan Quarterly Review*, *Sport Literate*, and *Georgia Review*.

ALLEN C. FISCHER, former director of marketing for a corporation, brings to poetry a background in business. His poems have been published in *Atlanta Review*, *Indiana Review*, *The Laurel Review*, *Poetry*, *Prairie Schooner*, *Rattle*, and *River Styx*.

ELIZABETH FOGLE is a lecturer in English at Penn State Erie, the Behrend College, and recently received her M.F.A. in Creative Writing at Georgia College and State University, with a thesis in poetry. She was a finalist for *Nimrod*'s 2008 Pablo Neruda Prize for Poetry.

MARVIN GLASSER is a retired academic—for thirty-five years, mainly at Pace University in New York City—and now a full-time poet. His work has been accepted by many magazines, including *Rattle*, *Main Street Rag*, *Hiram Poetry Review*, and *The Iconoclast*.

ROBERT HIGH GUARD studied poetry at Ohio University and has published poems in *Athens Magazine*. In the summer of 2007 he completed *The Kenyon Review* Writers Workshop led by Roseanna Warren; he is returning to Kenyon this summer for the poetry workshop led by David Baker. He was a semi-finalist for *Nimrod*'s 2008 Pablo Neruda Prize for Poetry.

LORRAINE HEALY is an Argentinean poet of Irish and Italian descent. Nominated for a Pushcart Prize in 2004, she received a M.F.A. from the New England College and a post-M.F.A. from Antioch University-Los Angeles. The most recent winner of the Patricia Libby First Book Award, her full-length manuscript is forthcoming from Tebot Bach Press.

LACEY JANE HENSON grew up in Champaign, Illinois, and spent some years in New Mexico before landing in Seattle, where she currently lives. She earned an M.F.A. from the University of Washington in 2006. Her stories have appeared or are forthcoming in *The Portland Review* and *MAKE: A Chicago Literary Magazine*.

LAURIE JUNKINS is a second-year M.F.A. student at Northwest Institute of Literary Arts (Whidbey Writer's Workshop) and has recently had poems published in *Apple Valley Review*, *Literary Mama*, and *Shark Reef*. She was a semi-finalist for *Nimrod*'s 2008 Pablo Neruda Prize for Poetry. She lives in New Jersey with her husband and children.

MARGARET KAUFMAN leads poetry workshops in Marin County, California, and edits fiction for *The Marlboro Review*. Her honors include a Marin County Artists' grant and the Anna Rosenberg Award. *Snake At the Wrist* is her first full poetry collection; Chronicle Books published a trade edition of *Aunt Sallie's Lament*. Limited letterpress editions of some of her poems have been published by *The Janus Press*, *Gefn Press*, and *Protean Press*.

PATRICIA GRACE KING's first published story appears here, inspired in part by her years in Guatemala, where she worked with Witness for Peace during the civil war. She holds a Ph.D. in English from Emory University and teaches at North Central College; she lives in the Printers Row neighborhood of Chicago, writing more stories and a novel.

JEANINE LIZETTE lives on the southern coast of Oregon in the Siskiyou National Forest. Her poems have won Honorable Mention in *The Paterson Literary Review*'s Allen Ginsberg Awards and *The Spoon River Poetry Review*'s Editor's Choice Awards, were finalists in *Margie*'s Editor's Choice and Strong RX Medicine Contests, and have also appeared in *The Ledge*.

MELANIE MCCABE received an M.F.A. in Poetry from George Mason University. Her work has appeared or is forthcoming in *Fourteen Hills*, *Quarterly West*, *Nimrod*, *Harpur Palate*, *The Evansville Review*, *The Georgia Review*, and *The Carolina Quarterly*. Her manuscript, *Dress-Up*, was a semifinalist for the Philip Levine Prize; in other versions, it was recognized as a finalist for Bright Hill Press's 2008 and 2007 Poetry Book Competition.

MELISSA MCNULTY, originally from Cape Cod, now lives and works in Washington, DC, and travels to Bolivia as often as she can. This September, she will attend the M.F.A. Program in Creative Writing at Hollins University.

JUDY ROWE MICHAELS is poet in residence and high school English teacher at Princeton Day School in Princeton, New Jersey, and a poet in the schools for the Geraldine R. Dodge Foundation. University Press of Florida published her first collection, *The Forest of Wild Hands*, and Word Tech is publishing her second, *Reviewing the Skull*.

KELLY MICHELS received her M.F.A. from North Carolina State University, where she won the Academy of American Poets Award in 2007. Her poetry also appears in the award-winning documentary *King Neptune: The Making of the Myth*. She was a finalist for *Nimrod*'s 2008 Pablo Neruda

Prize for Poetry. She lives in Raleigh, North Carolina.

MICHAEL MILLER's first book of poems, *The Joyful Dark*, won the Robert McGovern Prize and was published by Ashland Poetry Press. His poems have appeared in *The Kenyon Review*, *The Yale Review*, *The New Republic*, *The American Scholar*, *Ontario Review*, and other publications.

PATRICK MORAN's poems, translations, and essays have appeared in numerous publications, including *The New Republic*, *Iowa Review*, *Southern Review*, and *Margie*. He was a finalist for *Nimrod*'s 2008 Pablo Neruda Prize for Poetry. He is currently an assistant professor of creative writing at the University of Wisconsin—Whitewater. He lives in Fort Atkinson, Wisconsin, with his wife and three children.

RACHEL MORGENSTERN-CLARREN's work has appeared or is forthcoming in *New Delta Review*, *Upstairs at Duroc* (Paris), *Eclectica*, *The Oleander Review*, and *Glimpse Quarterly*. Earlier versions of the poems in this issue were part of a sequence awarded the 2007 Hopwood Award Theodore Roethke Prize at the University of Michigan. She was a semi-finalist for *Nimrod*'s 2008 Pablo Neruda Prize for Poetry.

MIKE NELSON received an M.F.A. in Creative Writing from the University of Maryland and is currently finishing a Ph.D. in English at Western Michigan University. His work has appeared in *The Penguin Book of the Sonnet*.

MATTHEW NIENOW is the author of *Two Sides of the Same Thing*, which won the 2007 Copperdome Chapbook Award from Southeast Missouri State University Press. Other new work has recently appeared or is forthcoming in *American Literary Review*, *Atlanta Review*, *Poet Lore*, *The Saint Ann's Review*, *Best New Poets 2007*, and elsewhere.

W. SCOTT OLSEN teaches English at Concordia College in Moorhead, Minnesota. His stories and essays have appeared in *The Kenyon Review*, *North Dakota Quarterly*, *Ascent*, *Willow Springs*, *Kansas Quarterly*, and other publications.

JOHNIE O'NEAL has been a finalist for the Pablo Neruda Prize for Poetry twice before, in 2002 and 2003. His work has appeared in *Nimrod*, *Mississippi Valley Review*, *Ironwood*, and *Fireweed*. He lives in Tulsa.

SEAN PRENTISS lives in the perpetual rain and snow of northern Idaho, where he teaches at the University of Idaho. During the summers, he lives in the sunshine and thin air of central Colorado, where he will soon build a rustic cabin on five acres of mountainside.

MAGGIE QUEENEY is a recent graduate of Syracuse University's M.F.A. Program in Poetry. She currently resides in Austin, Texas.

MARILYN RINGER, born in Oklahoma, now lives in northern California. Her poems have appeared in *Poet Lore, Porcupine, Eclipse, Slant, Left Curve, Reed Magazine, ellipsis, Westview, Phantasmagoria,* and *The Art of Monhegan Island* (2004), among other publications. She was a semi-finalist for *Nimrod*'s 2008 Pablo Neruda Prize for Poetry.

JAMES SILAS ROGERS is editor of *New Hibernia Review,* a journal of Irish Studies published by the University of St Thomas Center for Irish Studies. His chapbook *Sundogs* was published in 2006. In 2009, he will publish his mixed-genre book on cemeteries and sacred space.

MARY KAY RUMMEL's books of poetry include *The Illuminations, Green Journey Red Bird,* and *This Body She's Entered.* Her newest, *Love in the End,* was a finalist in the 2007 Bright Hill Press competition. Her poems have recently appeared in *RUNES, Whistling Shade, Bloomsbury Review,* and *To Sing Along the Way,* an anthology of Minnesota women poets through history. She was a finalist for *Nimrod*'s 2008 Pablo Neruda Prize for Poetry.

TANIA RUNYAN has published poems in such journals and anthologies as *Poetry, Willow Springs, Poetry Northwest, Southern Poetry Review,* and *A Fine Frenzy: Poets Respond to Shakespeare.* Her chapbook, *Delicious Air* (Finishing Line Press, 2006), was awarded the Book of the Year citation by the Conference on Christianity and Literature.

MICHAEL SALCMAN is a physician, brain scientist, poet, and essayist on the visual arts. Recent poems appear in *New Letters, Ontario Review, Harvard Review, Raritan, River Styx,* and *New York Quarterly.* His work has been heard on NPR's *All Things Considered* and in *Euphoria,* a documentary on the brain and creativity (2005). His first collection, *The Clock Made of Confetti,* and fourth chapbook, *Stones In Our Pockets,* were published in 2007.

RICHARD SANTOS was born in San Antonio, studied at the University of Texas—Austin and Georgetown University, and performed Shakespeare in London. Having worked as a telemarketer and a bouncer, he now works in politics and lives in Washington, DC. He is writing a novel and a short story collection, and he received an Honorable Mention in *Nimrod*'s 2008 Katherine Anne Porter Award for Fiction.

PENELOPE SCAMBLY SCHOTT's most recent books are a lyric collection, *May the Generations Die in the Right Order,* and a verse biography, *A is for Anne: Mistress Hutchinson Disturbs the Commonwealth.* She was a semi-finalist for *Nimrod*'s 2008 Pablo Neruda Prize for Poetry. She lives in Portland, Oregon.

TERESA SCOLLON received an M.F.A. in Poetry from the University of Southern Maine—Stonecoast. She has taught at Interlochen Arts Academy. Her work has appeared in *Wisconsin People & Ideas* and *The Dunes Review* and aired on Chicago's WBEZ. A frequent contributor and producer for Traverse City's community radio program *Radio Anyway*, she was a semi-finalist for *Nimrod*'s Pablo Neruda Prize for Poetry in 2008.

GLENN SHAHEEN recently received his M.F.A. from the University of Houston's Creative Writing Program. He was born in Halifax and currently resides in Houston. His work has appeared or is forthcoming in *Subtropics*, *Zone 3*, and *The Laurel Review*. He was a finalist for *Nimrod*'s 2008 Pablo Neruda Prize for Poetry.

ANIS SHIVANI is of Pakistani heritage, though he has spent most of his life in the U.S. His stories have been published as a collection, *Alienation, Jihad, Burqa, Apostasy*; a second collection, *Anatolia and Other Stories*, is forthcoming. His work has appeared in *Crazyhorse*, *Other Voices*, *Confrontation*, *Flyway*, and elsewhere; a novel, *Intrusion*, is nearing completion.

RICH SPENCER, a poet and fiction writer born and raised in Southern Ontario, Canada, was a semi-finalist for *Nimrod*'s 2008 Pablo Neruda Prize for Poetry. He has a B.A. in English Literature from Huntington College and an M.F.A. in Creative Writing from Hamline University, St. Paul, Minnesota. He currently lives with his wife in West Lafayette, Indiana.

GABRIEL SPERA's first collection of poems, *The Standing Wave*, was selected for the 2002 National Poetry Series and was subsequently awarded the 2004 Literary Book Award for Poetry from PEN USA-West. He received a 2009 Poetry Fellowship from the National Endowment of the Arts. He lives in Los Angeles.

LAURA HULTHÉN THOMAS teaches creative writing at the University of Michigan's Residential College. Her short fiction has appeared or is forthcoming in *Orchid: A Literary Review*, *Oleander Review*, *Epicenter*, and *Cimarron Review*. She wrote "Down to the Last Kopek" for the 2008 Dzanc Books Write-a-thon, a one-day write-in marathon fundraiser for Dzanc, a non-profit independent press based in Ann Arbor, Michigan.

TRACY THOMAS has been involved in the Phoenix poetry and art scene, dabbling in everything from performance poetry and art to painting, acid jazz and noise art. She recently discovered food and wine and proceeded to wreck her life with Cassoulet and Cahors. Currently she is attempting to repair the damage by applying to graduate school for an M.F.A. in poetry.

CECILIA WOLOCH is the author of four collections of poems: *Sacrifice*, a BookSense 76 Selection; *Tsigan: The Gypsy Poem*; *Late*, for which she was named Georgia Author of the Year in 2004; and *Narcissus*, winner of the Tupelo Press Snowbound Prize. A fifth collection, *Carpathia*, is slated for publication by BOA Editions in 2009. She is currently a lecturer in the Creative Writing Program at the University of Southern California.

JOSHUA JENNINGS WOOD is an assistant director and teacher at the Orange County High School of the Arts as well as an adjunct English instructor. He was a finalist for *North American Review*'s James Hurst Prize in Poetry in 2008 as well as a finalist for *Nimrod*'s 2008 Pablo Neruda Prize for Poetry. His work has previously appeared in *Zaum*.

LINDA WOOLFORD received an M.F.A. from Bennington College. Her work has appeared in *North American Review, Colorado Review, Cimarron Review, The Florida Review,* and *Bellevue Literary Review,* and has been nominated for a Pushcart Prize. A story has also been selected for inclusion in the forthcoming *What's Your Exit, A Literary Detour through New Jersey*.

JIM ZUKOWSKI's recent work appears in *Provincetown Arts Magazine, Northwest Review,* and *Water-Stone*.

DARREN DIRKSEN is an artist living in Locus Grove, Oklahoma. He is represented in Tulsa by Joseph Gierek Fine Art.

JUAN FRANCO, photographer, is a native of Colombia. He has explored and photographed all over the world, especially South America. He sees his work as providing a cross-cultural platform for discussion, interaction, increased understanding, and awareness, as well as offering a permanent record of people and places.

M. J. FLANAGAN is a native Tulsan whose work has been exhibited in many galleries, including the Alexandre Hogue Gallery at The University of Tulsa and the Philbrook Museum of Art. He has also taught photography and has had work published in several magazines.

JANAY HAMILTON is an eleven-year-old student at The Tulsa Girls Art School Project. Janay attends Carver Middle School and will enter sixth grade this year.

JEN HOPPA graduated from The University of Tulsa. She is a photographer who has taught photography and humanities classes at local colleges.

MANLY JOHNSON is a poet, teacher, and visual artist. He was *Nimrod*'s poetry editor for many years. His latest volume of poems is *Holding on to What Is: New & Selected Poems*.

JOHN MILISENDA's photography has appeared in over 125 shows and in publications including *Smithsonian* and *The New York Times*. His work is in the permanent collections of New Orleans Museum of Art, the Museum of Modern Art, and the Bibliothèque Nationale. He is currently working on a photography book of his family.

ANNE THOMPSON, who died in 2004, was a widely recognized photographer, in addition to her work as Court Administrator for the city of Tulsa.

M. TERESA VALERO, an Applied Associate Professor of Art at The University of Tulsa, is the co-founder and creative director of Third-Floor Designs, a student-run design studio. In addition to teaching, she is an award-winning photographer and graphic designer. Her photographs have been exhibited throughout the U.S., as well as in Venezuela, Lebanon, Syria, Spain, and Canada.

DANI WEFF is an eleven-year-old student at The Tulsa Girls Art School Project. She will enter sixth grade this year.

Nimrod gives thanks to The Tulsa Girls Art School Project, directed by Matt Moffett. The Tulsa Girls Art School Project (TGAS) is an after-school, non-profit program that teaches underserved girls in urban Tulsa. TGAS is starting its third year with twenty-five students. TGAS trains its students in visual arts genres including painting, ceramics, sculpture, fiber art, and black and white photography. Proceeds from art sales are split with each student and placed into a micro-bank account, so that each girl also learns the business aspect of being a visual artist. The two cover images in this issue were inspired by the 1956 French film *The Red Balloon*. They were recently exhibited at the Circle Cinema in Tulsa.

WORDS at PLAY

NIMROD INTERNATIONAL JOURNAL

Fiction Judge ROBERT OLEN BUTLER has published eleven novels and five collections of short stories, including *A Good Scent from a Strange Mountain*, which was awarded the Pulitzer Prize for fiction in 1993. His stories have twice won a National Magazine Award. His latest book is the novel *Hell*, set entirely in that place. His book on the creative process, *From Where You Dream*, is widely used in writing workshops. He teaches creative writing at Florida State University.

Poetry Judge MARIE HOWE's debut volume of poems, *The Good Thief*, was selected by Margaret Atwood as winner of the 1987 Open Competition of the National Poetry Series, and published in 1988 by Persea Books. Since then, she has published two more collections, *What the Living Do* and *The Kingdom of the Ordinary*. She edited (with Michael Klein) the anthology *In the Company of My Solitude: American Writing from the AIDS Pandemic*. Her work has been recognized with a fellowship at the Bunting Institute, as well as a Guggenheim Fellowship and a National Endowment for the Arts Fellowship. She currently teaches at Sarah Lawrence, New York University, and Columbia University in New York City.

Nimrod International Journal

The *Nimrod* Literary Awards
Founded by Ruth G. Hardman
The Katherine Anne Porter Prize for Fiction
& The Pablo Neruda Prize for Poetry

First Prize: $2,000　　Second Prize: $1,000

Postmark Deadline: April 30 of each year

No previously published works or works accepted for publication elsewhere. Author's name must not appear on the manuscript. Include a cover sheet containing major title and subtitles, author's name, full address, phone & email address. "Contest Entry" should be clearly indicated on both the outer envelope & the cover sheet. Manuscripts will not be returned. Entrants must have a US address by October of each year. Work must be in English or translated into English by the original author. *Nimrod* retains the right to publish any submission. Include SASE for results. The results will also be posted on *Nimrod*'s Web site in June: www.utulsa.edu/nimrod.　Poetry: 3-10 pages. Fiction: one short story, no more than 7,500 words.

Entry Fee: Each entry must be accompanied by a $20 fee. $20 includes both entry fee & a one-year subscription (2 issues).

- -

To subscribe to *Nimrod*:
Please fill out this form and send it with your check.

$18.50 for 1 year, 2 issues (outside USA, $20)
$32 for 2 years, 4 issues (outside USA, $38)

Name _____

Address _____

City_____ State_____ ZIP _____

Country _____

For more information, to submit, and to subscribe:
Nimrod Literary Awards
The University of Tulsa, 800 S. Tucker Dr., Tulsa, OK 74104
918-631-3080　nimrod@utulsa.edu　www.utulsa.edu/nimrod

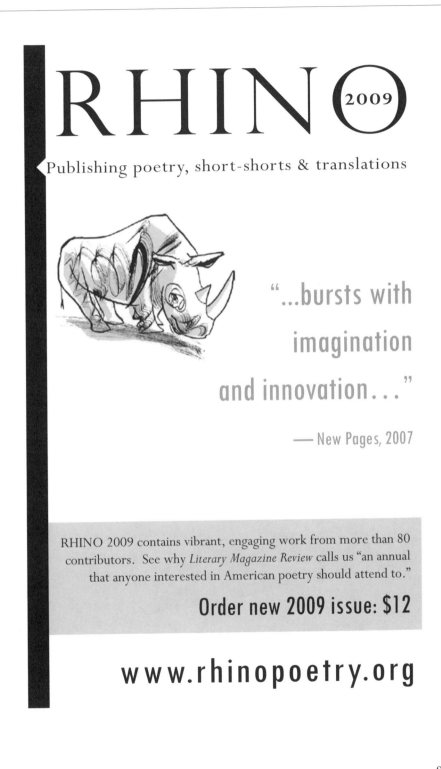

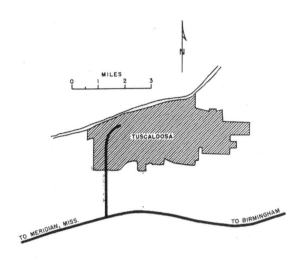

BLACK WARRIOR REVIEW

A preeminent literary journal founded in 1974 at the University of Alabama, *Black Warrior Review* publishes contemporary fiction, poetry, nonfiction, comics, and art by Pulitzer Prize and National Book Award winners alongsides work by new and emerging voices, in addition to a featured poetry chapbook solicited by the editors.

Please visit BWR.UA.EDU for more information, samples of published work, and web-exclusive content.